T0336787

Agent-based Spatial Simulation with NetLogo

Agent-based Spatial Simulation with NetLogo

Volume 1
Introduction and Bases

Edited by

Arnaud Banos
Christophe Lang
Nicolas Marilleau

First published 2015 in Great Britain and the United States by ISTE Press Ltd and Elsevier Ltd

Apart from any fair dealing for the purposes of research or private study, or criticism or review, as permitted under the Copyright, Designs and Patents Act 1988, this publication may only be reproduced, stored or transmitted, in any form or by any means, with the prior permission in writing of the publishers, or in the case of reprographic reproduction in accordance with the terms and licenses issued by the CLA. Enquiries concerning reproduction outside these terms should be sent to the publishers at the undermentioned address:

ISTE Press Ltd
27-37 St George's Road
London SW19 4EU
UK

www.iste.co.uk

Elsevier Ltd
The Boulevard, Langford Lane
Kidlington, Oxford, OX5 1GB
UK

www.elsevier.com

Notices
Knowledge and best practice in this field are constantly changing. As new research and experience broaden our understanding, changes in research methods, professional practices, or medical treatment may become necessary.

Practitioners and researchers must always rely on their own experience and knowledge in evaluating and using any information, methods, compounds, or experiments described herein. In using such information or methods they should be mindful of their own safety and the safety of others, including parties for whom they have a professional responsibility.

To the fullest extent of the law, neither the Publisher nor the authors, contributors, or editors, assume any liability for any injury and/or damage to persons or property as a matter of products liability, negligence or otherwise, or from any use or operation of any methods, products, instructions, or ideas contained in the material herein.

For information on all our publications visit our website at http://store.elsevier.com/

© ISTE Press Ltd 2015
The rights of Arnaud Banos, Christophe Lang and Nicolas Marilleau to be identified as the author of this work have been asserted by them in accordance with the Copyright, Designs and Patents Act 1988.

British Library Cataloguing-in-Publication Data
A CIP record for this book is available from the British Library
Library of Congress Cataloging in Publication Data
A catalog record for this book is available from the Library of Congress
ISBN 978-1-78548-055-3

Printed and bound in the UK and US

Contents

1

Introduction to the Agent Approach

1.1. Introduction

When we need to study a real system made up of interconnected elements, where each of these systems has its own dynamics, it is often impossible to foresee the emergence of a global dynamics for the system. In this case, what is in question is a complex system, because any one modification, even if it is marginal in terms of its one or several constituent elements, may lead to a dramatic change in overall operation of the system. It becomes clear that these phenomena may well be understood and observed only through the construction of a model. Even if in certain particular cases the model may be resolved analytically, as is the case for the Lotka–Voltera prey-predator models [VIA 11], computer simulation is indispensable in all other cases, i.e. in most thematically interesting cases. As such, agent modeling is one possible response for studying complex spatial systems.

Multi-agent systems (MAS) originally came into existence in the 1980s, at the crossroads of *Distributed Artificial Intelligence*[1] (DAI)

Chapter written by Fabrice BOUQUET, Sébastien CHIPEAUX, Christophe LANG, Nicolas MARILLEAU, Jean-Marc NICOD and Patrick TAILLANDIER.

1 DAI is concerned with the design of distributed IT systems which can solve problems using reasoning algorithms.

and *Artificial Life*[2] (A-Life) [FER 95], and are currently extremely popular. What is unique about them is their capacity to make apparent collective behaviors resulting from individual actions and interactions [JEA 97].

Within the domain, MAS are viewed as an entirely simulatory approach, which complements traditional techniques based on analytical, stochastic or other types of models [VAR 13]. As with the object concept [BOO 91], MAS engage a process of structuring thought which helps researchers or those involved in industry to solve the various problems they face. MAS are considered as the logical continuation of the object concept [FER 95, WOO 97] which brings increased modularity due to its ability to adapt, to learn and to be autonomous.

The fundamental principle upon which the multi-agent paradigm is based is that of breaking down complex objects into new, smaller problems, which are easier to model [BER 05]. Thus, the agent paradigm is "more a way of thinking than an implementation technique" [FOU 05]. It simply organizes our thought by analogy with the world around us. It is an elegant and intuitive way of envisaging and representing a complex phenomenon. In fact, this is one of the reasons why this approach has been adopted in a wide range of disciplines such as social sciences, ecology and finance, among others.

In this chapter, we will introduce the concept of the multi-agent system, beginning with a presentation of two examples of the use of such systems, in social sciences and soil sciences. We will then discuss the major trends in modeling and situate agents within the context of this work. Following this, we will formally define MAS before finally applying them to two concrete examples.

2 According to Christopher Langton in [LAN 89], "artificial life is the study of systems constructed by humans that exhibit behaviors typical to natural living systems" (definition taken from [REN 02]).

1.2. Two different MAS shown through examples

In order to illustrate the extraordinary expressive capacity of MAS, we have selected two concrete case studies which lead to two diametrically opposed models. The first case study, from social sciences, is concerned with the mobility between towns of town-dwellers, and the second case study, from ecology, studies soil sustainability.

1.2.1. *MAS in social sciences*

The agent paradigm is a modeling approach which is very well suited to the representation of the human being as an autonomous, intelligent individual, who is capable of learning and communicating with others. The agent approach also offers the advantage of providing a natural representation of the individual [SAN 05]. As a result, the model can be used to address a research question which may apply to a range of disciplines, such as the sustainability of a town, through one of its core components, daily mobility. If we consider a town to be a form of spatial organization, it is one that provides conditions which favor social interaction. As such, it follows that an ever-increasing number of daily transport journeys are required in order to achieve the objective of linking places. Urban spread, the functional specialization of urban areas and the low social value placed on mobility are factors that contribute to this trend and intensify its effects.

The right to a given level of mobility, linked to the desire for increasingly individualized and autonomous lifestyles, may result in significantly reduced accessibility of the town and its services. Given that "too much mobility kills a town", if a town's development has to be harmonious and sustainable, then researchers need to identify the conditions according to which daily and individual mobility do not prevent the town from fulfilling its role. This study must also take into account the management of urban growth, which nowadays causes many problems such as urban spread, congestion, energy consumption and production, and risks and dangers to the population.

Under these conditions, it is natural and logical to use the agent approach to model individuals who move around the urban zone according to timetables and certain socioeconomic characteristics: the city-dweller is an intelligent agent attempting to carry out a series of activities; the town is an environment regulated by transport and traffic rules. This approach is quite similar to a city-dweller/agent bijection.

1.2.2. *MAS in soil sciences*

The versatility of the MAS means that the approach is totally malleable, and its use may be adapted at will for the case study or research question to which it is applied: this approach may even be implemented for the study of soils.

Soil is a key component of ecosystems, which is the support for one of the main ecosystem services: the production of biomass (food, fodder, energy, wood and fibers). It is a critical resource, and one that is under threat. It is also non-renewable. As a result, it is essential to promote sustainable management practices both to halt its degradation and to foster its rehabilitation. New techniques for the rehabilitation of soil, such as soil building, are currently being developed. In order to evaluate the level of ecosystem service that a rehabilitated soil can provide, and in order to predict its development and sustainability, computer modeling and simulation tools are required. However, the multi-level character of soils and the overlapping of ecosystem processes involved within them mean that it is often difficult to model their complex systems using a classical macroscopic approach. In fact, soil is characterized by both biotic processes (linked to living organisms such as earthworms) and abiotic processes (linked to non-living elements such as the physics of the materials and the flow of liquids), which interact at various levels, from macro-fauna (such as termites and earthworms) or macro-aggregate (such as silt or clays) to microbes and the micro-structure (clay) of soil. Therefore, it is necessary to use modeling approaches which can handle this overlapping of various levels.

Agent-based modeling is particularly well suited to this context. For example, the Sworm model [MAR 08] describes a dynamic three-dimensional space in the form of a fractal made up of cubic cells. Each cell assumes the role of a soil aggregate with a particular behavior. As such, each cell can be represented by an agent with its own dynamics and its set of interactions, irrespective of its size. Its behavior can be driven by submodels such as the Mior model for the decomposition of organic material [MAS 07] or other models for water retention.

In contrast to the preceding model, the agents no longer represent individuals within a space under study, but rather they represent portions of space animated by biological processes. Due to the sheer number of microbes, it is technically impossible to represent each of them by an agent. Also, the current state of knowledge on microbial individuals means that it is impossible to define behaviors at their level.

1.2.3. *Summary*

It can be seen through these two examples, respectively, from social and soil sciences that MAS are malleable as a function of the context, the state of knowledge of the real system and the underlying research question. The fact that they are different helps our purpose, which consists of demonstrating the versatility of MAS. In this regard, the major challenge to design an agent-based model is not its computer-based implementation, but rather the identification of relevant elements to include in the model, and choosing how to represent them.

Quite apart from the capacity of an MAS to represent a system under study, its proximity to the real system means that it is intuitive and enables interdisciplinary dialogue. For the examples cited above, there is collaboration between mathematicians, geographers, economists and computer scientists, among others. The model becomes an element which brings them together, engenders ideas and favors the emergence of new research questions upon which all parties can agree. This does not at all conflict with the advancement of a particular research project within a particular discipline, which can quite feasibly happen alongside contribution to the common project driven by the model.

1.3. Agents and the major trends within spatial modeling

1.3.1. *Major trends in spatial modeling*

As has been the case in many other disciplines, the systematic and reasoned use of models has been developed over the last few decades with a view to understanding and modeling how spaces operate.

In 1999, the modeling group of GDR Libergéo was formed in order to take stock of all the spatial models developed in various French research centers. This group surveyed 20 or so models and classified them using a model comparison grid, with the aim of describing, classifying and comparing all types of models (e.g. graphic, statistic and simulation).

There are many different definitions of the terms "model". In 1973, Haggett defined models in the following way [HAG 73]:

> MODEL.– Models are schematic representations of reality, which are created to help us understand and explain reality.

A model may be considered as a formal representation of the theory of a system under study [WIL 74]. More generally, models may be viewed as an abstraction or approximation of reality which is created through a simplified vision of complex real-world relationships in order to make it possible to understand and manipulate them.

Nowadays, it is very difficult to define the position of one model in relation to another, mainly because models have been insufficiently categorized and formalized.

For over 30 years, geographers have been working with models of increasing complexity. From maps to computer models, through choremes and traffic management, forecast or optimization models: differentiating and categorizing models is not always a straightforward business. Whenever we use a map, graph theory or perhaps an optimization model for a town's public transport system, we are working with models and modeling.

In [BRI 00], Briassoulis cites various instantiations of models for the dynamics of territories. These can be classified into four major categories:

1) statistical and econometric models;

2) optimization models;

3) models of spatial interaction;

4) simulation models.

1.3.2. *Properties of modeling approaches*

1.3.2.1. *Statistical and econometric models*

The application of statistical techniques in order to derive the mathematical relationships between dependent variables (factors whose value is influenced by other factors) and independent variables is widespread in the modeling of socioeconomic systems and in other fields [ANS 98].

The most commonly used statistical technique is multiple regression analysis (and its variations such as regression in stages or two-stage least squares regression analysis), although other multivariate techniques are also widely used (such as factorial analysis or canonical analysis) [KLE 07].

Econometric models are applications of multiple regression techniques that are used to analyze economic questions. They are systems of equations which express the relationships between demand and/or supply and their root causes, and the relationship between demand and supply themselves (economic/market equilibrium) [BAT 76, WIL 74]. Generally known as econometric analysis, this set of specialized statistical techniques was developed in order to estimate their coefficients [JUD 88].

The work of Irwin and Bockstael [IRW 02] should be mentioned at this point: they use an economic model to describe to what extent it is worthwhile for the owner of an undeveloped plot of land to transform it into a site for building habitation, depending on the sale value of the land once it has been transformed into a usable site and the cost of achieving this.

1.3.2.2. *Models of spatial interaction*

These models, also known as gravity models, are used to model a variety of types of interactions which result from a multitude of human activities, such as commuting to work, shopping, traveling around town and mobility in general.

Haynes and Fotheringham [HAY 84] define spatial interactions in the following way:

> SPATIAL.– "Spatial interaction" is a general term which is used to cover any movement in space which results from a human process. This includes commuting to work, migration, information, and the flow of goods.

The study of spatial interactions usually implies the study of two interacting entities and the form of their interaction. In the case of the analysis of the dynamics of territories, the interacting entities are often people living within them or engaging in an activity (most often work or shopping), with origin and destination zones.

These interactions may assume various forms, such as displacements or flows of goods and information.

1.3.2.3. *Optimization models*

Optimization involves using operation research algorithms to minimize or maximize a given objective function. Constraints imposed within the system (such as availability of technologies and capacity levels) and hypotheses formulated concerning the exogenous variables are considered while this optimization is being achieved. Thus, it can be said that optimization models seek the solution to a limited number of problems under certain constraints.

The use of optimization models is generally focused on the improved use of resources available within the system. They are also used to facilitate the achievement of objectives by the entities within the system.

A well-known example of an optimization model is Schlager's *Southern Wisconsin Regional Plan Model* [SCH 65], which offers an objective function in order to minimize the cost of urban development within a given zone of the territory under study, provided that land is available.

1.3.2.4. *Simulation models*

Batty [BAT 76] states that "all mathematical models which include the large scale use of computer systems are considered to be simulation models". However, even though we consider "simulation" to be a modeling technique, it also has a more precise meaning. Wilson [WIL 74] suggests a more comprehensive definition and a precise usage framework for simulation models: simulation techniques involve "a set of rules which make it possible for a set of numbers to be actioned simultaneously, generally through the use of computer systems, though the rules for and the consequences of their application cannot be transcribed in the form of algebraic equations. Sometimes the simulation technique naturally lends itself to solving a particular problem. This happens, for example, when the basic theory is comprised of a set of relationships which imply certain probabilities. Thus, it is necessary to use simulation techniques for situations that are too complicated to be manipulated with direct algebraic techniques".

In this chapter, we take a simulation model to be the animation of a model with a view to gain understanding, insights and even a forecast of future events.

Simulation models are generally categorized according to the level of spatial analysis (level of spatial detail) they refer to, because there is a close link between the spatial level of the analysis and the theoretical level of the aggregation used (or that is possible). A distinction should be made between three scales of models, depending on the reference system under study. For example, if we consider the study of a country:

– local level simulation models (for example, a town or municipality);

– regional level simulation models (a state, county or region);

– global level simulation models (the country as a whole).

A distinction should also be made regarding the level of analysis of the individuals: there are different aggregation levels for models (e.g. individuals, households and social groups).

1.3.3. *How to model a system*

Obviously, in order to model a system, the distance between the model and the system being modeled needs to be made as small as possible. This is a challenging exercise for several reasons. In fact, a very good knowledge of the system being modeled is required, suitable modeling tools need to be found, and the model needs to be created with these tools, while the constraints inherent in the system that is being modeled also need to be observed.

A model always seeks to address a research question. This is a precondition required for the identification of the constituent elements of the target system. To achieve this, it is necessary to reveal the active elements, the interactions between them and the surrounding elements, and to characterize the autonomous entities and their behaviors. The place is also of prime importance, and its topology and properties must be considered. Relationships have a great significance in the process. They are often the key to the complexity of systems. Thus, the model does not need to aim to cover all of the aspects of the modeled system. Rather, it can concentrate on its particularities.

Model validation is a complex stage in this process. How can we ensure that the model is representative of the simulated system? Indicators built into the model may be used as a basis for this investigation; they may be compared to the real-world experimental values. Researcher expertise is also invaluable in supporting this stage: simulation experiment results can be compared with knowledge gained on the ground.

The step-by-step method that we suggest is presented here:

1) definition of the scientific questions that the model aims to address;

2) identification of the target system's constituents;

3) collection of data required to construct the model;

4) definition of the agents and the environment. Definition of the interactions between all the model's elements;

5) implementation of the model;

6) calibration of the model through successive simulations;

7) exploration of the model which answers the scientific questions, or redefinition of these questions.

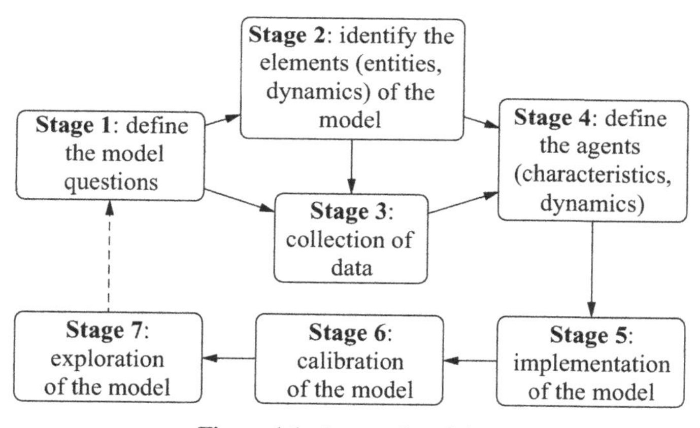

Figure 1.1. *Stages of modeling*

1.4. The agent paradigm

Let us now provide a more formal introduction of the concepts from the world of agents.

1.4.1. *Basic concepts*

One of the most influential definitions of the concept of agent, which is used as a reference point by the French research community, was suggested by Jacques Ferber in [FER 95]. According to this definition, the agent is:

> CONCEPT OF AGENT ACCORDING TO J. FERBER.– a physical or virtual entity:
>
> – which is able to act in an environment;
>
> – which can communicate directly with other agents;
>
> – which is driven by a set of tendencies (in the form of individual objectives or a satisfaction, perhaps even survival function, which it aims to optimize);
>
> – which possesses its own resources;
>
> – which is capable of perceiving its environment (in a limited manner);
>
> – which has only a partial representation of this environment available to it (it may even possibly have no representation of it);
>
> – which has skills and offers services;
>
> – which may possibly be able to reproduce;
>
> – whose behavior tends to satisfy objectives, while taking the resources and skills at its disposal into account, and as a function of its perception, representations, and the communications it receives.

This definition states the minimum properties that an entity must have in order to be considered an agent. These characteristics may be summarized in four words [WOO 97]:

– *autonomy*: ability to evolve according to its own behavior without external intervention;

– *reactivity*: ability to react to external events;

– *proactivity*: ability to make decisions in a more or less developed way in order to achieve its objectives;

– *sociability*: ability to interact with other agents.

In the same spirit as the above definition, Jacques Ferber interprets the concept of a multi-agent system as [FER 95]:

CONCEPT OF MULTI-AGENT SYSTEM.– being composed of the following elements:

– an environment E, i.e. a space which has a metric;

– a set of objects O: these objects are situated, i.e. for each object, for a given moment, they can be associated with a position in E. These objects are passive, i.e. they can be perceived, created, destroyed and modified by the agents;

– a set of agents A, which are particular objects ($A \subseteq O$), which represent the system's active entities;

– a set of relationships R which brings the objects (and thus the agents) together with each other;

– a set of operations Op which makes it possible for the agents from A to perceive, produce, consume, transform and manipulate the objects from O;

– operators responsible for representing the application of these operations and the world's reaction to this modification attempt, which we will call the laws of the Universe.

This definition can be summarized using four core concepts [OCC 01]:

– *agents*: set of active entities in the system which have their own behavior;

– *environment*: medium in which the agents evolve. Its structure depends on the domain of application. However, it is often spatialized; in other words, it is accorded a metric;

– *interactions*: set of languages and exchange protocols between the agents. These are sometimes low level, originating from physics models, or high level, like language acts;

– *organization*: set of groupings of agents with federating entities where all the agents have a common goal.

This summary has been the subject of a modeling approach named Vowel after the A,E,I,O [DEM 95, DEM 97, DEM 03]. These four components define the concept of multi-agent system in a general manner. There are currently a very large number of formalisms and run-time environments based on this type of approach. Therefore, we will now address the question of whether a multi-agent system is a process for reflection or an implementation tool.

1.4.2. *Interactions*

The richness of MAS lies, to a large extent, in the interactions that occur between agents. These interactions can be expressed in many ways.

The organization Foundation for Intelligent Physical Agents (FIPA) has published a set of rules and standards regarding these interactions. These rules can be summarized as follows [FAP 00]:

– agents can communicate with each other;

– an agent provides a set of services and makes them available to all other agents in the system;

– each agent is responsible for limiting its accessibility to other agents;

– each agent is responsible for defining its relationships, contracts, etc., with other agents. Thus, an agent directly "knows" (through its set of knowledge) all the agents with which it can interact;

– each agent knows, with its name, the way in which it can be accessed from outside the system. As a result, the agents are supposed to interact autonomously and without constraints.

The medium through which these interactions are conducted is variable. The agents can exchange through sending messages, which generally have standardized contents. A large number of works have examined the creation of oriented languages, commonly known as Agent Communication Language (ACL). Some of the best known languages are FIPA-ACL [FOU 02]. This type of communication means that exchanges can take place from point to point or that an agent can be transmitted toward a community of agents.

Another technique is that of the blackboard, which consists of allowing agents a board where they can read or write in order to communicate with the community of agents. This is a transmission pattern.

Finally, there is the type of communication which we will call diffuse. The agents can, through mechanisms of perception and action respectively, perceive a change in others or in the environment, and can act on others and on the environment. This is also a form of communication.

1.4.3. *Types of agents*

All those with an interest in agents agree on the fact that, for pedagogical purposes, there are two main categories of agents [FER 95]: *reactive* and *cognitive*. The first category of agents is based on simple behaviors which correspond to a *stimuli-action* strategy. In contrast, the second category of agents has genuine faculties for reflection and adapting its behavior.

Many agent architectures for representing spatial phenomena have been suggested in the literature. In this context, the belief desire intention (BDI) approach describes a humanized decision-making process for agents [RAO 91]. This architecture is based on a simple idea: the achievement of a *desire* is made through carrying out intermediary *intentions* which are identified through an analysis of the agent's *beliefs* about its world.

We might be tempted to state that the BDI architecture is ideal. However, the decision-making process for purely cognitive agents (such as BDI agents) demands high use of computer resources (processor calculation time and memory, for example). Their wide-scale use creates performance issues. Brownian agents seem to be a solution, given that they combine the properties of reactive and cognitive agents [SCH 03, SCH 02]. In fact, their behavior derives from the evaluation of a set of variables combined with pure analytical or stochastic laws. In this way, Brownian agents maintain the simplicity of reactive agents, but also have at their disposal behavior imitative of cognition, through the stochastic functions that are a part of them. These kind of agents are suitable for the representation of the movement of a large number of humans, as is proposed in [GLO 04].

In reality, agents and multi-agent systems are designed on a case-by-case basis in order to simulate complex phenomena as much as possible; they are often at the crossroads of reaction and cognition, bringing together internal variables of state and memory, reactiveness and cognition, or determinism and stochasticity of behaviors. As a result, they often present a hybrid architecture which combines:

– *reactive behavior rules* which are based on stimuli received or perceived by the agent (events, messages, observations or stochastic laws); the reactive behavior rules may apply some actions or call some high level cognitive functions;

– *cognitive behavior rules* which use developed algorithms and the agent's knowledge, for example a shortest route algorithm based on a mental map of the space structured in the form of a graph.

This general architecture is developed in more detail as a function of the case study in question, in particular, through the inclusion of an agent architecture (e.g. BDI or adaptive), or even through the definition of an organizational model.

1.4.4. *MAS organization paradigms*

Like all distributed systems, there are two main types of control in MAS: centralized control, in which a master agent manages work, organizes solutions and mediates conflicts, and distributed control where the system is said to be evolutive and where each agent has a total or partial plan of action. In practice, we find totally centralized architectures, totally distributed architectures or architectures that combine both these approaches.

As outlined by J. Ferber [FER 03], during the development of a multi-agent environment, two possibilities are available to us: a development focused on agents or a development focused on the organization. Agent-centered multi-agent systems (ACMAS) are modeled in terms of the mental states of the agent and are very useful in the case of highly cognitive agents. In the case of a complex system, it is impossible to be fully aware of the development and the behavior of the system as a whole solely on the basis of the behavior of the various agents. Their interactions need to be taken into account, and an overall point of view needs to be taken, which is why an ACMAS is not recommended for modeling a complex system.

We will further describe the organization-centered multi-agent systems approach (OCMAS) and the Agent/Group/Role model (also known as an AGR or Aalaadin model [FER 98]).

1.4.4.1. *General principles of OCMAS*

If we consider matters in terms of organization, this provides us with a new approach toward describing the structure and the interactions which appear within an MAS. The organizational level (also called social level in [JEN 00]) is located at a level above that of the agents, which is the only level that is considered in ACMAS.

The organizational level describes the structural and dynamic aspects of the organization. It is based on three principles summarized as follows:

PRINCIPLE 1.1.– the organizational level describes the *what* and not the *how*. It imposes a structure on the actions of the agents, but does not describe the way in which they behave. In other words, the organizational level does not contain a code which can be executed by the agents, but rather it provides specifications regarding the limits and the expectations it is possible to have on agent behavior.

PRINCIPLE 1.2.– no description of an agent and no mental state are present at the organizational level. This level states nothing regarding the manner in which agents will interpret it. A colony of ants is considered an organization in much the same way as the board of a company. The organizational level of mental states such as beliefs, desires, intentions or goals is not discussed.

PRINCIPLE 1.3.– an organization makes it possible to break a system down. Each part (or group) provides a context for interactions between the agents. A group provides the boundaries agents belonging to the same group can interact freely. On the other hand, a group is completely inaccessible for agents that do not belong to it.

These three principles have the following significance:

1) an organization may be viewed as a dynamic structure, whose agents are various components. Joining a group or playing a role may be viewed as integration;

2) modeling a system at the organizational level may leave the implementation choices open, such as the fact that a specific agent plays a specific role;

3) it is possible to create truly "open systems", where the internal architecture of the agents is not specified;

4) it is possible to create secured systems through using groups in a "black box" method, where whatever happens inside cannot be seen from outside. It is also possible to define a security policy in order to exclude "undesirable" agents from joining a group.

1.4.4.2. *The agent group role (AGR) model: an example of OCMAS organization*

The AGR model is based on three primitive concepts: *agents*, *groups* and *roles*, which are structurally connected and cannot be defined by other primitives. These concepts satisfy a set of axioms that unify them.

– *Agent:* an agent is an active communicative entity which can play several roles and can be a member of several groups. An important characteristic of the AGR model, which is in agreement with the second principle described above, is that there is no constraint placed on the architecture of an agent or on its mental capacities. An agent can be as reactive as an ant or as cognitive as a human, without any restriction.

– *Group:* groups are the atomic aggregation sets for agents. A group is formed from a set of agents which share common characteristics, and is used as a context for activities, making it possible to divide organizations into different sections. Following the third principle, two agents can only communicate if they belong to the same group; but an agent may, however, belong to several different groups. This makes it possible to define organizational structures.

– *Role:* the role is an abstract representation of the function, service or identification of an agent within a group. An agent must play at least one role within a group. Roles are local to groups and must be solicited by an agent. Several different agents may play the same role.

The groups may overlap because an agent may be a member of several groups at the same time. This overlap property for groups makes it possible to conceptualize a world where all the agents are at the same level and are not organized in a fixed manner into a rigid structure. Organization and hierarchy occur at the group level and can thus change over time.

The three above-defined concepts of agent, group and role are linked by a set of five axioms:

1) each agent is a member of (at least) one group;

2) two agents can only communicate if they are members of the same group;

3) each agent plays (at least) one role in a group;

4) an agent is a member of the group within which it plays a role;

5) a role is defined with a group structure.

The AGR model makes it possible for us to define a dynamic organization of the agents. The organization of agents within an MAS is an element which structures the process. When the system being studied is considered at different scales, it needs to be possible to see or represent the fact that a group of interacting agents can behave in a specific way and, at another level of abstraction, can act as if they were a single entity.

1.4.5. *Agent platforms*

The current strong position of agent-based modeling has in part been made possible by the development of new platforms which allow modelers, including those who have no information technology (IT) background, to define this type of models with ease. There are nowadays many platforms available for the definition and simulation of agent-based models, some of which are open source. These platforms may be divided into two non-exclusive categories on the basis of the type of languages used to define the models.

The first category of platforms defines models using a generic programming language, such as Java, C++ or Python. These platforms are generally intended for IT engineers and are often more suitable for the development of large models. The best-known open-source platforms for this category are Swarm [MIN 96], Cormas [BOU 98], Mason [LUK 04] and Repast [NOR 13].

The second category of platforms uses a dedicated modeling language to define models. These models are generally easier to use than those in the first category and are therefore intended for a wider range of users. However, the user is required to have algorithmic skills. The best-known open-source platforms in this category are NetLogo [TIS 04] and GAMA [GRI 13].

Platforms in the final category define models using a graphic modeling language. In general, users of these platforms need only have very little knowledge of algorithms, or sometimes even nothing at all. An additional advantage of these models is that they facilitate dialogue between modelers and thematic modeling technicians. However, they are limited to the definition of simple models and do not provide the same rich resources as the other categories of platforms. The platforms in this category include StarLogo TNG [RES 96] and MAGeo [LAN 13].

It should also be noted that there is a current trend to integrate several ways for defining models within a platform. For example, in the latest version of the Repast platform, there are three possible methods for defining models: in Java, in Relogo (where the language from the NetLogo platform is used in a Repast model) and by graphic modeling. Cormas and GAMA also offer graphic modeling tools in their latest versions.

Among all the platforms, NetLogo ranks first because of the simplicity of its use. Even if this platform does not offer the possibility of defining models as complex as those that can be defined with GAMA or Repast, it has the advantage of being very easy to use, even for those who are modeling for the first time, or who have a low level of algorithmic knowledge. Another advantage of this is that many of the other platforms currently available have adopted some of its concepts. This means that it can be a good way to start working with these concepts before moving on to more complex platforms such as GAMA or Repast.

1.5. Observing a phenomenon through agents

Before simulation occurs, MAS are also involved in explicating knowledge linked with the initial research question. There are various possible approaches for structuring the modeler's thought and the formalization of the problem. First, we might mention mathematical approaches such as ordinary differential equations (ODE) and partial differential equations (PDE), stochastic methods (such as Bayesian networks and Markov chains). After this come IT approaches (through simulations), such as cellular robots, individual-based approaches and MAS. In this context, MAS play a very particular role due to their proximity to reality and their adaptability to all contexts.

We will first present a method for modeling a real phenomenon using agents. We will illustrate our explanation with an example from social sciences concerning inter-urban dynamics.

1.5.1. *Two agent approaches to a real phenomenon*

With regard to MAS as modeling tools, there are two major trends [EDM 04]. The first trend is parsimonious modeling, known as keep it simple stupid (KISS), where the observed system is reduced to its simplest representation in order to highlight its dynamics. Thus, we speak of a comprehension model for KISS. The second modeling trend is keep it descriptive stupid (KIDS), in which the observed system is described in all its complexity on the basis of field data, particularly using geographic information systems (GIS), in order to describe the real system as accurately as possible. In this case, we speak of a descriptive model. Typically, in order to understand the difference between the above-cited approaches, we add the following details.

The KISS approach aims to simplify the model as much as possible in order to construct an intelligible controlled environment focused on the system's dynamics which is under study. This can be seen through microscopic or macroscopic observation of the system by simulation. If an example from epidemiology is simplified, the acquired immune deficiency syndrome (AIDS) model from the NetLogo library is obtained. This model describes a homogenous space with infected or healthy individuals, with random circulation patterns, where there is an infection at each meeting. KISS modeling makes it possible to understand the dynamics observed by simulation, taking a certain number of parameters into account. Due to the short timeframe of these experiments, the modeling may be interactive. It is thus possible to define serious or multi-actor games for an almost exhaustive exploration of the value of the parameters, or potentially for the identification of scenarios which might be simulated as a next step, using a KIDS model. The aim of the KIDS approach is to describe the system in the finest possible detail. For example, the individuals in the AIDS model mentioned above would, through this approach, have a realistic circulation behavior (such as pendulum movement, or movement linked to place of residence) which is linked to field studies conducted. Therefore, KIDS modeling comes into its own when what is required is an appreciation of a system's future or a method for evaluating and decision-making policy on the ground. However, the number of parameters involved is often very high, and the calculation time may be as long as several hours, or even several days. This means that KIDS models cannot be used interactively. Before any simulation, the scenario needs to be thought of carefully because it is impossible to completely explore this type of model.

In order to provide a clearer idea of the KISS and KIDS approaches, we will provide a concrete example of their use in the section that follows.

1.5.2. *Agent modeling through an example: the MIRO project*

The *Modélisation Intra-urbaine des Rythmes quOtidiens* (MIRO) project (financed by *Programme de Recherche Et D'Innovation dans les Transports terrestres* (PREDIT) 2004-2007, *Agence Nationale pour la Recherche* (ANR) 2009-2013, *Ministère de l'Ecologie, du Développement Durable et de l'Energie* (MEDDE) 2014-2015) aims to explore, through computer simulation, the possible impacts of urban policies on the spatiotemporal accessibility of a town to citizens, and the consequences that these policies have on the daily mobility of the citizens. It also aims to establish territorial diagnostics (local gains and losses in terms of accessibility) and social diagnostics (populations which are favored or disadvantaged by the different tested policies). Finally, it facilitates the exploration of the possible global impacts of the modification of individual behaviors, which focuses more on the bigger picture than on the maximization of one individual useful feature. The agent approach makes it possible to see the town through various points of view through scenarios that modify its structure, its services and its inhabitants with the aim of observing the new dynamics which result from these changes.

From this point of view, a comprehension model (of the KISS type) and a descriptive model (of the KIDS type) which show the same dynamics, but with different modeling goals, would complement each other perfectly.

1.5.2.1. *The SMartAccess model*

SMartAccess is a pedagogical comprehension model which allows the user to construct an imaginary town and to test urban planning hypotheses.

The synthetic character of this model means that it is perfectly suited to testing urban structures (such as compact towns or urban villages); it is also suited to defining, in an iterative and interactive manner and based on a large number of macroscopic and microscopic indicators, urban configurations that meet certain sustainability criteria. One of its aims is to help users become aware of how difficult it is to take charge of the development of a complex urban system; this becomes even more difficult when we want to achieve several goals, some of which are mutually incompatible.

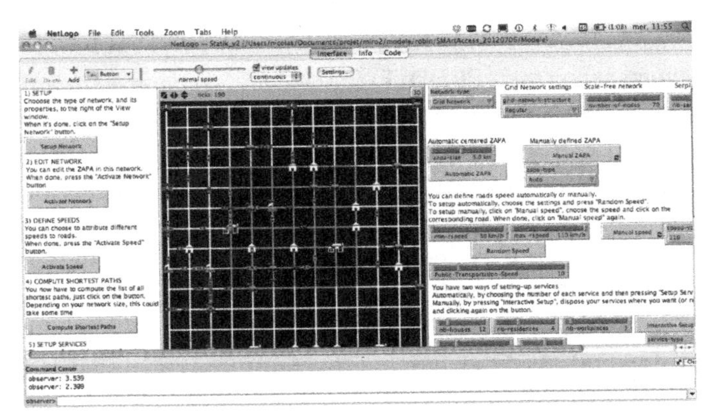

Figure 1.2. *Screenshot from the SMartAccess model. For a color version of the figure, see www.iste.co.uk/banos/netlogo.zip*

1.5.2.2. *The GaMiroD model*

GaMiroD is a descriptive model which has been applied to the towns of Dijon and Grenoble. It was developed using the GAMA platform [DRO 13], which allows the simulation of several hundred thousand inhabitants. In contrast to the SMartAccess model, the GaMiroD model attempts to describe the towns of Dijon and Grenoble, and their dynamics, as accurately as possible.

This model has been developed in line with the available field data, which are:

– *structure*: the road network is built using the geographic information systems of Dijon and Grenoble, which address not only the existing physical network but also the rules for circulation on it (e.g. direction of movement and speed restrictions);

– *description of services*: most of the two towns' services are described following the classification categories of Siren data. As a result, each building in each town is classified according to one or several functions (e.g. residential, school, shop and supermarket) and opening hours are indicated;

– *population*: population of the models mirrors the real population of 120,000 and 400,000 individuals, respectively, for Dijon and Grenoble. This "synthetic" population is built using INSEE data from 1999 and a survey on household mobility from 2009.

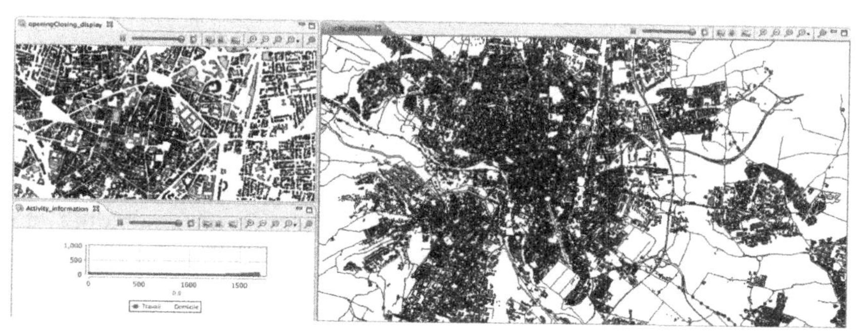

Figure 1.3. *Screenshot from the GaMiroD model. For a color version of the figure, see www.iste.co.uk/banos/netlogo.zip*

The aim of these two case studies was to enable testing of scenarios involving change in the urban environment. The studies were also linked to local public policy actions arising from a desire to achieve sustainable development: (1) the construction of a dedicated infrastructure for public transport and (2) the implementation of an urban regulated traffic zone to reduce pollution. Applying the GaMiroD prototype for both sites facilitated the detailed verification of whether it would be possible to reproduce the protocol, and made it possible to test the model's calculation abilities for two towns of differing sizes.

1.5.3. *Critical analysis*

Through the SMartAccess and GaMiroD experiments, we can clearly see the approach's level of expressiveness: one problem can be tackled from several points of view, with an extended scale and detail of description. The closeness of the approach to the real system and available field data enable the exchange of knowledge and skills between modelers and field experts. The agent model can thus become a basis for discussion. It plays the role of an intuitive representation of a complexity being studied, while also playing a role in the integration of all of the contributions of the various actors involved. It links a simple idea on the system with theories and concepts, all the while using field data. This centralizing role of the agent model makes it possible to capitalize on the experience and skill of all the disciplines which are collaborating in the project. Discussions and negotiations lead to the controlled emergence of a model whose simulation provides a virtual reproduction of the modeled realities through a scenario which needs to be observed. The observation of this scenario thus leads to the validation/invalidation of an initial collective understanding of the real system and makes new phenomena, which had not yet become apparent, observable. Bringing all the points of view together and opposing them with each other guarantees the quality of the modeling process and the simulation results, even though there is no formal framework. Experience has shown that the MAS which correspond to the method supported in this book are rarely very far from reality.

In fact, the extreme versatility of MAS makes them an approach which is fit for many purposes, and which can be adapted to any situation. However, the high level of flexibility of MAS may also be a point of weakness: the permissiveness of such systems is a source of modeling errors and of uncertaincy in the models. It may lead to conditions favorable to uncontrolled increase in complexity and combinatorial uncertainties. This, in turn, leads to difficulties in the verification and validation of data.

As a result, one of the primary concerns of a modeler is the production of a model which can be trusted, where the simulations based on the model really do simulate the system which is under study. To achieve this, modelers must pay much attention to the modeling hypotheses, data and inevitable simplifications. For example, for the modeling of road traffic within a town, one of the first simplifications for modeling would be to break down the sections of the road network into cells of the same size. Vehicles then move from cell to cell over time. Another simplification might be to define a temporal budget and to carry out the circulation around the model in line with this budget.

The greater the distance traveled, the larger the expenditure of the vehicle in terms of the budget. If the goal is to study interactions between vehicles, for example to make it possible to observe an "accordion" phenomenon on a portion of the network, the first modeling assumption discussed will be well suited to this purpose, because it shows the space that the vehicles occupy (each cell is occupied by one vehicle at the most). However, the second simplification makes it possible to ensure that a vehicle will reach its destination within a given time, but it does not allow the observance of friction between vehicles. Thus, we have two models of traffic, where one describes the interaction between vehicles and the other is concerned with journey time. The second simplification would be suited to studying the accessibility of a town's services.

The choice of one modeling strategy over another is made through intuition and modeling experience or through a trial and error method based on experiment plans. To return to the above example, if we try to study accessibility using the first simplification, we will notice a significant error in the time of travel in relation to the theoretical journey times; these errors will disappear if we use the second approach. Additionally, tests also facilitate the refinement of the model constants, such as the spatial size of a cell for the first simplification.

Thus, validation and verification of the model are a significant and essential part of the modeling–simulation process. As we have previously stated, validation requires broad experimental experience acquired through a large number of simulations (several thousand, or even several hundred thousand), where results must be compared to field data. Verification is more formal. It cannot be envisaged for the model as a whole, but can only be applied to certain individual aspects of the model such as exchange protocols between the vehicles, or that a vehicle never leaves the road. It should be remembered that any model is a point of view on a reality, but it is never actually real in itself.

Modeling strategy and modeling validation are addressed in sections 2.5 and 4.4, respectively.

1.6. Summary

This chapter has presented the basic concepts of MAS. We have introduced the core definitions and the organizational paradigms. We have also presented the key trends in spatial modeling in order to place agent models into context. The examples that we have provided have also shown the rich expressiveness of these systems when it comes to creating models of complex distributed systems. However, before we can build models and explore them through simulation, we need to address the question of description formalisms in agent models.

The next chapter will aim to demonstrate how to manipulate these various formalisms.

2

Description Formalisms in Agent Models

2.1. Introduction

This chapter will aim to present good practice in, and the benefits of, formalization in modeling multiagent systems (MAS). To achieve this, the authors will first reiterate the usefulness of modeling systems, while placing the paradigms associated with a multiagent approach in context. Then, they will argue that the use of graphic modeling languages enhances the exchanges between the parties involved in the design of an MAS. Following this, two types of graphic models based on the same semantic base are presented: *Unified Modeling Language* (UML) and *Agent Modeling Language* (AML). The first graphic model is intended for general use and facilitates its users to analyze the ontology and dynamics of the modeled system. The second graphic model uses paradigms specific to agents and facilitates its users to create a design which is closer to the MAS which will be produced. After having discussed the relative merits of each of these graphic model types and presented some possible extensions, the chapter discusses the utility of, and a method for, documenting a multiagent model. In order to do this, the *Overview, Design concepts, Details*

Chapter written by Fabrice BOUQUET, David SHEEREN, Nicolas BECU, Benoît GAUDOU, Christophe LANG, Nicolas MARILLEAU and Claude MONTEIL.

(ODD) protocol, which guides the modeler in the creation of a documentation of the objectives, constitutive elements and specific properties of the model, is presented.

We illustrate each of the concepts presented (UML, AML and ODD) through their application to an example which will be a recurrent theme in the remaining of this chapter.

2.2. Recurrent example

Many applications exist which have clearly demonstrated the utility of the agent approach for modeling complex phenomena. These involve numerous domains, such as ecology, social science or epidemiology. We have chosen to address the domain of epidemiology because, first, this theme takes in several other domains, in particular ecology and social sciences, and second, a wide range of multiagent concepts can be involved in modeling complex phenomena such as these.

As such, this chapter, and those that follow it, will be thematically linked through a recurrent modeling example which is based on an epidemiological phenomenon. The phenomenon in question is the geographic dispersion of an epidemic transmitted to humans by mosquitoes. The aim of the model is to understand and measure the impact of the pendular journeys people take (moving from home ↔ work) on the development and spread of a contagious disease.

We have decided to study malaria, which is present in many African countries, and we apply this to the Maroua subregion of Cameroon (see Figure 2.1).

The only way in which malaria is transmitted to humans is through the bite of an infected anopheles mosquito. A healthy mosquito becomes infected when it bites an infected person. People cannot pass the disease on to other people, and mosquitoes cannot pass the disease on to other mosquitoes. By itself, the mosquito has a very small movement radius, of approximately 50 m a day, but it is present throughout the territory.

However, the real vector for the spread of the disease seems to be people because they need to travel over large distances to conduct their daily activities.

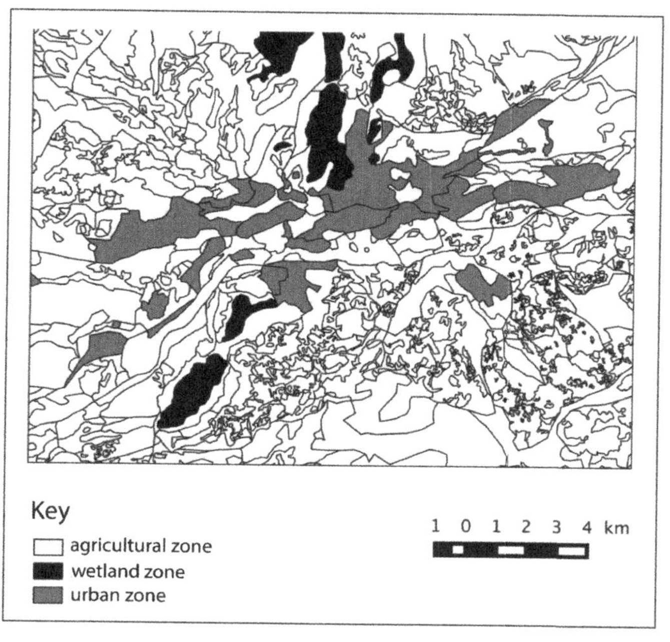

Figure 2.1. *Map of the Maroua subregion (Cameroon)*

Most of the inhabitants of the Maroua live in urbanized areas (black in Figure 2.1). The crop farmers of the region travel in a pendular movement between their homes (in town) and the area that they farm, outside the town (white and gray areas in Figure 2.1). The wetland zones correspond to wet areas where the mosquitoes can lay their eggs.

In the following, this system will be modeled using UML (section 2.3.1), and then AML (section 2.3.2), and will be documented using the ODD protocol (section 2.4). In this way, the readers will discover the different forms of model description through an example of each.

2.3. Formalization of agent models

In this section, we will first detail the reasons for formalizing MAS, and then we will present two tools designed to aid this formalization – UML and AML – which we will illustrate using our recurring example.

Formalization is a process which has three goals. The first goal is related to the system under study. A tool is required that is suitable for gaining an understanding of the system concerned. The second goal is connected with abstraction, which helps us to not be restricted by technical considerations linked to the simulation components. The third goal is the generation of a code, which will make it possible to transition from model to implementation. In addition, graphic formalizations, such as UML and AML, also allow us to streamline communication about the content of the model among several people. These languages have the advantage of being able to synthetically show, using one or several diagrams, complex mechanisms and structures. The graphic nature of these diagrams simplifies their understanding for non-programmers.

In this chapter, we have chosen to concentrate on UML and AML; the latter is an extension of the former, and it is more specifically dedicated to the agent paradigm through its formalization of the description of agent behaviors and interactions.

The various diagrams developed from UML may also, of course, be used for model development. However, its generic nature causes certain problems when it comes to using it within a specific context. Thus, for spatialized simulations, it is necessary to use a language which can represent space and its constraints, such as the representations underlying Geographic Information Systems (GIS) [CHI 13].

2.3.1. *UML*

In the 1970s and 1980s, there was disagreement between those who believed in modeling data and those who believed in functional modeling. In this period, the use of flow and relational diagrams was generally considered to be mutually exclusive.

These two camps finally came to an agreement at around the end of the 1980s, and realized that most projects could benefit from the use of both model types. This reconciliation was followed by the emergence of numerous object-oriented analysis and modeling methods. However, each method had its own specific notation and definition of terms such as object, type and class. There was no common standard. The number of modeling languages increased from less than 10 to more than 50 between 1989 and 1994.

At the end of 1994, Grady Booch and Jim Rumbaugh announced their collaboration on the development of a *Unified Method*. They were later joined by Ivor Jacobson. In the end, after several years of experimentation with various notations and concepts, the group established a semantics for object-oriented concepts and agreed on a common notation on the basis of several of the notations and concepts with which they had experimented.

During 1996, the *Unified Method* developed into the UML. This new name was designed to emphasize the fact that UML was a modeling language and not a method. Its aim was to provide an expressive notation to define a semantics for implied concepts, and to leave the development process choice open. In the end, UML, developed from the combination of the three methods of object modeling, Object Modeling Technique (OMT), Booch and Object Oriented Software Engineering (OOSE), became an essential standard. Originally created to enable a developer to represent, specify, analyze and visualize the structure of a project in object-oriented programming, UML is today used in a large number of fields.

The development of UML is quite like the development of software in that there are *major* versions as well as improvements and extensions. The current version of UML is version 2.0 [OMG 05], which is divided into four parts:

- *UML 2.0 Superstructure*: diagrams used for modeling;
- *UML 2.0 Infrastructure*: foundations shared with MOF 2.0;
- *UML 2.0 OCL*: the language of constraints;

– *UML 2.0 Diagram Interchange*: makes it possible for exchange of diagrams between tools to take place (including from a graphic point of view).

UML Superstructure contains various types of diagrams:

– *six structure diagrams*: classes, objects, composite structures, components, deployments and packages;

– *three behavior diagrams*: activities, use cases and state machines;

– *four interaction diagrams*: sequence, communication, overview of interactions and timing.

2.3.1.1. *Formalization of model structure (static diagrams)*

This section presents the descriptive aspect of UML modeling. This is also known as the static part, or the structure. Here, we will only present two of the six structure diagrams: class diagram and object diagram. These are the diagrams that are most widely used in UML modeling. The class diagram is also used for meta-models (models of models), also known as ontology.

2.3.1.1.1. Class diagram

The UML class diagram allows us to model the structure, i.e. the static part of a system. Classes are essential in that they define an abstract type which will later make it possible to instance objects in the object diagram. Figure 2.2 presents the complete class diagram for our recurring example. We can see the class `Entity`. This class possesses the Boolean-type attribute `is-infected` and a function `infect()` which makes it possible to infect another `Entity`. Furthermore, this is a situated entity, and thus possesses the attribute `CurrentPosition` which is the location in which it is found, and the method `move`. In this diagram, classes are not isolated. There may be links between them, known as relations. There may also be relations between classes for various reasons:

– *Heritage* allows one class to inherit all of the attributes and methods of the mother class from which it is descended. This relation is represented by a bold arrow. Thus, the classes `Mosquito` and `Human` inherit the attribute `is-infected` from the class `Entity`. In addition to attributes and inherited methods, the class `Mosquito` also possesses the attribute `patient0`. This represents the mosquitoes that are contaminated at the initialization of the simulation, known as patient zero. This patient is represented by a Boolean which is true in this case and would otherwise be false.

– *Association* makes it possible to link two classes. It may be named and may contain information on multiplicity (cardinality) and navigation (direction of the relation). In the example, we have shown the association `Has contaminated` which is connected in a specific way, because it links `Entity` and itself (reflexive association) to indicate the chain of infection, showing who has `contaminated` and the `infected` entity. The *cardinality* "*" indicates that an entity can be the contaminator of zero or several entities, and the cardinality "`0..1`" at the other end of the association indicates that an `entity` has been infected by zero or a single contaminator. There are two special association cases: *aggregation* and *composition*. These are represented, respectively, by an empty and a filled-in diamond on the aggregate side. In our example, a composition relationship links the places (the class `Place`) to their `Territory` (aggregate).

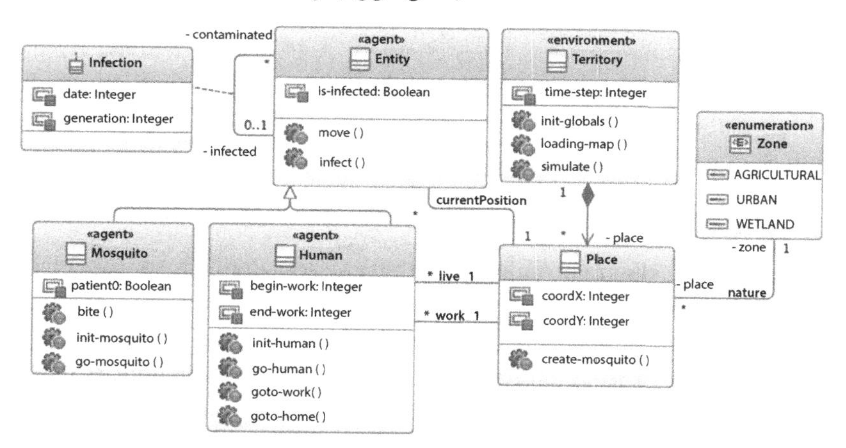

Figure 2.2. *Representation of the class diagram from the recurring example*

2.3.1.1.2. Representation of the recurring example with UML

In the UML model, we have grouped the common elements of the mobile entities (mosquitoes and humans) together in a class `Entity`. We represent the concept of contamination between entities with an association which has attributes, called “Infection”. The information does not appear in the diagram (because we have not presented the constraints), but an entity cannot be infected by an entity of a different subtype. For this reason, information regarding the source is maintained through association, and information concerning the date and generation is also maintained through the association attributes.

The `territory` is made up of elements from the class `Place` which corresponds to the various possible soil occupation zones, specified through the attribute “nature” in the class `Place`. This is an enumerated-type attribute, whose various modalities are specified in the class `Zone`. Furthermore, in our representation, the `Territory` also plays the role of environment for the system and contains the representation of time (`time-step`) in the simulation and the entire management part of the system. We find these same elements of simulation management for beginning the simulation after the various components have been initialized and the card has been charged. A `Place` is denoted by its coordinates, which represent the center of the zone. Initially, it needs to be possible to create infected mosquitoes. This is performed by the method `create-mosquito`.

2.3.1.1.3. Object diagram

The object diagram facilitates the classes defined in the class diagram to be instanced as real objects. This diagram is useful for giving an image of the state of the system at time t. In order to model the initial state of the system, for example, an object diagram is used. In Figure 2.3, we have represented three entities, two of which are mosquitoes (a zero patient and an uncontaminated mosquito) and the last one is a human. At time t, the communication chain is limited to the zero patient. It is possible to give object values to all or part of the attributes. In the example, we have not shown all of the objects and relations. For example, the agents are situated and they should be in a relation with the instances of the class `Place`. Furthermore, we have only represented one `Place1-3`.

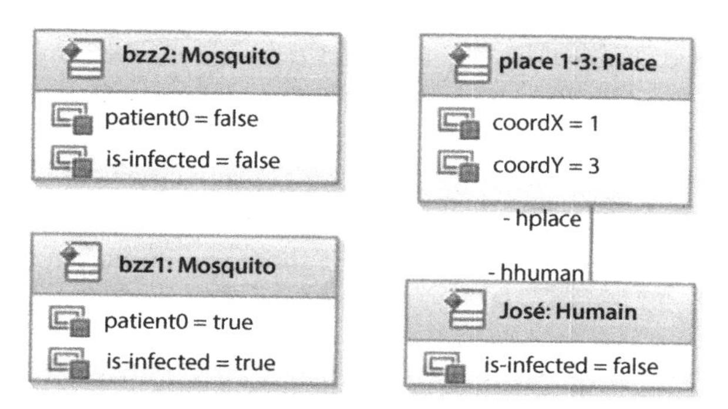

Figure 2.3. *UML object diagram*

2.3.1.1.4. Meta-model

A meta-model is a modeling language which makes it possible to describe another language, much like grammar which is used to describe real language. In UML, the class diagram represents all of the elements permitting the description of a UML model. This means that the language can represent or define itself by itself, and can also define a new framework for modeling. In this way, it becomes possible to extend or specialize UML, as suggested by the creators of AML. We will observe this in much detail in the section that follows.

2.3.1.2. *Formalization of model operation (dynamic diagrams)*

This section presents the analytical diagrams, which are also sometimes known as dynamic diagrams, because they enable the description of the dynamic aspect of the system. It brings together all of the behavior diagrams and the interaction diagrams. Of the seven possible diagrams, we will only present three diagrams here: activity diagram, state-transition diagram and sequence diagram. We will conclude by discussing the coherence verification features. Coherence verification can be carried out on the basis of meta-modeling elements, and using all of the information provided by the various diagrams.

2.3.1.2.1. Activity diagram

The UML activity diagram is one of the diagrams which allow the modeler to represent the behavior of an object using nodes (of activity, action, control or objects) and transitions. Activity diagrams are suitable for specifying sequential or concurrent treatments. They provide an overview of the control flows from one activity to the other. In Figure 2.4, we show activity linked to the movement of a mosquito. This can be seen as an activity related to the method `go-mosquito`. Thus, the mosquito moves about and, if there is a human in the area, it bites them.

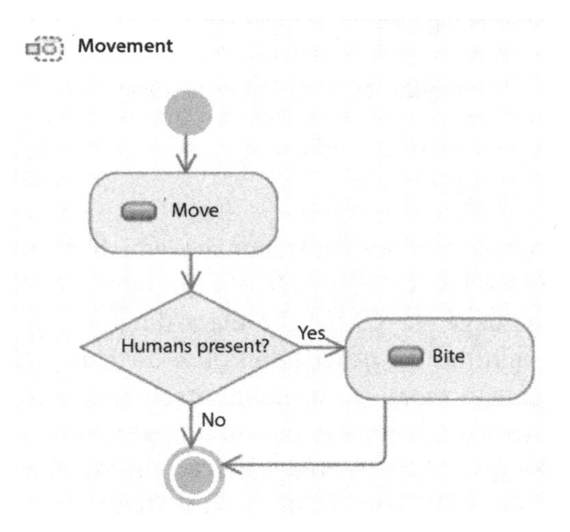

Figure 2.4. *UML activity diagram*

2.3.1.2.2. State-transition diagram

The role of the state-transition diagram is to represent finite-state automata (i.e. entities that are characterized by a set of states which, at any given moment, are in a specific state) in the form of a set of transitions, which may or may not be labeled. A state is characterized by the value of the attributes of a system at a time t. A transition represents the transition from one state to another; such a transition is generally triggered by an event. This triggering may be automatic, when the event that triggers the change is unspecified. It is also possible to condition the triggering of a transition using *guards*: these are Boolean expressions, expressed in natural language or in *Object Constraint Language (OCL)*, for example. In Figure 2.5, we show the lifecycle of a mosquito. It begins its life and moves around until it dies or is killed by a human. If this does not happen, it lands on a person and biting them each time is possible. During the exchange of fluid, one or the other of the entities involved may become infected with malaria. It should be noted that the mosquito never rests and as soon as it is in the same place as a human, it will bite the human.

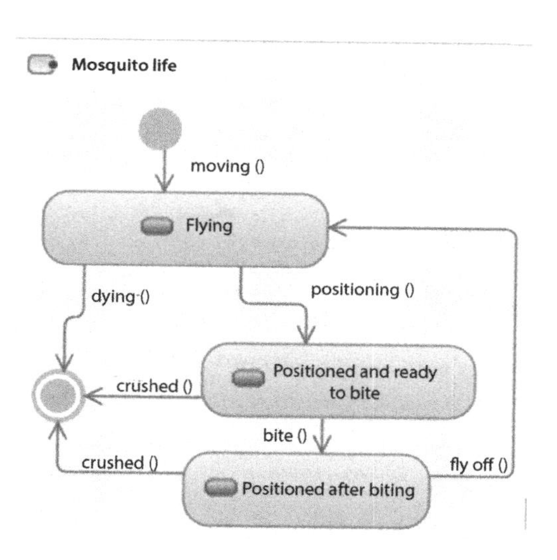

Figure 2.5. *UML state-transition diagram*

2.3.1.2.3. Sequence diagram

Sequence diagrams are used to represent interactions between the modeled system's entities (actors or objects). It makes exchanges (synchronized or non-synchronized) visible. There is a composition language available, which means that parallel treatments can be expressed using interaction frameworks which may contain algorithms. In Figure 2.6, an exchange is shown between the three entities of the object diagram, showing a contamination cycle.

2.3.1.2.4. Consistency checking

As with any representation, it is important to check the consistency of the model. Currently, there are tools available which can help make these checks, such as ATL. ATL[1] is a model transformation language, which works at the meta-model level, and has been in development since 2003 at the University of Nantes. It aims to make it possible to express model transformation rules and to execute them. Since January 2007, ATL has been part of the Eclipse *Model-to-Model* (M2M) section, and thus it is recommended for use as a tool for transforming one model into another. In addition, it is integrated as a *plugin* to the design platform Eclipse. To achieve this, a meta-model needs to be defined, which enables the representation of a model, as shown in Figure 2.7.

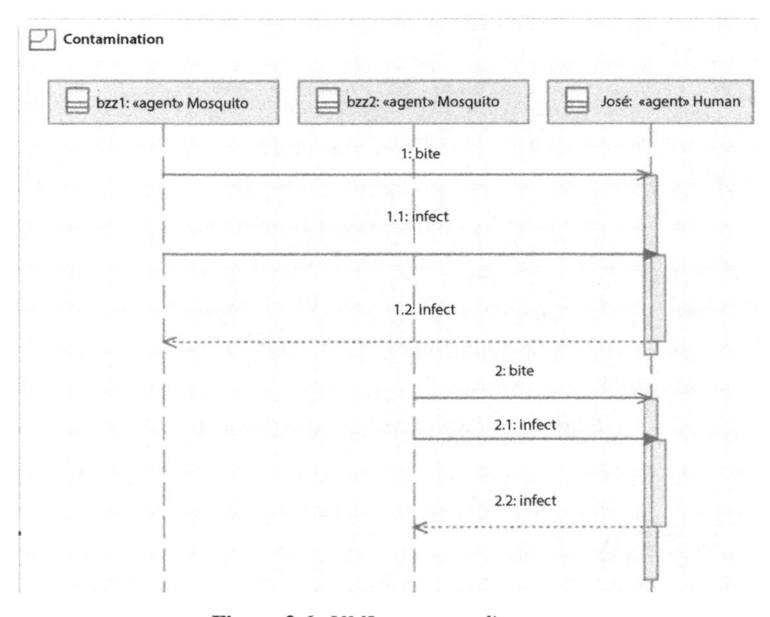

Figure 2.6. *UML sequence diagram*

This meta-model contains a meta-class `Problem` and a meta-list `Severity`. This meta-model allows us to instance problems detected

1 ATL is an abbrevation of ATLAS *Transformation Language*.

in the model in order to identify their source (attribute `location`), description and severity. Their severity lets us know whether the error is critical for code generation. If this is the case, then no code is generated. On the other hand, if there are only warnings and not critical errors detected, then code generation takes place.

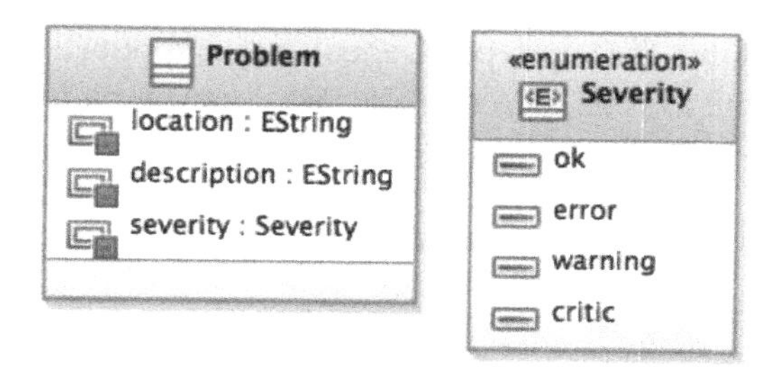

Figure 2.7. *Problem meta-model*

Modeling like this can be carried out using standard UML; however, when it is conducted in this way, it would be initially difficult to understand and could not be used as a tool for communication.

This is why the following section discusses the AML extension which has been added to UML.

2.3.2. *AML*

Since the UML language is very general and is oriented toward object programming, much work has been conducted on the development of a suitable graphic formalism, which might perhaps even be dedicated to the agent paradigm.

The development, since the mid-1990s, of MAS design methods (e.g. Gaia [ZAM 03], TROPOS [BRE 04] or Prometheus [PAD 02]) has naturally been accompanied by the development of various dedicated graphic modeling languages (e.g. Agent UML (AUML) [BAU 01b] or AML [CER 07]) which are more or less based on UML, and which aim to supplement UML with concepts specific to the domain of MAS. Of these languages, we will be particularly concerned with

AML [TRE 05, CER 07]. AML is a semi-formal language for modeling and documenting applications based on MAS. It was developed as an extension to UML 2.0 [OMG 03]. The main aims of the designers of this language are to include and bring together the preexisting concepts from various agent architectures (in particular, *Beliefs Desires Intentions* (BDIs)), and preexisting languages and modeling methods. Thus, AML seeks to be suitable for any type of agent-based applications and to be independent from the methodology and development platform used and from the case to which these are being applied.

2.3.2.1. *Formalizing model structure (agent-group-role)*

2.3.2.1.1. Agents

This section emphasizes the description of the model structure, which in UML is conducted mainly by using class diagrams. In contrast to UML, with which only classes may be defined, by using AML we can refine and represent various types of entities involved in MAS and agent-based simulations. Figure 2.8 is a fragment of a complete AML meta-model. It presents the hierarchy of AML entities on a general level. A more detailed description will not be given here. Similarly, the concepts and formalisms used in the structure model are lower level concepts. For example, we will directly use the concept of agent without reference to the fact that it is a specialization of *AutonomousEntityType* which is descended from the entities *BehavioredSemiEntityType*, *MentalSemiEntityType*, etc.

The principal entities are the agents (autonomous entities which can perceive, interact and have a certain behavior within their environment; these also have mental attitudes and social abilities), the resources (entities without their own autonomous behavior, which are used by agents; their availability is an important characteristic) and the environments (the entities within which the other entities develop). AML also makes it possible to define the entities' role and organization, which are linked to the social capacities of the agents. These two concepts are close to those presented in the Agent, Group, Role (AGR) model [FER 04]. An organization also means that a set of agents which are considered at a higher level as a single agent can be represented.

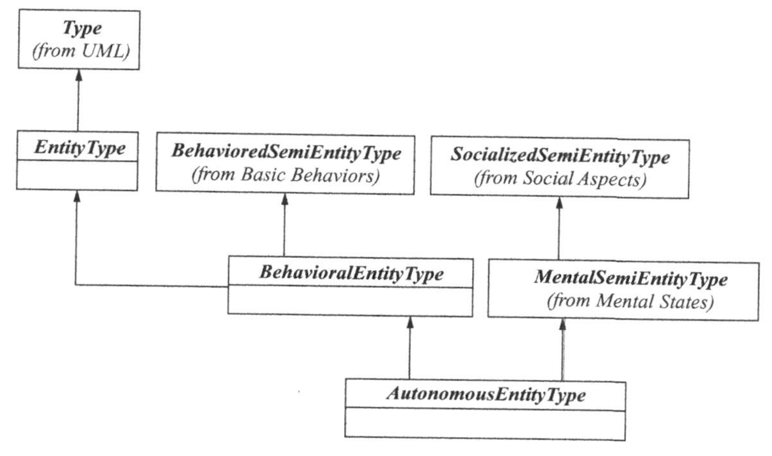

Figure 2.8. *Entity hierarchy in AML*

Each entity is represented, graphically speaking, by a UML class with a stereotype unique to the entity and/or an icon, which specifies to which type the entity belongs. Figure 2.9 depicts the entity. It is characterized by a list of attributes, a list of operations, the elements which composes it (the field part in UML 2), and behaviors. The *parts* are particularly useful for specifying which agents make up an organization. Behaviors are complex actions composed of operations or perhaps even other behaviors. The way in which these are conjugated for different types of entities is shown in Figure 2.10.

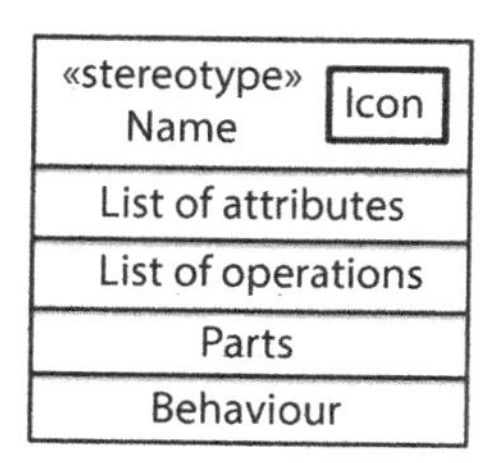

Figure 2.9. *Description of an entity in AML*

Finally, the AML formalism is very open and it is possible to describe the same element of the system within the modeled system in several ways. Thus, in the description of the formalism that follows, we will detail the methodological choices that we have made. We will present AML modeling based on the AGR approach.

Type of entity	Stereotype	Icon
Agent	«agent»	
Environment	«environment»	
Resources	«resources»	
Organization	«organization unit»	
Role	«entity role»	

Figure 2.10. *Stereotype and icon for each type of entity*

The agent is the central element of the modeling. At the lowest level, it is described as in Figure 2.9. At higher levels, it is possible to refer to an agent that has already been described, simply by using its name and the *agent* icon.

An agent is identified by a name, and for a given agent there may be several instances, and thus several agents of the same *type*. It is, therefore, important to make a distinction between the agent *type* (which is close to the UML class concept) and the agent itself, which will be present within the system (instance).

As shown in Figure 2.9, following this we find the list of agent attributes and the list of its operations (the actions that it can carry out). The *parts* part of the agent will always remain empty within this chapter. In fact, for the purposes of this work, we consider that an agent cannot be made up of other agents (as is the case in an implementation in NetLogo)[2]. The final part, *behaviors,* contains the *fragment behaviors*. These make it possible to describe the *complex* behaviors that the agent

2 In contrast to NetLogo, other agent-based modeling and simulation platforms (such as GAMA [GRI 13] or Cormas [LEP 12]) allow for the definition of agents as being made up of other agents.

can accomplish by breaking down them into several simpler actions. *Fragment behaviors* can also be used to describe reusable actions by other agents. As described in section 2.3.2.2.2, this part of the agent is fulfilled only if the agent is able to conduct complex actions. This concept will be described in much detail in the interaction model.

2.3.2.1.2. Groups

The concept of group does not exist as such in AML. In its place are *organization units*. These are used in AML to describe organizational structures, environments which specify social arrangements between the entities in terms of interaction, roles, constraints, etc. This approach is relatively close to the notion of group as it is introduced into the AGR model. As a result, we have decided to use *OrganizationUnitType* to describe the groups of our MAS. In the same way as for agents, it is essential to make a distinction between the group as a structure and the group as an instance.

In the AGR approach, the group is an abstract notion, allowing us to bring together the agents which share characteristics or resources. As it stands, the AML formalism shown in Figure 2.9 is too rich. In fact, a group, as defined in the AGR model, has neither attributes nor methods. This formalism nonetheless allows us to model the notion of an agentified group.

Our model must actually be able to describe the fact that a set of agents may be considered as a unique entity at a higher level of abstraction. We represent this in AML using *OrganizationUnitTypes* and a specific role of *leader* for each group. This role will always have the name of leader followed by the name of the group to which it is attached.

In a model, a group will have its empty *attribute list*, *operation list* and *behavior* parts. The *parts* part is the only one that will be full: this is the part that makes it possible to describe the group's structure, that is to describe what it is made up of. A group may be made up of agents, other groups or possibly both. In this part the various roles which the group's agent may play are also found, with the specific role of *Leader* which is present in each group.

2.3.2.1.3. Roles

According to the AGR model, a role belongs to a group. In our structure model, we represent this by placing all of a group's roles in the group's *parts* part.

In AML, a role is described as shown in Figure 2.9. The concept of role is as defined by Ferber [FER 98] for the AGR mode. Thus, a role cannot be made up of other roles, and for this reason, the *parts* part is always empty. The three other parts may or may not be empty, depending on whether the role gives access to attributes, simple methods or complex methods.

The systematic existence of the specific *Leader* role for each agentified group should be noted. For this role, the *attribute list* part (respectively, *operation list*) allows us to describe the list of attributes (respectively, methods) of the agentified group, that is the agent playing the role of the group leader. The *behaviors* part makes it possible to describe the complex actions that the agentified group (and thus the agent playing the role of *Leader*) is capable of carrying out. As with a more classical role, these parts may be empty.

According to the definition of role in the AGR model, two more things need to be modeled: the fact that some roles require prerequisites to be carried out, and that some roles may make it possible to direct other agents. As AML is based on UML 2 and is compatible with it, the prerequisites may be described using OCL constraints on the relation of *"playing a role"*; the graphic representation of this is shown in Figure 2.12. The hierarchy between the roles is expressed using links between the roles, as shown in Figure 2.11.

There are two types of relationships between entities: "peer-to-peer" relationships and "master/slave" relationships. There are three types of links between two roles in order to show these types of relationships. "Peer-to-peer" (a) relationships are shown by black and white triangles. These "peer-to-peer" relationships are the relationships between entities of the same social status and that have the same level of authority.

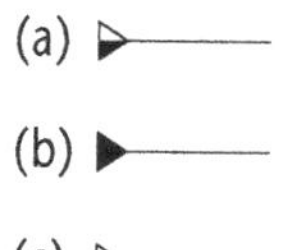

Figure 2.11. *Types of link between roles in AML*

Relationships of the "master/slave" type are shown by the links (b) and (c). The link (b), a black triangle, represents the leader (or *superOrdored* in AML). A leader can control the behavior of the agents under its command. On the other side of the relationship is the link (c), made up of a white triangle, which represents the subordinate. An (a)-type link is always associated with another (a) link, and the (b)-type link is always associated with a (c)-type link.

Now that we can link the roles with each other, let us see how we can link the roles to agents.

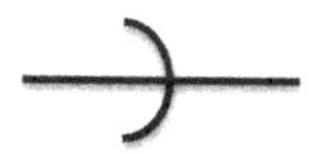

Figure 2.12. *Playing a role in AML*

Figure 2.12 shows the association between a role and an agent, which means that the agent plays the role in question. The half-circle faces toward the role. We can also specify the role's multiplicity, that is the maximum number of agents which can play this role in this group at the same time.

We have now shown the three essential components of the AGR model, which are the agents, the groups and the roles. There are, however, two further entities which are used in the structure model: environment and resources.

2.3.2.1.4. Environment and resources

The environment is a logical and physical entity which surrounds all the system's entities. Its AML representation is shown in Figure 2.9. There is a maximum of one unique environment in the structure model. The environment may not be present if it does not contribute anything to the model.

We have assumed that the resources are connected to the environment, as this is the global entity in our system. Thus, the *parts* part, renamed *Resource List,* contains the system's resource(s). The three other parts of the environment may be used. From the environment, we only consider the system's global variables (such as temperature) and the operations which make it possible to modify these.

The resources are physical entities (for example, raw materials in a production system) or computerized entities (for example, a database). *Simple* resources are accounted for in our system: these are not made up of other elements. As such, a resource will never have any *parts* in its representation (see Figure 2.9). A resource may possess one or several attributes (such as a capacity). Finally, in the case of an information technology (IT) resource, it is considered that this may contain simple or complex operations. In the case of a knowledge bank, for example, these operations may be used by agents which have access to it.

2.3.2.1.5. Representation of the recurrent example with AML

In the AML representation of the recurrent example, we have chosen to take the opposite of the UML representation for the formalization of the link between infections. In fact, because AML allows us to adopt the AGR approach, we have decided to use this to represent the infection. Here, we have two roles. The first role is concerned with the `contaminator`. This is a specific role within a group, which allows us to find out the source of the contamination for all of the infections of the group `Infection`. The second role is concerned with the `infected` entity. It indicates, when an entity is infected, the date of the infection and where it came from. It also makes it possible to acquire the infection capacity (operation `infect()`) and for it to become, in turn, a contaminator of the group `Infection`. The second group `patient0` makes it possible to manage mosquitoes that are infected at the system's initial state. As for the rest of the system, the same elements are present as with the UML model. One small variation is that complex behaviors based on other operations or system behavior, such as `goto-work`, which uses `movement` to go from a specific `Place` to another, from home to work, can be highlighted (using the circular arrow).

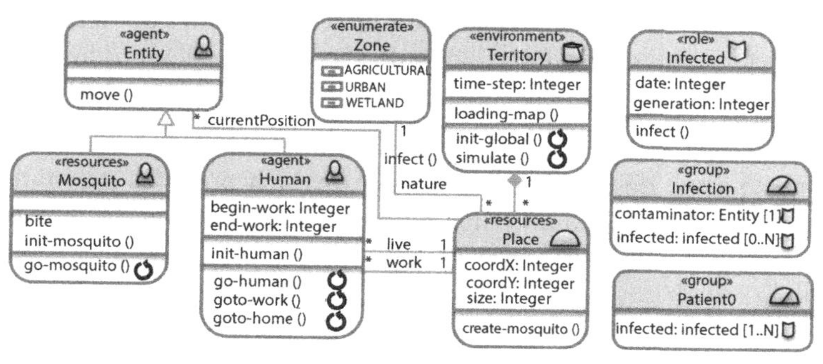

Figure 2.13. *AGR representation with AML for the recurrent example*

This concludes the descriptive part; let us now focus on the analytical part, which contains the interactions and the actions.

2.3.2.2. *Formalization of model operation (interactions and actions)*

In this section, we will present the modeling elements which allow us to describe the dynamic part of the models, in particular interactions and actions.

2.3.2.2.1. Interaction model

There are two types of interaction: interactions between an agent and one or several other agents, and interactions between an agent and its environment, which is where the agent and its resources are based. Here, we will consider several interactions, which can be classified into five major types:

– *communication*: three types of communication may be listed: sending messages, using a blackboard and communication with markers (such as pheromones). A message may also have several consequences for the agent: it may change its state, it may make it send a reply or it may make it carry out a particular action;

– *reaction*: a distinction is made between actions and agents, and the effects that these actions produce. An action carried out may have consequences on one or on several agents, as well as on the environment;

– *cooperative and/or complex actions*: some actions cannot be carried out by one agent alone, and require cooperation between several agents. Also, some complex actions may be broken down into several simpler actions. This is especially the case for the actions known as *at a high level of abstraction*, which will be discussed later in more detail;

– *scheduling*: due to the action model, which provides the starting and ending dates for each of the actions carried out, we can check if a scheduling is possible or not. Additionally, we can produce a naive scheduling if we are lacking this. In this way, it is possible to check that an agent does not complete an action before one which precedes it has been completed (by it or another agent);

– *knowledge and learning*: agents are able to memorize, learn and modify their basic knowledge as the system develops. As this part is in itself a very important subject, these two concepts are very minimal in our model, and their further development is one of the possible ways in which the system may develop.

2.3.2.2.2. Actions

The AML formalism is open with regard to modeling choices, and thus the same model, even a very simple one, may be described in several ways with this formalism. We will, therefore, specify and detail certain modeling choices.

It is possible to describe the actions and capacities of agents on different levels. Therefore, the choice of modeling is made on the basis of the type of action. The discriminating factor is the fact that there is no *special* precondition or postcondition. We consider a condition to be special if it does not relate uniquely to the capacity and knowledge of the agent regarding the accomplishment of the action.

Thus, a simple action is an action without any special preconditions or postconditions. It will be described directly in the organizational part of the agent.

2.3.2.2.3. Complex actions

Cooperative actions and complex actions are described in the structure model using the AML concept *fragmentBehavior*.

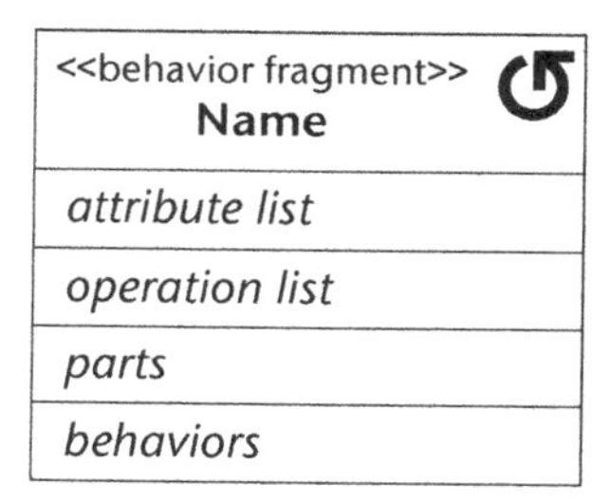

Figure 2.14. *Description of a behavior in AML*

Figure 2.14 shows what is known in AML as *fragment of behavior*. These are used in two cases: for describing behaviors which could be reused and for breaking down a complex behavior into several simpler behaviors. In the first case, this means that we make several behaviors correspond to a fragment of behavior. In this way, an agent which has this fragment of behavior has these operations. We do not use them as they are, but rather we use them to describe the actions that may be described as *complex*. Also, the parts *attribute list* and *parts* always remain empty. If the complex action may be divided into several simple actions, these will appear in the part *operation list*. If the complex action may be divided into several actions which are also complex in themselves, then these will appear in the part *behaviors*.

2.3.3. *UML versus AML*

UML is very widely used. Its expressiveness means that it is a modeling and communication system which is suitable for our needs.

It can be used alongside other languages and/or formalisms, or can also have extensions added to it as necessary. OCL also allows us to express the properties of the system.

The UML approach in an MAS implementation can lead to additional complexity. In particular, this occurs when the model needs to include those MAS paradigms that it does not allow to be suggested natively (such as AGR). In this case, it is necessary to redefine these or to add information to link these with the implementations.

The risk that this approach leads to is the loss of illustrative and intuitive aspects. Thus, the complexity is not due to the system under study, but rather it is due to the modeling elements.

For example, how can the different levels of abstraction of which a system is comprised of be expressed? How can the autonomy of entities at each of these levels be expressed, with perception, knowledge, capacities and access to various resources?

Obviously, AML formalism, which has been defined for this very purpose, does offer these concepts. Those who do not like it argue that it is unfortunately not widespread. This comes partially from the fact that there are only a few tools which support the use of this language.

It is important to note that AML is extremely powerful and modular; this is in part due to the fact that it is descended from UML. However, AML is not easy to grasp as a whole. In addition, all of its complexity is not necessarily useful in the context of agent-based simulation. In this chapter, we have not presented an exhaustive list of all the concepts which exist in AML, but rather we have limited ourselves to those that seem relevant to the domain of agent-based simulation, and which have been used in the example. For a more complete overview of the concepts available in AML, the readers may refer to the reference work on AML [CER 07].

In this chapter, we will be concerned with the link between the models, in particular between UML and the tool NetLogo.

2.3.4. *Other variations of UML*

Although there are other ways of modeling MAS, these methods are for the most part focused on a particular field, and cannot be used in a more general case. However, we should highlight several of the works which propose a modeling or specification language: Agent Communication Language specification from the Fondation for Intelligent Physical Agent (FIPA ACL) [FOU 97], Knowledge Query and Manipulation Language (KQML) [FIN 94], Taming Agents and Objects (TAO) [SIL 03], Object-Process Methodology for Multi-Agent System (OPM/MAS) [STU 03], AUML [ODE 00, BAU 01a] and [ODE 01].

The most developed and successful of these approaches is the AUML approach. AUML [ODE 00, BAU 01a] suggests mechanisms for modeling interaction protocols in MAS. In order to achieve this, a new diagram class has been introduced in UML: protocol diagrams. These extend UML state and sequence diagrams in several ways. The specific extensions introduce the agents' roles and their simultaneous execution sequences, extend the messages' semantics and model the interaction protocols.

AUML was put forward and accepted for inclusion in the standard FIPA'99. However, AUML does not offer a graphic solution to the problem of agentified groups.

2.3.5. *Formalizing changes in behavior in UML*

The concept of role which we outlined in the AGR approach is also useful for specifying a behavior which will change over time at the level of the same entity. Although this concept is directly available in AML, it is not when the modeler decides to use a UML formalization. In this section, we will show how modelers can structure their model to show changes in behavior; this is achieved through the use of a *Design Pattern* such as Actor-Role [COA 97].

The Actor-Role design pattern involves representing the attributes and actions linked to a behavior within a specific class (the class role), and which is associated with the Agent class. As Bommel explains: "when we concern ourselves with the representation of humans or animals which can evolve, transform, and change behavior throughout their life, it is useful [...] to associate a specific behavior with the agent that plays this role, [...] in order to allow it to change role (and thus behavior) over time" [BOM 09]. In this way, when an entity changes behavior, no major modification needs to be done to the entity, and all that needs to be done is to associate a new behavior to it. When this logic is applied to spatial entities, we more readily refer to state rather than role. The application of this pattern thus consists of specifying a distinctive class to which the spatial entity pertains, along with the actions and attributes linked to a certain state. This structure proves itself to be particularly relevant in the modeling of occupations of space, to which states bring specific dynamics. It also makes it possible to organize these dynamics clearly, and thus to communicate more effectively with regard to the content of the model.

We propose to extend our recurrent example to present the application of the Actor-Role pattern to the dynamics of spatial entities. Thus, we will illustrate its use on a well-known case in the study of change in soil occupation.

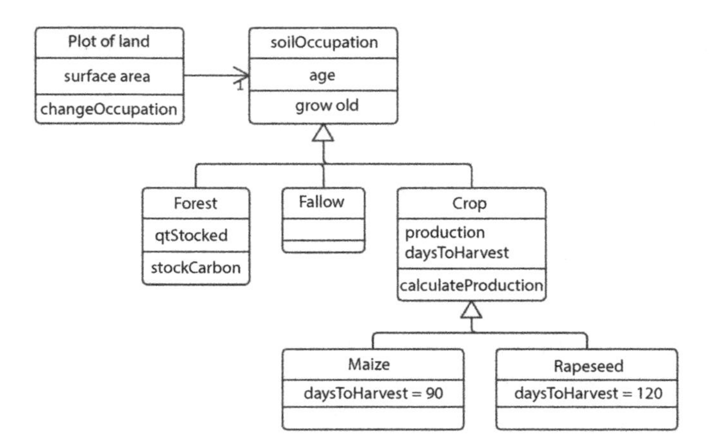

Figure 2.15. *A class diagram for modeling changes in soil occupation (figure adapted from [LE 05])*

In the example in Figure 2.15, the Agent-Role pattern is found at the level of the association between the plot of land and its occupation of the soil. In this model, an instance of plot of land does not change over time: its surface area remains constant. However, its soil occupation may change. Several types of soil occupation are possible, each of which possesses its own dynamics. A soil occupation of the type cultivation (specialization) can calculate production once its age has reached the number of days before harvest. As for a forest, within this model it has the function of a carbon sink. Using this structure, the operation of a third agent, which uses for cultivation purposes a plot of land previously used as forest, consists of replacing the association of the plot of land to an instance of the class forest with an association to an instance of the class Rapeseed, for example.

Although this architecture is clearly advantageous in terms of its clarity, implementing it within NetLogo can be difficult because only one level of inheritance is possible in this platform, and this level of inheritance is reserved for the *turtle* class. In practice, the modeler is often obliged to specify the attributes and code the operations of all the types of occupation (or roles) for a class, and then to add the conditions which ensure that the entity cannot execute methods which correspond to another type than the one it belongs to at the current time. Also, the modeler needs to ensure that the attributes of a type are correctly reinitialized each time the soil occupation changes.

The above discussion illustrates the difference, however excellent the design, between a model which makes it possible to take all of the paradigms into account and the reality of implementation. This implementation needs to be conducted in an environment or using languages which require a certain vigilance regarding the concepts, or even profound adaptations of these, such as the absence of the concept of objects.

2.4. Description and documentation of agent models

This section addresses the question of describing and documenting a multiagent model. Section 2.4.1 will remind the readers of the roles that the documentation and standardization of a model fulfill, which are, among many others, making it easier to understand and explain the structure and operation of the model, to spread information about it and communicate about it with others, to compare it, replicate it, to use it for other purposes and to reuse it, and to ensure that it is complete. Section 2.4.2 presents a protocol in detail, which has become a *de facto* standard for describing multiagent models: the ODD protocol [GRI 06, GRI 10]). A brief history of this protocol will be given, outlining the goals that underlied its creation. The various elements which define the ODD protocol (in its revised version) are then discussed: (1) the model's aim, (2) entities, state variables and scales, (3) general operation of the model and process scheduling, (4) underlying design concepts, (5) initialization, (6) input data and (7) submodels. Section 2.4.3 will then illustrate, using various examples, ODD implementation, while highlighting frequently occurring usage or interpretation errors. This section also shows the link which exists between the diagrams created during the model's design phase and the protocol's components.

2.4.1. *Why describe and document?*

The definitions of models and modeling given by Jean-Louis Le Moigne [LE 90] emphasize intelligibility as one of the most important properties of a model:

– A model is an intelligible, artificial, symbolic representation of situations in which we are involved.

– Modeling is the act of intentional development and construction of models, which are likely to render intelligible a phenomenon perceived as complex, and to amplify the reasoning of the actor by projecting a deliberated intervention within the phenomenon; the particular aim of this reasoning is to anticipate the consequence of possible plans of action.

In this way, a model builds an organized set of knowledge which represents a complex system. Questions are being asked about this system; its current operation needs to be understood, and also, possibly, the way that it has developed in the past. Also, its future possible development needs to be known, along with how it is impacted by various scenarios, and this development needs to be influenced to lead it toward some desirable outcome.

The documentation of a model thus becomes fundamental in the mobilization, understanding and sharing of the knowledge which it brings, and the efficient use of this knowledge. The documentation must make it possible to describe the model in an instructive, explicit and unambiguous manner, which is relevant for as wide a public as possible.

2.4.1.1. *Instructive description of knowledge obtained using the model*

The instructive character of the documentation of a model is in its capacity to address progressively the model's different levels of description, from the most general down to the most detailed. This is because we cannot directly go into the detail or the code of a complex model. As a result, it is essential to have an overview to understand the model's context and aims, to understand what the model is doing before understanding how it is made, and then to focus little-by-little on its global components, and their interactions. Following this, we can progressively move on to the detail of the manipulated data and modeled processes. It is precisely to this end that the ODD protocol was developed. This protocol will be described in the section 2.4.2.

2.4.1.2. *Explaining the structure and operation of the model without ambiguity*

For a model considered stable, none of the aspects should remain implicit or vague to the extent where a knowledge gap exists in understanding the model or rendering it operational. This is a difficulty that frequently occurs when a model is being conceptually refined so that it can be transformed into an operational computerized model. It is this stage which generally makes gaps, ambiguities or incoherencies apparent, which then require a return to the conceptual model and the further redetailing or redefinition of certain aspects of this model. There is a sort of dialectics between the conceptual model and the computerized model which means that several cycles are necessary in order to elicit the knowledge carried by the models progressively. The main difficultly clearly lies in the manner in which the model's documentation takes the organization of the modeled system into account, the interactions between its components and the properties which emerge from an organizational level in relation to the underlying level(s), all the while managing a record and justification for the decisions taken along the path for attaining a stable version of the model.

In the context of this modeling process, ambiguity takes on a particular character. At the beginning of the model design process, it may be useful to accept some ambiguity in order to avoid undue focus or time spent considering a point which might lead to problems between those parties involved in the modeling. However, it is also important to remove the ambiguity later in the refinement of the design by specifying the conditions which lead to accepting or refusing it. Temporary ambiguity may thus contribute flexibility which is useful for the modeling process, particularly in the case of a process which is being conducted together by several parties.

2.4.1.3. *Taking the multiplicity of model users into account*

The documentation of a model must be relevant to its users at different stages of its development and implementation. Therefore, the model must be made comprehensible to the various stakeholders in the modeling process, which may comprise people with specific knowledge bases (such as scientific, institutional, technical or empirical) and discipline-related interests (thematic or computer-related). A model must be understandable to the various types of users who contributed to its development, as well as to people other than the initial stakeholders, who may wish to use or further develop the model. This involves several levels of documentation, which are not necessarily hierarchical. The use of different forms of documentation (written, graphic, diagram, video, etc.) may also favor the comprehensibility of the model to a varied public. It is necessary to take several points of view into account when building a model of a complex system, and similarly the documentation of a model must make it possible to observe and understand these different points of view.

2.4.1.4. *Including mobilized meta-knowledge when building the model*

The documentation must also explain why certain aspects have been included in the model, and why others have not. Grimm [GRI 99] has remarked that one of the advantages of individual-centered models is that they can integrate empirical knowledge, with all the difficulty of defining the criteria making it possible to decide whether certain empirical knowledge should or should not be fed into the model. It is a requirement of relevant documentation that it should make these criteria clear.

Thus, documenting a model involves more than the mere description of the knowledge it contains; it also requires the description of the meta-knowledge which led to the elicitation of this knowledge (i.e. the model's hypotheses).

2.4.1.5. *Making it possible to replicate the model*

The documentation associated with a model should make it possible to replicate the model. Starting from an analysis of several examples of replication, Bommel [BOM 09] highlighted the inadequacies of descriptions of many models, with particularly weaknesses in specifications relative to the management of time and interactions. He considered this stage of replication to be necessary, and that it should be executed as far as possible by modelers other than the initial designers to enhance the reliability of the simulators and allow a true refutation of models. Literature on the topic has only recently become preoccupied with this question in relation to multiagent models [GRI 06]. A particular reason for this is that their usage has undergone considerable development in several disciplines which handle complex systems. By suggesting a protocol such as ODD, a first stage is available which makes it easier to write and read multiagent models, resulting in a description of these systems which is sufficiently comprehensive to allow them to be replicated. The first revision of this protocol was published in 2010 [GRI 10], and had a basis in the experiences of the many researchers who had begun to use the protocol.

2.4.1.6. *Working alongside the model development cycle*

The question of writing and reading a model has a particular connection with two aspects of its lifecycle: first, how the creation of the model can be facilitated (effective writing), and second, how to facilitate its use and integration into other models (effective reading). These two aspects are not separated in time, but rather are closely linked to each other. Indeed, the writing phase presupposes the involvement of a certain number of people who must be able to share the state of development of the model as it develops, and thus must be able to read the model as effectively as possible. Similarly, once the model is considered to have reached a certain level of completion, being able to read it conditions the writing of new developments of it, or its integration into more comprehensive models.

Complex models can often be divided into a set of submodels which mutually interact, each of which makes up a model in itself, potentially of a nature different from the others. The integration of several models thus requires good description of each of them, which in particular renders the definition of information communication interfaces between them as effective as possible.

2.4.1.7. *Developing relevant forms for visualizing a model*

How can the most relevant possible forms of visualization be developed for making the constitutive processes of the model clear, and for presenting, analyzing and interpreting outputs from the model simulations? Visualization is not only involved in making the conceptual model operational, but it also makes it possible to elicit knowledge for building the conceptual model [BEC 03]. Thus, developing a graphic visualization of a mathematical law associated with a submodel makes it possible to explain and visualize the effects of this law in light of various hypotheses, and, using this as a starting point, to calibrate the model more effectively, or even to alter its structure when required. In this way, comprehension is enhanced by making it possible to find the basis for the results, and to examine the chain of causalities and interactions which led to these, to be able to see the reason for them, and thus to gain a better understanding of the system under study. Graphic interfaces promote communication between the partners, and can potentially serve to mediate if there is some difficulty in reaching a shared vision. They contribute to the transparency of models, that is to say they help them to be understood quite easily by a wide range of people [WAL 77].

Analysis and understanding of the behavior of models is one of the key factors in their validation. Here, the word "validation" is taken to mean "acceptable for its intended use because it meets specified performance requirements" [RYK 96] and "are well designed and justifiable" [SIN 00].

Visualizing a model entails visualizing the knowledge that it contains, and in particular the knowledge pertaining to its dynamics and organization: static documentation is insufficient for these. In other words, the visualization of a model may be considered to be a dynamic form of documentation. UML and AML, which we have previously discussed, are very good examples of this.

2.4.2. *How can models be described and documented?*

In response to the recurrent difficulty of obtaining complete and homogenous documentation of multiagent models, a protocol has recently been suggested for the description of these models in a more formal manner. This is the ODD protocol suggested by Grimm *et al.* [GRI 06]. ODD offers a predefined documentation structure, which means that modelers can specify an aim for the model, its components and the way in which the properties specific to the MAS are taken into account (e.g. emergence or adaptation). The first version of the ODD protocol was published in 2006 [GRI 06]. After testing within the research community, a revision was offered in 2010 [GRI 10, POL 10, RAI 11]. Today, ODD has become a *de facto* standard for describing and communicating an agent model. It has been adopted by many modelers (e.g. [POL 08, NAI 10, CAI 13]).

2.4.2.1. *ODD protocol components*

ODD describes a multiagent model by making a distinction between three major parts (Table 2.1): the elements that provide an overview of the model, the design concepts and the model details. We will present each of these elements below in the order recommended by the protocol.

2.4.2.2. *Overview*

The first part of ODD aims to provide a synoptic vision of the modeled system, from the point of view of its structure as well as its dynamics. It is made up of three main elements.

ODD (in English)		*ODD (in French)*	
Overview	1. Purpose	Vue d'ensemble	1. Objectif
	2. Entities, state variables and scale		2. Entités, variables d'état, échelle
	3. Process overview and scheduling		3. Processus et ordonnancement
Design concepts	4. Design concepts – Basic principles – Emergence – Adaptation – Objectives – Learning – Prediction – Sensing – Interaction – Stochasticity – Collectives – Observation	Conception	4. Eléments de conception – Principes – Émergence – Adaptation – Objectifs – Apprentissage – Prédiction – Perception – Interaction – Stochasticité – Coopération / Agrégation – Observation
Details	5. Initialization	Détails	5. Initialisation
	6. Input data		6. Données d'entrée
	Submodels		7. Sous-modèles

Table 2.1. *ODD protocol components divided into three categories (as per Grimm et al. [GRI 06, GRI 10])*

2.4.2.2.1. Purpose

The purpose of the model is indicated in a concise but precise manner. What is it for? What is the modeling question that is being addressed? The protocol component defines the "What?".

2.4.2.2.2. Entities, state variables and scale

Once the purpose of the model has been declared, its various components are specified. Which entities are represented? What are the attributes that characterize these entities? What spatial and temporal scales are used? In other words, "of what" is the model made?

The entities involve all the categories of the model (agents and groups of agents, spatial entities and global environment). These are described in terms of properties, known as state variables in ODD, which have values that may or may not evolve during the simulation (e.g. an agent's name, the behavior strategy of a group of agents, the modality of soil occupation of a plot or the global rate of harvesting of a resource). The initial values are provided at the model's initialization. These state variables (quantitative, nominal qualitative or ordinal) should not include derived or aggregate variables, whose values result from a combination or a calculation conducted by using other variables (e.g. total quantity of food consumed during the simulation, average animal density per hectare or distance to the nearest neighbor).

As for the choice of spatial and temporal scales, this involves, on the one hand, specifying the spatial resolution of the patches or the area actually covered by the patch and, on the other hand, the temporal resolution or the real duration represented by a time-step in the model. The temporal horizon is also specified (duration or planned length of the simulation).

2.4.2.2.3. Process overview and scheduling

Following the structure, the model dynamic is described. How do the entities behave at each time-step? How does the environment change? What order is the simulation organized into? The set of processes and the way they are scheduled are mentioned.

Processes are designated by verbs (e.g. moving, fleeing and updating the quantity of grass consumed) and they refer to the submodels listed in the third part of the protocol. The operation properly speaking of the processes is thus not provided at this level. The list of actions carried out and the order in which they occur are all that are provided at this stage.

The actions are those carried out by the models entities (the agents or the patches) and also those carried out by higher level entities such as the model itself or the observer (for updating global indicators and the associated graphics).

The ODD protocol does not impose any particular formalism for the presentation of this varied information. However, it is advisable to use a UML class diagram to describe the model's structure (see section 2.3.1.1). The scheduling of the process may also be described using a UML activity diagram (see section 2.3.1.2).

2.4.2.3. *Design concepts*

Elements of documentation which are important for interpreting results are information on the emerging properties of the model, the hypotheses put forward and the capacities of certain agents (e.g. adaptation or learning). These elements are often not particularly formalized. In this part, ODD suggests a list of 11 items which provide information, not on the operation of the model, but on the way in which the concepts specific to the modeling have been taken into account. All of these concepts can be made explicit through answering the various questions suggested by the protocol, which are in the form of a checklist [GRI 10].

The ODD protocol makes it possible not to provide information about all of the concepts suggested in this part because some of these concepts may not be appropriate to the model that is being developed. Also, it is possible to add certain concepts unique to the user. However, in this case, it is advisable to explicitly specify that these are not elements that are provided by the standard.

2.4.2.4. *Details*

After a sketch of the model, with its main dynamics, has been created, this third part addresses the technical details which should make it possible to reimplement that model as a whole. ODD offers information provision at this level for three elements: initialization, input data and submodels.

Principles	What are the concepts, hypotheses or theories underlying the model design? At what are level are they integrated into the model?
Emergence	What are the emerging concepts not foreseen by the model, which result in interactions between or adaptations among agents? What are the expected emergent phenomena which result from the rules introduced into the model?
Adaptation	Do the agents always retain the same behavior? Are they able to adapt during the simulation? Do they have the choice to behave according to several alternatives? What are the decision-making rules which regulate this choice? What are the conditions for a potential change in behavior?
Goals	Do the agents seek explicitly or implicitly to reach a goal in relation to their adaptive behavior? What is this goal? What is its indicator/criteria? What is the usefulness/fitness function?
Learning	Does the experience acquired by the agents during the simulation make their decisions change? Are they able to learn? How are these learning mechanisms implemented?
Prediction	Can the agents evaluate the consequences of a decision that they might make? How do they predict the effect of their decision? Are they able to do this?
Perception	To what information do the agents have access? What are the state variables that they perceive or receive from other agents (internal variables or variables relative to the environment)?
Interaction	What direct or indirect interactions are integrated into the model? Upon what mechanisms present in the reality of these interactions are they based? Are they local or global interactions? Does the model allow the agents to communicate? In what form?
Stochasticity	Which model processes or variables introduce a random element? Why is this random element represented?
Co-operation / aggregation	Is there an organizational level in the model which is made up of groups of agents? Are these group products of an emergence phenomenon or explicitly defined because they share common properties (notion of breeds in NetLogo)?
Observation	What are the indicators observed during the simulation for the understanding and the analysis of the model's behavior? What are the outputs (e.g. data or graphs)?

Figure 2.16. *The key questions ODD proposes in order to specify the agent model's design elements (taken from [GRI 06, GRI 10])*

2.4.2.4.1. Initialization

The documentation should specify all the simulation's initial conditions. How many agents are there? How are they distributed in space? What are the initial values of the variables and the parameters? What is the state of the environment? Are the initialization conditions constant and based on reference data, or are they stochastically fixed? The idea here is to provide all the information required for the reproduction of the results of a simulation.

2.4.2.4.2. Input data

The dynamics represented in the model may be based on auxiliary data (for example, an imported predefined spatial environment), they may be modulated by forcing factors (for example, relief, surface temperature and quantity of precipitation) or they may integrate an existing model (for example, the growth curve of a plant species). If this is the case, this is the level where it should be mentioned. If not, the protocol recommends that it should be explicitly indicated that the model does not call for particular input data. It should be noted that this documentation element does not concern the value of parameters or state variables, which may also come from external files.

2.4.2.4.3. Submodels

The processes that make up the model and their order of execution were specified in the first part of the ODD. In this part, the operation of each of them should be precisely indicated, as well as the reasons why certain hypotheses were adopted, and how these submodels were calibrated, along with any usage limitation they may have. The submodels may be composed of equations, algorithms or specific rules, all the parameters of which must be explained and justified. If the submodels are based on theories or methods that have already been published, these publications should be referenced.

2.4.3. *ODD documentation of the recurrent example*

In order to illustrate the use of the ODD protocol, the recurrent model will be presented below, documented according to this standard.

2.4.3.1. *Overview*

2.4.3.1.1. Purpose

The aim of the model in the recurrent example is to explore the propagation conditions for malaria in the subregion of Maroua (Cameroon) in light of the pendular mobility patterns of farmers, who make a daily journey between their homes (in town) and their plots of land (outside town). The goal is to understand and measure the impact of these journeys on the spread of the illness.

2.4.3.1.2. Entities, state variables and scale

The model is made up of two agent categories: humans (farmers) and mosquitoes. These two types of entities are characterized by a state of infection (`is-infected?`) and an attribute which indicates whether the agent is a source of the epidemic or not (`is-infection-exterior?`). Each agent is also located in space (attributes `xcor` and `ycor`). Human agents also know the place where they work and where they live (attributes `home` and `work`) as well as the time when work begins and when it ends (attributes `beginning-work` and `end-work`).

The environment in which the agents are situated is made up of a set of places (spatial units) which are characterized by a soil occupation (attribute `nature` of the class Place) linked to a color (attribute `pcolor`). For each place, it is specified whether the place is a dwelling place or not (attribute `place-dwelling?`). The spatial units correspond to 50 m x 50 m cells which form a rectangular grid, representing the territory (dimension: 523 x 424 cells). These dimensions are imposed by the map taken as input data (see the Initialization of the ODD description part).

As for temporal resolution, the simulation time-step is set at 10 min (which makes 240 simulation steps per day). The model is built to carry out simulations of up to 30 days.

Several variables are also defined as model parameters: the number of mosquitoes present in the environment (`number-mosquitoes`), the number of farmers (`number-humans`), the distance from which a mosquito can reach farmers to bite them (`distance-contamination`) and the home–work distance for each farmer (`distance-home-work`). The model makes provision for an activation or non-activation of mosquito reproduction (`reproduction-mosquitoes?`) as well as for possible contagion between farmers and mosquitoes during the journey between home and work (`contagion-transport?`).

A simplified presentation of the model structure is given in the UML class diagram (Figure 2.2). The set of state variables is reproduced in Table 2.2.

2.4.3.1.3. Process and scheduling

At each time-step, the processes are conducted in the following order: (1) the mosquito agents act by moving randomly through space, biting a human present in the radius of contamination (procedure `go-mosquitoes`) and (2) depending on the time of day, the humans go at work (procedure `goto-work`), stay at work and go back at home at the end of the day (procedure `goto-home`). These farmer actions are included in the procedure `go-humans`. Within each set of agents, the simulation platform chooses the order in which the agents carry out their tasks. At the end of each time-step, the simulator updates the different output indicators: the number of mosquitoes and farmers infected according to the time.

The dynamics of the patches is limited to the creation of new mosquitoes (`go-patches`).

Entity	*Variable name*	*Possible values*
Human and mosquito	`xcor`	[0,523]
	`ycor`	[0,424]
	`is-infected?`	{true,false}
	`is-infection-exterior?`	{true,false}
Human	`home`	one patch
	`work`	one patch
	`start-work`	[0,240]
	`end-work`	[start-work,240]
Patch	`pcolor`	[0,240]
	`place-dwelling?`	{true,false}
Global	`step-time`	[0,2400]
Parameters	`number-mosquitoes`	[0,1000]
	`number-humans`	[0,2000]
	`distance-contamination`	[0,10]
	`distance-work-home`	[1,500]
Patch	`contagion-transport?`	{true, false}
	reproduction-mosquitoes?	{true,false}

Table 2.2. *Summary of the different state variables and parameters*

2.4.3.2. *Design concepts*

2.4.3.2.1. Principle

It is hypothesized that the human agents perform a pendular movement: during the day, they begin traveling to their workplace, remain immobile at the workplace in order to work and then return to their homes. In addition, various studies have shown that mosquitoes are present throughout the territory and that their range of movement remains very local. This is why the hypothesis that they move randomly within a limited radius is realistic.

2.4.3.2.2. Emergence

A spatial propagation phenomenon for the disease is observed, which follows the movement of the human agents.

2.4.3.2.3. Perception

The mosquitoes have the capacity to perceive nearby farmers (that is those who are present within a radius that is less than the parameter `distance-contamination`). As for the farmers, they are aware of time, and this helps them decide whether it is time to go to work, to stay in work or to go home. However, they cannot perceive the other farmers or the mosquitoes.

The cells know whether the mosquitoes are located on them (in order to decide they are producing a new mosquito agent or not).

2.4.3.2.4. Interaction

The only interactions present in the model are the interactions between a human agent and a mosquito agent. When a mosquito perceives a farmer within its contamination zone, it will bite that farmer. If one of the two agents is a carrier of malaria, the other will be infected. If both agents are in the same state of contamination, the bite will have no effect.

2.4.3.2.5. Stochasticity

The model contains a share of stochasticity, both in the initialization and in the dynamics. In particular, the position of the mosquitoes in space (with respect to the humans) is random for one of the cells (with respect to dwelling places). The position of the human workplace is also random among the cells that are not dwelling zones. The first infected mosquito is also chosen at random. During the simulation, two dynamics include an aspect of randomness. During the creation of a new mosquito, it is placed onto one of the neighboring cells (chosen at random) of the wetland cell that "produces" the mosquito. In addition, the movement of the mosquito is also partially random: it moves at a constant distance but in a direction that is chosen at random.

2.4.3.2.6. Observation

The main display of the simulator is a map showing the land occupation types (black cells for dwelling places, blue for wetlands and black for farming land), along with the mosquitoes and humans. This display is updated at each time-step, allowing the observer to see the dynamics of the movements. In addition, the graph of interactions between humans and mosquitoes (bites) is also displayed, and is updated at each time-step.

During the simulation, the development of the number of mosquitoes and humans can be seen through a curve which shows these values over time.

The simulator can also calculate and display (when this is required by the user) the average number of human–mosquito interactions (i.e. the number of mosquito bites) which have occurred before a human is infected.

2.4.3.3. *Details*

2.4.3.3.1. Initialization

The first stage of simulation initialization is the loading of the map, which sets the color (and thus the usage type for the soil) for the different cells. Following this, the mosquitoes are randomly created throughout the space with a healthy infectious status (`is-infected?` and `is-infection-exterior?` are initialized at false). The human agents are then randomly created at dwelling zones, with a workplace chosen randomly in the non-dwelling zones and a healthy infectious status. Finally, an epidemic is created: one of the mosquitoes is chosen at random and becomes infected. It is also noted as being the source of the epidemic (`is-infection-exterior?` is set as true).

2.4.3.3.2. Input data

As an input, the models take a map of soil use in the Maroua subregion, in the form of a raster image. Only three types of soil use are shown on this map: dwelling place (in black), wetland (in blue) and farmed land (in white).

2.4.3.3.3. Submodels

We can make a distinction between three submodels within the model, which correspond to the three main dynamics of the model:

pendular movement: the behavior of the human agents is limited to their pendular movement – each day, they go to work in the morning, work (and thus remain immobile) during the day and then return home in the evening. The choice between these categories is made as a function of the simulation step during the day (i.e. as a function of the simulation step). We have refined this model to allow for infection during the journey (parameter `contagion-transport?`): when `contagion-transport?` is false, in order to avoid any contact between humans and mosquitoes during the journey, we consider that the human displacement is instantaneous (whereas, it takes several simulation steps when `contagion-transport?` is true);

demography of the mosquitoes: we have introduced a very simple reproduction dynamics for the mosquitoes, based on the fact that they lay eggs in water and spend the start of their life (as an egg, larva and nymph) in the water: each day (and thus every 240 simulation steps), the wetland cells (which are blue) will create a mosquito agent if another mosquito agent is present in the cell;

infection: at each simulation step, all the human agents who are within the contamination radius of a mosquito are bitten. For each mosquito–human interaction, if the infectious state of one of the two agents is infected and the other is healthy, then the healthy agent becomes infected. If both are either healthy or infected, their infectious state remains unchanged.

2.5. Discussion on documentation

Nowadays, modelers have many languages available to them for formalizing and documenting their MAS.

UML is well suited to the description of the structure and the behavior of the model. It remains more widely used and offers a semantics which is rich enough to describe many MAS. In the case of models which include more complex organizations or actions, the use of AML, enriching the UML notation, can be particularly useful. In any case, an MAS should be described at the very least by a class diagram, which describes its structure, and by activity or state-transition diagrams, which model the behavior of the entities.

As for the documentation, the ODD protocol is becoming increasingly widely used by modelers, especially for presenting multiagent models in research literature. It is gradually becoming a recognized standard, on the same level as UML. It may also be noted that the ODD descriptions include increasingly UML class diagrams for explaining the structure of models being presented graphically and synthetically, which demonstrates the complementarity of the tools. ODD offers predefined documentation structure (the packaging), whereas UML allows the production of a part of the content in the form of diagrams.

The designer's attempt to formalize and document the model is essential in the lifecycle of the MAS. It makes it possible to use the model in a more reliable and enlightened way, so the users can gain a better understanding of the questions it attempts to contribute to answering and can see precisely what structure and operation of the representations are use to achieve this. However, much more remains to be done in this field not in terms of the design, but in terms of the use of models, first, in order to increase their reliability and, second, to facilitate informed use of them:

– *make models more reliable to use*: this will involve the transition from a documentation of a model as the result of a modeling process to a documentation of the modeling process itself. It will include the justification of choices made and test methodologies used to ensure that insofar as possible the computer implementation of the model is faithful to the conceptual model that was developed. This aspect also includes a quality documentation of the usage conditions of a model so that it is used advisedly to address the question that has been targeted throughout its development, and so that the risks of abusive use to resolve problems to which it is not suited are avoided;

– *make models easier to use*: it is also becoming important to facilitate the uptake and analysis of a model's results, for example, by the definition of the different usage scenarios and a detailed analysis of the results obtained.

Recent studies have shown that this question is beginning to be addressed, for example, with the development of the tool *Transparent and Comprehensive Ecological modeling documentation* (TRACE) [GRI 14], which offers standardization of the documentation associated with the models' objectives, with their design and with their implementation.

It is now more important than ever to provide conditions which favor the establishment of connections between the designers and users of models, in a process of mutually working alongside each other.

3

Introduction to NetLogo

3.1. Introduction

NetLogo is a programming environment which allows for the construction and exploration of agent-based models. Developed at the Center for Connected Learning, the software currently draws from StarLogoT[1], which is available for Mac OSX, and StarLogo[2], which was developed at MIT's Media Laboratory. It is the latter that has had the greatest influence on the programming language used by NetLogo, known as Logo[3], which was itself inspired by the Lisp programming language family. The history of Logo allows for a partial understanding of NetLogo's philosophy.

3.1.1. *A little history*

When NetLogo is presented in workshops, the first advantage expressed is that of how easy it is to pick up and use. This stems both from its graphical interface and the programming language used,

---

Chapter written by Frédéric AMBLARD, Eric DAUDÉ, Benoît GAUDOU, Arnaud GRIGNARD, Guillaume HUTZLER, Christophe LANG, Nicolas MARILLEAU, Jean-Marc NICOD, David SHEEREN and Patrick TAILLANDIER.

1 http://ccl.northwestern.edu/cm/StarLogoT/.

2 http://education.mit.edu/starlogo/.

3 http://el.media.mit.edu/logo-foundation/index.html.

which is known as Logo. This language was created in 1967 by a collaborative effort between Wallace Feurzeig and Seymour Papert. Papert was largely inspired by the constructivism of Jean Pigaet with whom he had worked several years before. With the advent of the first computers in the 1980s, researchers began to ask themselves about their utility within an educational context: how were computers to be used to enable the teaching of dynamic and complex worlds? Computers needed to be a medium that bridged the difference between the learner's need for knowledge and the world to be explored, which implied a need for a language permitting the learner and the computer to communicate. However, none of the programming languages available at the time were adapted for use by young learners. It is from the observation of this fact that the premise for Logo came about, a language that was intuitive for the learner and close to natural language as a result of being interactive, modular and flexible.

Logo is an interpreted programming language, which means that each line (containing a particular command) inputted by the user is immediately executed. These commands are interpreted by Logo as an order (e.g. the `jump 10` command results in the turtle moving by 10 steps), which will send back an error message if the command cannot be carried out. The language is modular, which means that commands can be grouped to form more complex sequences that can be made into new terms and are combined to form the complete program. This modularity allows for the construction of large projects. Finally, Logo is flexible as it does not require the direct input of the figures used. Type assignment is done based on the data used in the instructions. Even though this might be slightly perturbing for those used to other programming languages, the choice to not require direct input was made as it is closer to the way that non-programmers think. This choice is also found in other programming languages such as Caml[4] or Python[5].

There is only one single syntactic rule used in Logo: that of prefix notation. A command must always be placed before any eventual

4 http://caml.inria.fr/caml-light/index.en.html.

5 https://www.python.org/.

variables. Thus, the `jump` command followed by the variable `10` which makes the turtle move by 10 steps is written as follows: `jump 10`. To this rule is added that of the left–right analysis of instructions. Therefore, for the `jump random sqrt 4` command, the evaluator begins by reading the `jump` command, which receives the single variable `random`, which receives the single variable `sqrt`, which, in turn, receives the single variable 4. In practice, this leads to first executing the square root of 4, with the other instructions being put on hold, while the value of their respective variables is being calculated. Next, the `random` command is executed with the value 2 as a variable. Finally, the `jump` command is executed resulting in a jump of a number of steps corresponding to the result given by the `random` command with 2 as its input variable.

3.1.2. *Purpose of the chapter*

This chapter aims to help readers new to programming to discover the NetLogo modeling and simulation platform in an educational manner. The final aim is for such an individual to be able to write their own models and simulate them within NetLogo by the end of the chapter. So as to accomplish this, the reader will be instructed in the development of a simple model which will be expanded upon later. This first experience of developing a multiagent model is simplistic but remains nonetheless complete and enables us to understand and grasp the main concepts and techniques useful for defining models and simulations.

The remaining chapter is organized into five sections. In the first section, we will see that, using its metamodel, the NetLogo platform is particularly well-adapted for representing spatial phenomena. In the second section, we will present the tool interface used in NetLogo. In the third section, we will develop a simple model step by step, while referring to the metamodel viewed previously. The fourth section introduces the interaction model used for the behaviors of the agents. Before concluding, we will put forward a brief presentation of the additional functionalities offered by NetLogo.

3.2. Metamodel of NetLogo

The NetLogo platform corresponds to a simulation approach said to be “in time-discrete intervals”, which means that it makes a collective group of entities evolve in successive time intervals of equal length[6]. The corresponding modeling approach therefore consists of identifying the entities that are to be incorporated into the model and then defining the behavior of each one across each time interval. This approach is centered on the entities involved, otherwise known as agents. NetLogo’s metamodel identifies three different types of entities which can be modeled: 1) the environment: this is a rectangular space modeled in the form of a regular grid of n x m square tiles (*patches*); 2) the mobile agents (*turtles*): these move within the environment and interact with it and each other; 3) the links: these are dynamically created inbetween the *turtle* agents.

Finally, there is a specific agent known as the *observer*, which exists outside of the model. Its role is to control and monitor the execution of the simulation. This agent creates all the entities within the model (*patches, turtles and links*) and controls their simulated behavior.

NetLogo proposes a particularly useful functionality for the manipulation of agent-based models. It allows us to give instructions to groups or subgroups of agents, or *agentsets*. As a result, it is possible to collectively control all of the *turtles* as well as to pick a smaller subset and give it instructions that are not followed by the remaining agents. So as to do this, it is possible to create species or *breeds* which can be manipulated as groups of agents.

3.2.1. *Patches*

The environment is a rectangular space made up of a grid of n x m squares that are known as *patches*. Each *patch* corresponds to a square of the grid, within which movement is impossible. Each *patch* also has a corresponding position within the two-dimensional (2D) space of the

---

6 In NetLogo, a unit of time is known as a `tick`.

environment. All *patches* are also autonomous agents with their own state and behavior that is independent of that of the surrounding *patches*.

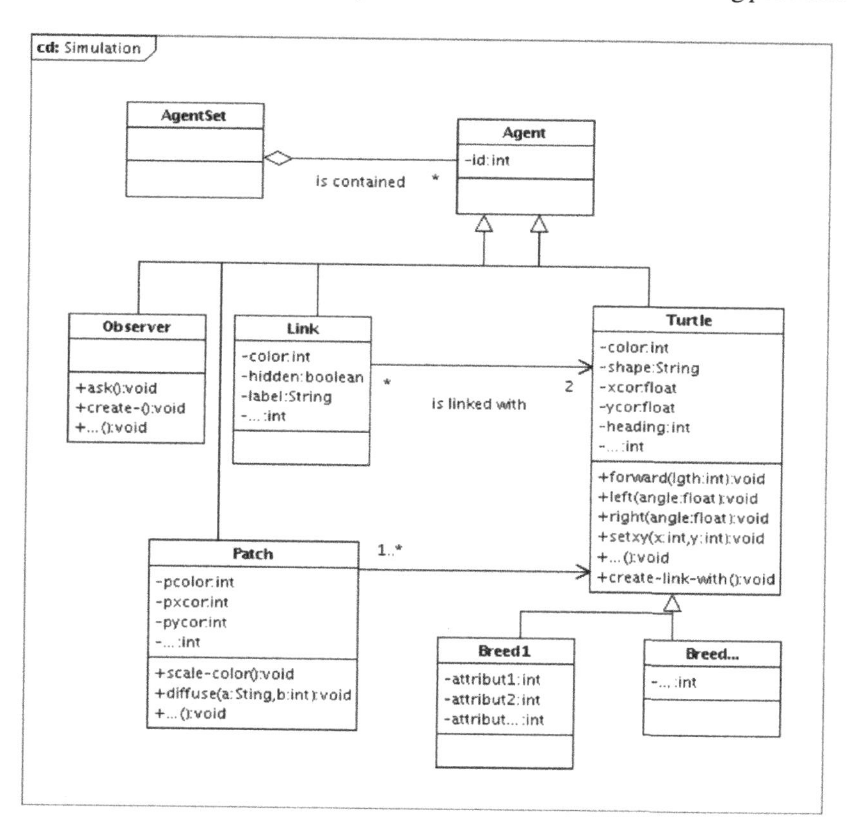

Figure 3.1. *A NetLogo model's corresponding metamodel*

3.2.1.1. *Topology of the environment*

The modeler has the possibility, by use of the interface, to choose the topology of the environment, by determining whether the grid should be horizontally or vertically continuous. To do this, all that is needed is to edit the large black square on the *Interface* tab. Making the grid horizontally continuous means that the first and last columns of *patches* are effectively next to each other. Therefore, two *patches* belonging, respectively, to the first and last columns of a single line become neighbors. In the same manner, making the grid vertically continuous means that the first and last lines of *patches* become adjacent. By default, the environment is continuous along both axes, which corresponds to a toroidal topology. When the environment is only continuous along a single axis, its topology is a cylinder, either horizontally or vertically oriented. If the environment is not continuous along either axis, then its topography is that of an enclosed, 2D square.

This same interface also allows the user to divide the simulation space into *patches* of different sizes, effectively changing the resolution used. It must, however, be noted that all *patches* must be rectangular in shape. If the modeler requests a higher number of *patches* along a particular axis, then the space is not sectioned into smaller segments but instead, the size of the environment is increased along the axis in question. This leads to a simulated environment that is rectangular in shape.

3.2.1.2. *Patch variables*

The state of each *patch* is defined using a certain number of predefined variables to which any number of additional variables can be added.

The most commonly used predefined variables are the `pcolor` variable, which defines the color of the *patch* and the `pxcor` and `pycor` variables, which, respectively, define its *x* and *y* coordinates. Since the position of the *patch* is fixed within the grid, its coordinates can only be read, not edited. On the other hand, their color can be modified. Other than their position and color, *patches* can be linked with a text label (`plabel`) to which a numerical value or string can be added, and whose color can also be defined (`plabel-color`). The size of the *patches* and the size of their labels can only be indirectly modified via use of the interface.

3.2.1.3. *Patch primitives*

Patches can be manipulated using primitives defined within NetLogo. Below are some of the most commonly used primitives:

– `neighbors`: enables access to its neighbors;

– `distance`: returns the distance between the agent that called the function and another agent given as a variable;

– `sprout-<breeds>`: creates a certain number of agents of the `breeds` species on the patch that called the command;

– `diffuse`: this command is a little particular as it is a primitive of the *observer*. It allows for the spreading of variables to its neighbors; etc.

3.2.2. *Turtles*

The *turtles* are the mobile agents in the simulation. They are designed to move around the environment and therefore on and across the *patches*. They are spatially located within the environment and are visible on the grid. The *turtles* can view their environment and the other agents within it. They have an action capacity, a characteristic that is essential for an agent. It is possible to define more detailed agent types than the simple *turtle*s with the keyword `breed`. They can then be assigned specific attributes and a unique behavior.

3.2.2.1. *Turtle variables*

Just as with the *patches*, the state of each *turtle* is defined using a certain number of predefined variables to which any number of additional variables can be added. The *turtles* share certain variables with the *patches* such as color (`color`) as well as having their own location coordinates on the *patch* grid (`xcor` and `ycor`). Equally, labels can be assigned to them, as well as the color of these (`label` and `label-color`). The `size` variable allows us to modify the *turtle's* size and `who` returns the *turtle's* identity (`id`).

3.2.2.2. *Turtle primitives*

Turtles can be manipulated using primitives defined within NetLogo. Here again, some of the most commonly used variables are listed below:

– `distance`: returns the distance between the *turtle* that called the function and another *turtle* given as a variable;

– `die`: kills the *turtle*;

– `hatch`: creates a given number of *turtles* that are daughters of the selected turtle. The children are created identical to the mother and are placed at the same location as it;

– `forward`: moves the *turtle* forward a given number of steps;

– `move-to`: the *turtle* moves to the location of an agent given as a variable;

– `left, right`: allows the *turtle* to turn left or right, respectively, by a given number of degrees;

– `<breeds>-here`: returns a group of agents containing the *turtles* that are on the patch of the agent that called the command; etc.

3.2.3. *Links*

The *links* are also agents but they have the particular function of linking two *turtles* together. The *turtles* are then known as nodes. The *link* is clearly represented by a line linking the two *turtles*. As a result of this, *links* are not located on the *patch* grid. There are two types of *links*: directed and undirected. Just as with the *turtles*, the modeler can define their own *link* types.

3.2.3.1. *Link variables*

As with the other agents, the state of each *link* is defined using predefined variables to which any number of additional variables can be added. Again, certain variables described earlier can also be used: `color`, `label` and `label-color`. Also useful are `end1` and `end2` which describe the nodes at either end of the *link*.

3.2.3.2. *Link primitives*

Links can be manipulated using primitives defined within NetLogo. Once again, some of the most commonly used primitives are listed below:

– `create-links-to, create-links-from, create-links-with`: these are different ways of creating *links*;

– `link-with`: returns the *link* between the *turtle* calling the function and another *turtle* given as a variable;

– `my-links`: returns a list of all the undirected *links* that are connected to the *turtle* calling the function;

– `link-neighbors`: returns a group of agents. It contains all the *turtles* found at the other end of *links* connected to the *turtle* calling the function;

– `my-in-links`: returns a group of agents. It contains all the directed links leading to the *turtle* calling the function;

– `my-out-links`: returns a group of agents. It contains all the directed links leaving from the *turtle* calling the function; etc.

3.2.4. *The observer*

The *observer* is located outside the simulation space and controls and monitors its progress. It allows for the sending of instructions to all the agents in the simulation. It is the link between the user and the agents.

3.3. The NetLogo software interface

The NetLogo interface is centered around three tabs: *Interface*, *Information* and *Code*. This allows for rapid switching between the development and simulation aspects of a model, and therefore allows for an incremental modeling process which alternates between development and testing phases.

It is these three tabs (Interface, Info and Code) that the user is presented with upon first launching the NetLogo software application, all of which have specific roles within the modeling process.

The *Info* tab is used to document the model. NetLogo provides a basic framework which can be modified (with the *edit* button) to be perfectly suited to the needs of the modeler. The description can, for example, be an Overview, Design concepts, Details (ODD) description of the model. It should be noted that this documentation is saved along with the model and will, as such, be transmitted along with it.

The *Code* tab mainly contains an editable text field within which the modeler writes their NetLogo code. Notably, it contains a *Check* button which is activated whenever the file is saved. It allows for the detection of syntactic mistakes in the NetLogo code entered in the text field. This check also occurs automatically whenever the user switches between tabs. If a mistake is discovered, a yellow band appears above the tab. The tab also contains a scrollable list that contains the different procedures contained in the model, for quick and easy access.

Finally, the *Interface* tab contains the graphical interface of the simulator. When a new model is created, a default environment is displayed. This environment can then be easily modified by the modeler, who can add control elements to the simulation (such as *buttons*), elements which allow for control more than various input values of the simulation variables (*sliders*, *switches*, *choosers*, etc.) or to display returned values and other simulation indicators (*monitors*, *plots*, etc.). At the lower end of the *interface,* tab can be found the *Command Center*, which contains the console that displays all of the messages produced during the simulation. However, this is not the extent of its utility; the user may also choose to use it to execute NetLogo code on the spot, which most notably allows for the testing of a currently running simulation. They may also choose within what context this code is executed, determining which specific entities (*observer*, *turtles*, *patches* or *links*) are to be affected by it.

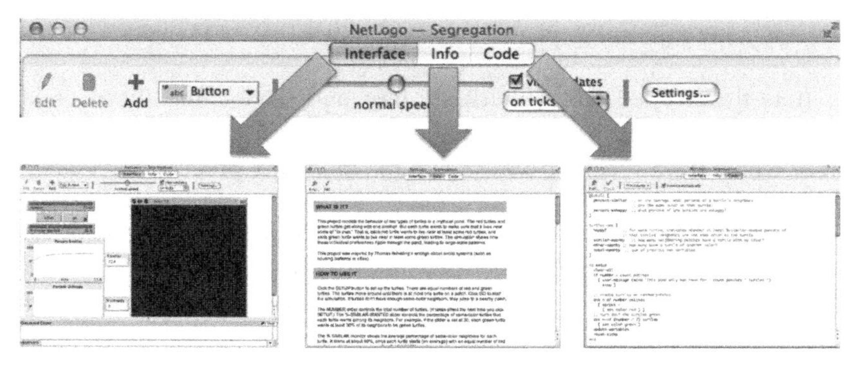

Figure 3.2. *The NetLogo software interface, with details of each of the three tabs*

3.4. Step-by-step creation of a simple model

A NetLogo program is a sequence of procedures which permits the simulation of the behaviors of created objects (agents and environment) during their execution. As seen in the previous chapter, a multi-agent system (MAS) is characterized by a static architecture (the environment and species) and individual behaviors which determine the dynamics of the system, the interactions therein and, as a result, can show emergent behavior. The dynamics of the system are largely determined by the initial situation which can be calibrated in order to receive interesting results.

Therefore, the development of a NetLogo model is centered around defining the following elements:

1) the model's structure, which involves defining the model's global variables, the structure of the environment and the species within it;

2) an initial state, with variables defined in the user interface;

3) the behaviors of the agents and environment using procedures;

4) the model's outputs.

Figure 3.3 proposes a suggested setup of a NetLogo model, which is as follows:

– expressing and defining the structure of the world to be simulated, of the global variables and species;

– defining an initial state described within a set of procedures with the `setup` prefix (of which there should be one per species). These procedures are called in by a general procedure conventionally named as `setup`;

– defining the agents' behaviors;

– defining the agents' lifecycle and of the environment within a set of procedures with the go prefix (again, there should be one per species). These procedures are called in by a general procedure conventionally named go;

– defining procedures that will be used for the model's outputs, notably in the form of charts and/or tables.

COMMENT 3.1.– The NetLogo language can be expanded by means of extensions (e.g. for the manipulation of geographical information systems (GIS) data). It is mandatory to declare the extensions used when creating a program, prior to defining global variables and species. The program can then be organized in a logical manner, based on the temporal order in which various elements will be executed when running the program. This begins with the initialization procedure, followed by the actions of the various agents, the sequencing within each iteration of the simulated world and finishes with the outputs, such as charts, tables or other graphical representations of data.

In the case of a large model, it is possible to split the model into several files. The `includes` primitive adds new tabs which allow for quick access to any additional files included in the model. This primitive must link to files in the NetLogo file extension format (.nls).

3.4.1. *Creating the structure of the world and defining its initial state*

The modeler's first task is to create and initialize the world which will function as an environment for the simulation's agents. This is done both with the use of NetLogo's graphical interface and by writing code.

3.4.1.1. *Defining the simulation space*

NetLogo allows for the creation of a single modeling and simulation space per case study. It is this space that can be edited from the *Model Settings* window (Figure 3.1). The topology of the simulated area (*World wraps*), the origin of the x and y coordinates (*location of origin*) and its dimensions (`pxcor` and `pycor`) are selected from this window. In the example of Figure 3.4(a), the origin $(0, 0)$ is placed in the center of the space, its topology is toroidal and the space is made up of 10,201 *patches* spread over 101 lines and 101 columns.

A *patch* is characterized by its position in the simulation space which is identified from the coordinate system chosen. Figure 3.4(b) represents the layout of the environment's *patches* in the form of a matrix; the *patch* $(-4, 5)$ corresponds to the cell with coordinates $x = -4$ and $y = 5$ in the matrix.

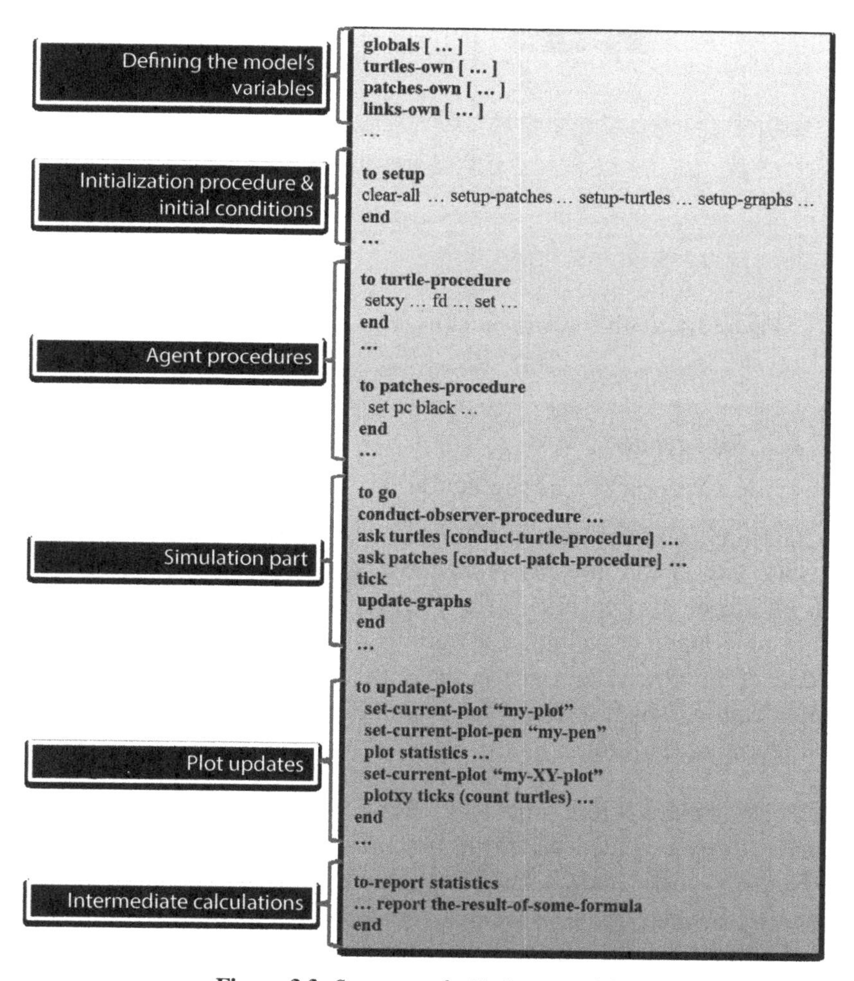

Figure 3.3. *Structure of a NetLogo model*

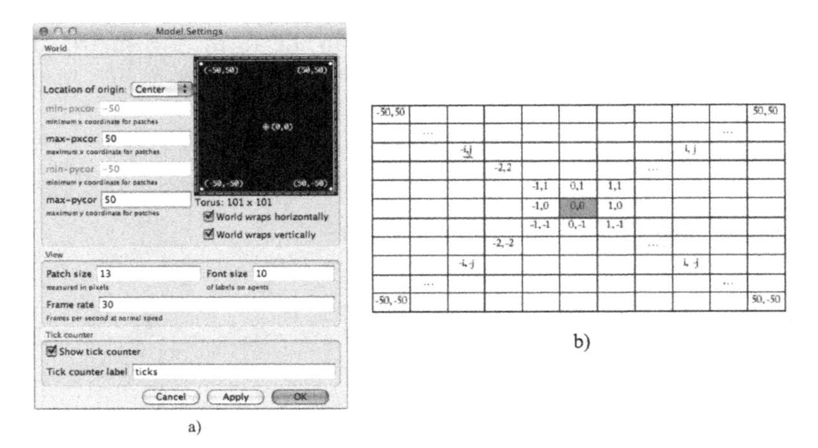

a)

b)

Figure 3.4. *a) World configuration interface and b) representation of the environment in matrix form*

3.4.1.2. *My first procedure*

3.4.1.2.1. Creation of a `setup` button

The only way for a user to launch a simulation, that is to say, to execute any of the model's procedures, is to activate a button within the interface. A right click in any empty space on the interface will bring up a menu containing the various different elements that can be added, from which the user can make their choice. Start by creating a single button, which will prompt a window to open with options for its configuration (Figure 3.5).

The *Commands* text input field allows the modeler to describe the actions to be executed when the button is activated, which is written in NetLogo code. Buttons are most commonly used to call a procedure from the model. For this to happen, the procedure name must be written within this field. In Figure 3.5, clicking on the button launches the `setup` procedure (which we will define in the following paragraph). The button's text appears in red if there are any errors detected in the code assigned to it or within any procedures the button may call. The name of the button corresponds to what is written in the *Display name* field, and will default (if said field is empty) to the text in the *Commands* field.

A procedure is always executed in a specific context (that of the *observer*, the *turtles*, the *links* or the *patches*). For example, executing a procedure in the context of a *turtle* allows for the usage of *turtle*-specific variables (e.g. `color`) within the procedure, the variables that do not perhaps apply to *patches* (which have a `pcolor` variable, but not a `color` one), *links* or the *observer*. The scrollable *Agent* list allows the user to define within which context the *Commands* code is executed: if *patches* is selected, then the code is applied to all the *patches* in the model.

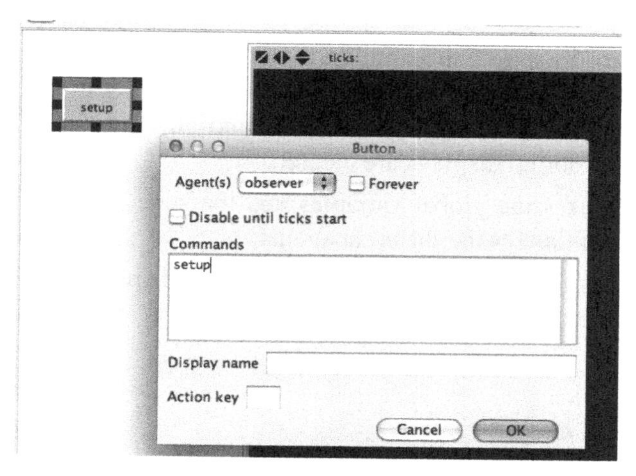

Figure 3.5. *Button creation*

3.4.1.2.2. The `setup` procedure

Once the `setup` button has been created, the modeler must write the corresponding `setup` procedure. A procedure always has the same form in NetLogo:

```
to nom_procedure
     [NetLogo code instructions or
     calls of procedures defined within the model]
end
```

We want to write a procedure called `setup` which displays the message "model initialization" in the *observer*.

```
to setup
    show "model initialization"
end
```

COMMENT 3.2.– The instruction `show` displays (in the *observer*) the message entered as a variable. This message can be a character string (which is written in between inverted commas), a numerical value or a color, such as `show "my message"`, or `show 3.14`.

A `setup` procedure also always has the same form in NetLogo:

– it begins by setting the simulation back to its initial state, due to the `clear-all` primitive: the values of all variables are set to their defaults (parameters, *patch* variables), all *turtles* and any remaining *links* are killed and all output displays are cleared;

– it initializes the global variables and the state of each *patch* and creates and initializes the different agents;

– it resets the tick counter and sets the output displays to their values at the initial state (`reset-ticks` primitive).

```
to setup
    clear-all
    [global variable initialization]
    [agent creation and initialization]
    reset-ticks
end
```

3.4.1.2.3. Initializing the environment: loading an image

One of the tasks of the `setup` procedure is to initialize the environment and therefore to define the initial state of all *patches*. In the example we have been using throughout the text, we will start by initializing the environment to represent the studied region. So as to accomplish this, we have a map of land use in the subregion of Maroua at our disposal, in the form of a raster image named as landuse87NBB.BMP. This image has a resolution of 523 by 424 pixels. Each type of land use is characterized by a particular color. So as to import the data available within this image, we use the import-pcolors primitive. This command scans the image, resizes it to the scale of the environment and then assigns each patch the color of the corresponding pixel (pcolor variable of the *patches*). Figure 3.6(a) displays the result of importing an image into an environment with a lower resolution, that is to say a lower number of *patches* than there are pixels contained in the image and Figure 3.6(b) shows the result of importing an image of equal resolution to that of the environment.

```
to setup
      ...
      show ''Model initialization''
      import-pcolors ''landuse87NBB.BMP''
      ...
end
```

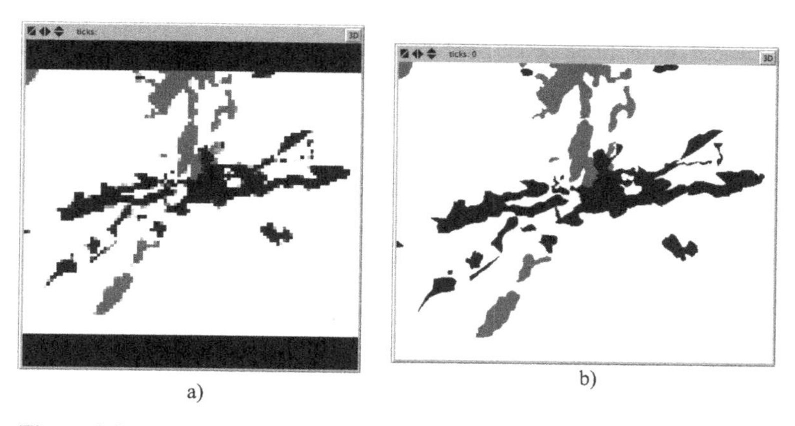

Figure 3.6. *Importing a same image into an environment of a) 50 patches by 50 patches and b) of 523 patches by 424 patches*

3.4.1.3. *Diversifying the world*

By default, NetLogo only recognizes three agent types in its simulation models: *patches*, *turtles* and *links*. Yet, it is often useful, or even necessary to be able to create different agent types with specific attributes. In NetLogo, new agents are created using the keywords breed (for new *turtle* types) and directed-link breed or undirected-link breed (for new *link* types). These keywords are assigned by several variables: the name of the new agent group (in the form of an *agentset*) of this species as the first variable and the name of an individual agent of the species as the second variable[7].

As presented in the Unified Modeling Language (UML) diagram of our example, we need to create two different new *turtle* agent types: mosquitoes and humans. The term *mosquito* is therefore the name of the species, and the term *mosquitoes* indicates the collective group of all existing *mosquito* agents. Furthermore, to represent the infection class that links two agents, we have created an additional *link* type: *infection*.

```
breed [mosquitoes mosquito]
breed [humans humain]

directed-link-breed [infections infection]
```

The defining of species also creates global variables: for example, `mosquitoes` will be able to be used within the model and will contain all agents of this species (which would, for example, be useful for ordering all the mosquito agents to move). The term will also be able to be used with primitives: for example, `create-<breeds>` is used to create mosquito agents by replacing `<breeds>` by `mosquitoes`: `create-mosquitoes 50` will create 50 mosquitoes. Many other primitives can adopt this ability, such as `<breeds>-at` and `<breeds>-on`.

It should be noted that each agent type created in this fashion possesses any variables that the current *turtles* own (such as `xcor`, `ycor`, `color`, `heading`, etc.). Similarly, new link types will be given the variables of existing *links*. Nonetheless, it is possible to give additional variables to both the basic agent types in NetLogo (*patch*es, *turtles* and *link*s) and any and all new species created by the modeler. Importantly, when a variable is added to the *turtle* agent group, this variable will also be added to any other existing *turtle* species.

---

7 Conventionally, the first variable is the pluralized form of the second variable (mosquitoes/mosquito or wolves/wolf as in the classic predator-prey model in the NetLogo model library.

The modeler can add new variables to the *patches*, *turtles* or *links* as well as all other breeds, by using the keywords `patches-own`, `turtles-own`, `links-own` or `<breeds>-own`:

```
patches-own  [pvar1 pvar2 ...]
turtles-own  [var1 var2 ...]
links-own    [lvar1 lvar2 ...]

<breeds>-own [bvar1 bvar2 ...]
```

This command, which will be executed before any other event in the procedure, allows for the creation of additional variables belonging to the *patches* (`pvar1`, `pvar2`, etc.). Each agent that is created (whether a *patch*, *turtle*, *link* or other species) is as a result given an instance of these variables which can be locally modified, independently from the other agents.

In the example that we have been studying, we wanted all the agents (mosquitoes and humans) to have an infectious state. Therefore, we add an `is-infected?` variable to the *turtles*, and as a result, to all species (in this case, humans and mosquitoes) so as to avoid having to add this variable to both species manually. Nonetheless, the mosquitoes and humans each have their own personal variables: the mosquitoes have the variable `is-infected-external?` which specifies whether a mosquito has been infected by another agent during the simulation or if it was a source of the epidemic, infected prior to the launch of the simulation.

```
turtles-own    [is-infected?]
humans-own     [house work begin-work end-work]
mosquitoes-own [is-infected-external?]

patches-own    [location-home?]

infections-own [date generation]
```

3.4.1.4. *Populating the world*

We will now create and initialize the different agents which we want to be present in the model. When the agents are created with the setup procedure, the create-<breeds> primitive must be used[8]. This primitive creates new agents of this breed, the number of which is given as a variable, and calls the commands in between the brackets for each of the agents, respectively.

```
create-<breeds> number [
    [grouped commands which apply to all the
    newly created agents]
]
```

These commands usually serve to initialize each of the agents' variables. To modify the value of an *existing* variable (or, more generally speaking, of an individual variable), the modeler uses the set primitive which gives the variable (given as a variable of the primitive) the value of an expression:

```
set variable expression
```

The set command can only be used for existing variables. It is sometimes useful to define local variables, that is to say variables which exist only for the current procedure, such as to store the results of intermediate calculations, for example. So as to accomplish this, the modeler must use the let primitive, which will both create a new variable (given as a variable of the primitive) and assign it the value of the following expression:

```
let variable expression
```

For example, the following code (inspired by our running example) allows for the modeler to write a procedure init-humains which creates 50 human agents and gives them each a position, a color, a size (inherited from the *turtles*) and the is-infected? and home variables.

---

8 When creating a new *turtle* breed, the primitive hatch-<breeds> number [commands] must be used; on the other hand, if a new *patch* form is being created, the primitive sprout-<breeds> number [commands] must be used.

```
to init-humans
     let list-houses patches with [locationHome?]
     create-humans 50
     [
        set home one-of list-houses
        setxy [pxcor] of house [pycor] of house
        set size 24
        set is-infected? false
        set color green
    ]
end
```

For each of the 50 human agents who are created, the program initializes the `size` variable (set to 24), `is-infected?` (set to `false`), which means that the agent was not infected at the start of the simulation, and `color` (set to `green`). To initialize the `home` variable, we begin by selecting all the *patches* which are houses and can be homes:

```
let list-houses patches with [locationHome?])
```

and we store the list of these *patches* within the `list-houses` variable. The `with` variable carries out a search within an *agentset* (a list of agents) so as to put together a new *agentset* containing all the agents that satisfy the expression run in the variable that is to its right (in this case `[locationHome?]`, which is to say that their `locationHome?` variable has the value `true`).

Then, we initialize the `house` variable with respect to one of the *patches* of this *agentset* with the `one-of` primitive.

The `setxy` primitive assigns a value to the agent's position variables (`xcor, ycor`). Here, we give the agent the coordinates of its `home` variable as it is initial position: the `of` primitive returns the value of the variable given as a variable to the left of the agent that is placed on the right (`[pxcor] of home`).

3.4.1.5. *Influencing world creation: modifiable variables*

The modeler may consider that the initial number of *human* agents should be a variable of the model. This may be so that it can be modified by the user during the simulation or so that it can be modified so as to explore the model in full detail. In such cases, the modeler has the option of adding an element to the interface, such as a *slider*, so as to make the variable manually modifiable (Figure 3.7).

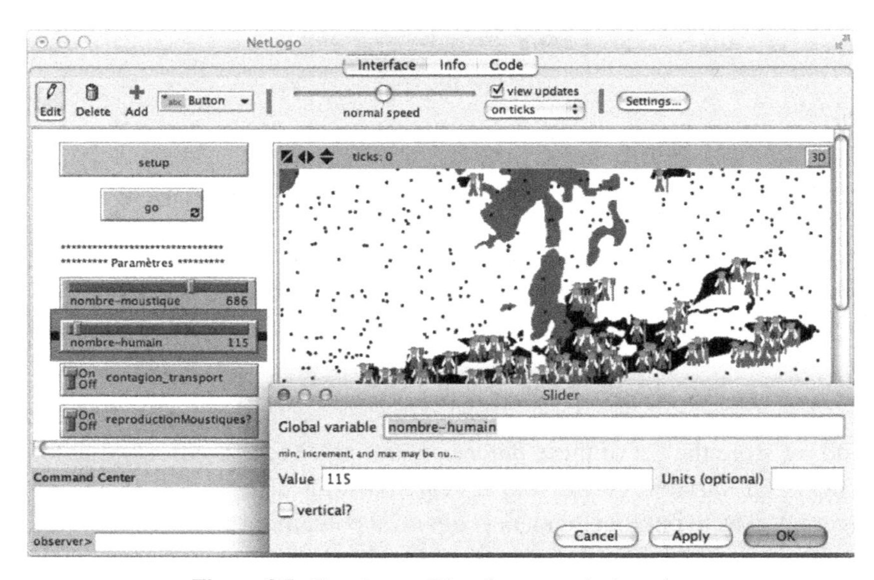

Figure 3.7. *Creating a slider that controls the value of the* `number-human` *variable*

Adding a *slider* to the interface means that a new global variable must be created and initialized (within the *Global variable* field), which will be able to be used within the model, for example, for the creation of as many new agents as the user should want.

```
to init-human
    ...
    create-humans number-human [ .... ]
    ...
end
```

3.4.2. *Introducing environmental behaviors*

3.4.2.1. *Simulation lifecycle*

The simulation's lifecycle is managed by a procedure usually named as go (see Figure 3.8). It successively describes the behavior of the environment and the agents for each time frame (*tick*). This procedure is called into action by clicking on a button or by somehow modifying another element of the interface.

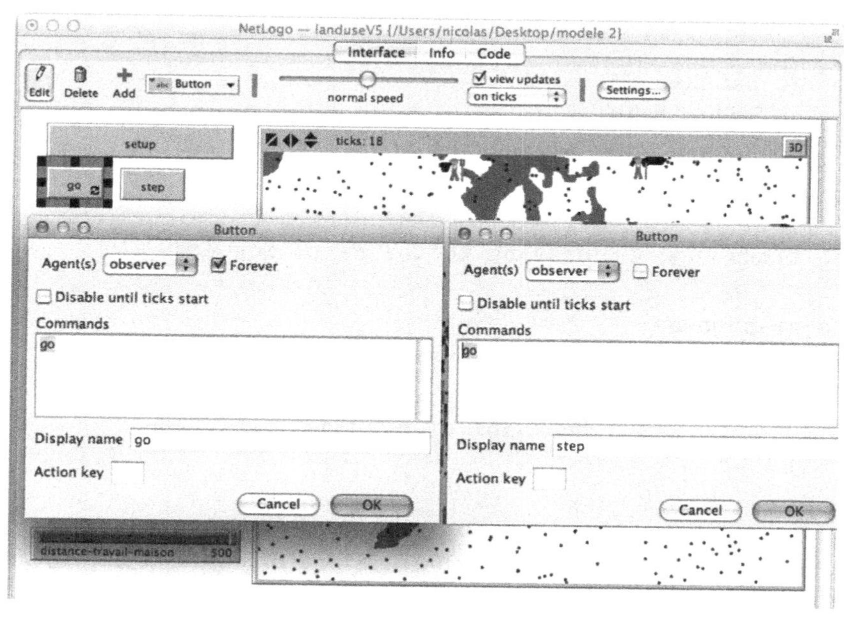

Figure 3.8. *Illustrating different button modes*

Two different execution modes of the model can be identified with the interface: a step-by-step mode (*step* button) and an automatic mode (*go* button) are available. To define a step-by-step mode, a simple button that calls the go procedure is created within the interface. Every time that this button is clicked, a single *tick* passes. The automatic mode requires the creation of a similar button that also calls the go procedure. However, in this case, the check box next to *forever* must be ticked.

When this button is first clicked, it remains activated and calls the go procedure at regular intervals, until clicked again.

The go procedure activates the behavior of the grid's cells (*patches*) and the different agents (*mosquitoes* and *humans*). In practice, this means that the go-patches, go-mosquitoes and go-humans procedures are called and executed. The go procedure finishes with the ticks command, which ends the current *tick* and incrementally increases the *tick* counter.

```
to go
   go-patches
   go-mosquitoes
   go-humans    ; calling the go-humans procedure
                which models the human
                agents' behavior
   ticks        ; passing to the next tick end

to go-humans
   ask humans
   [
            ... ; behavior of a human
   ]
end
```

COMMENT 3.3.– The ask command is one of the most important available in the NetLogo language. It asks all of the agents contained within a list (list_of_agents) given as its variable to execute the commands defined within the section enclosed by square brackets ([...]). In other words, this command can be read as saying: for *EACH* agent contained within list_of_agents, *EXECUTE* the instructions contained within the bracketed section.

```
      ask listofagents
      [
  ... ; commands detailing all actions
      ; to be carried out by an agent.
      ]
```

3.4.2.2. *Environmental behaviors*

Introducing a behavior within the environment serves to model the phenomena which apply at the spatial level rather than at the level of the individual, for example, the spreading of a forest fire, the dispersion of a virus by winds or the pollination of a space. In the case of the example we are using, the environmental behaviors enable us to model the proliferation of mosquitoes.

In an environment represented in grid form (as in NetLogo's case), giving it dynamic behaviors effectively models a phenomenon of the studied system that is composed of a simulated environment within which the *turtles* evolve. As a result, each *patch* agent within the simulation space has a specific behavior associated with it. Furthermore, each *patch* behaves individually by evolving its internal state and acting within the world.

The behavior of the *patches* is usually controlled by a procedure that is assigned this job alone. It is known as `go-patches` by convention. This procedure analyses all of the *patches* and executes each of their respective behaviors. So as to do this, it uses the `if` and `ask` operators as well as the other operators associated with *patches*, as listed in the documentation.

In our running example, the mosquito proliferation is periodic if and only if this behavior is activated by the `reproductionMosquitoes?` variable that is present on the interface. In this case, a conditional order is used.

In the NetLogo language, the *if-then* command is different from the *if-then-else* command. The `if` command executes the instructions located in the associated section if the condition is satisfied. The `ifelse` command adds an alternative section which is executed when the condition is not satisfied.

```
...
; Previous instructions
if condition
```

```
  [
  ... ; group of instructions to be executed if
          condition is satisfied
      ; (condition = true).
  ]
;  Following instructions
...
```

```
...
 ; Previous instructions
ifelse condition
 [
 ... ; group of instructions to be executed if
          condition is satisfied
      ; (condition = true).
 ]
 [
 ... ; group of instructions to be executed if
         condition is not satisfied
     ; (condition = false).
 ]
; Following instructions
...
```

In NetLogo, a condition is a Boolean expression which has a `true` or `false` value. Such an expression is made up of, among other things: 1) equality operators (=), inequality operators (<>) and relational operators (>, <, <=, >=) between different variables (numeric or alphanumeric); 2) binary Boolean operators such as and or `or` and 3) the unary operator `not`.

As we have seen before, the mosquito proliferation is periodic. It is also a function of an activation variable within the interface which allows for the activation of the mosquito proliferation phenomenon. As such, the activation condition of the cell behavior `(if (reproductionMosquitoes?) and (ticks mod timeStep = 0))` is split into two parts:

– reproductionMosquitoes?, a variable defined within the interface as part of a *switch* element (interface element allowing for a choice between only two options);

– ticks mod timeStep, where ticks is a NetLogo variable that indicates the number of *ticks* that have passed since the beginning of the simulation and timeStep is an interface variable that determines the number of *ticks* between two proliferation events. When ticks is a multiple of timeStep, the result of the ticks mod timeStep calculation is equal to 0.

COMMENT 3.4.– mod gives the remainder of a euclidean division between two whole numbers. For example, 10 mod 8 returns 2.

When combined, the ask command and the with operator allow for the assigning of a specific behavior to a reduced agent population depending on the modeling hypotheses. In our example, two hypotheses are adopted: 1) only the humid areas (in blue), where stagnating water is present, allow for the proliferation of mosquito larvae – (pcolor = blue); 2) mosquito proliferation can only take place if they are locally present, that is to say when their number is 1 or greater – (count moustiques-here >= 1).

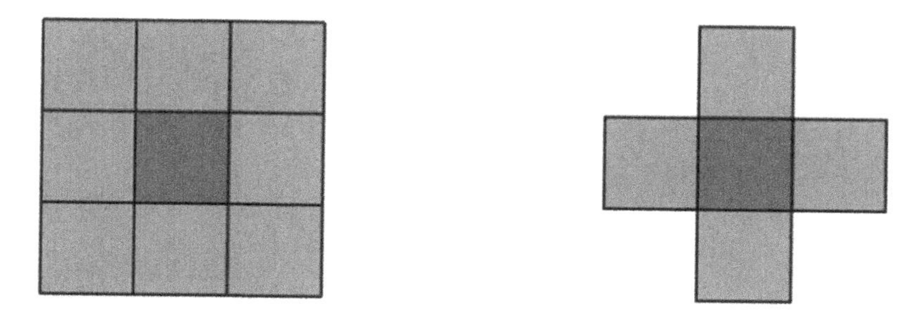

Figure 3.9. *Cells selected (in light gray) with the neighbors and neigbors4 commands*

Each selected cell creates a new mosquito agent and places it somewhere in its surroundings. Initially, a cell is randomly chosen (with the one-of operator) from the adjacent cells: whether the 8 that surround the selected cell (neighbors operator), or whether the 4 that share a side with the currently selected cell (neighbors4 operator). Then, a mosquito agent is created with the sprout-mosquito command.

The sprout-<breeds> and hatch-<breeds> commands allow for the creation and initialization of *turtles* of a given species in the same way as the create command (as discussed in section 3.4.4.1). However, these three commands distinguish themselves by the context in which they are used: create is used in the general context by a procedure called by the interface or by the user; hatch can only be used for *turtles* and sprout can only be used for *patches* (see example below). The sprout-<breeds> and hatch-<breeds> commands are nonetheless used in the same way as the previously discussed create-<breeds> command:

```
ask patches [
   sprout-<breeds> number [
   ... ; set of instructions which apply to each agent
       ; created for its initialization]
    ]
]
```

OR

```
ask <breeds> [
   hatch-<breeds> number [
   ... ; set of instructions which apply to each agent
       ; created for its initialization]
    ]
]
```

In our example, the newly-created mosquito is placed in the center of the myNeighbor cell by the following command:

```
setxy [pxcor] of myNeighbor [pycor] of myNeighbor
```

Finally, the complete go-patches procedure is as follows:

```
to go-patches
  if (reproductionMosquitoes?) and (ticks mod
       timeStep = 0)
  [
  ask patches with [(pcolor = blue) and count
       mosquitoes-here
                      >= 1)]
  [
    let myNeighbor one-of neighbors
     sprout-mosquitoes 1
    [
      setxy [pxcor] of myNeighbor [pycor] of myNeighbor
      set size 5
      set shape "butterfly"
      set isInfected? false
      set isInfectionExternal false
      set color black
      ]
   ]
 ]
end
```

3.4.2.3. *Turtle agent behaviors*

Defining *turtle* behavior is done in the same way as behaviors are added to *patches*: a procedure go-<breed> is usually implemented for each species. Apart from the commands detailed in the previous section, a *turtle*'s behavior will often use movement commands to enable the agent to move within the environment.

A *turtle* agent is considered to be a self-supporting entity that has an x, y position (within the xcor and ycor variables) and an orientation (heading). This direction is represented by an angle α in degrees measured between the *y*-axis and the tangential trajectory of the agent (its speed vector).

So as to move, the *turtle* agents perform commands which modify their position and orientation. These are limited to:

– `forward` Δ or `fd` Δ $\rightarrow$ moves the turtle a distance of value Δ (forward motion);

– `back` Δ or `bk` Δ $\rightarrow$ reverses the turtle a distance of value Δ (backward motion);

– `move-to` Ω $\rightarrow$ moves the turtle to the center of an agent Ω;

– `setxy` xy $\rightarrow$ moves the turtle to the coordinates given by x and y;

– `left` α or `lt` α $\rightarrow$ turns the turtle to the left by an angle of α in degrees (anticlockwise rotation);

– `right` α or `rt` α $\rightarrow$ turns the turtle to the right by an angle of α in degrees (clockwise rotation);

– `face` Ω $\rightarrow$ makes the turtle face an agent Ω;

– `facexy` xy $\rightarrow$ make the turtle face the coordinates given by x and y.

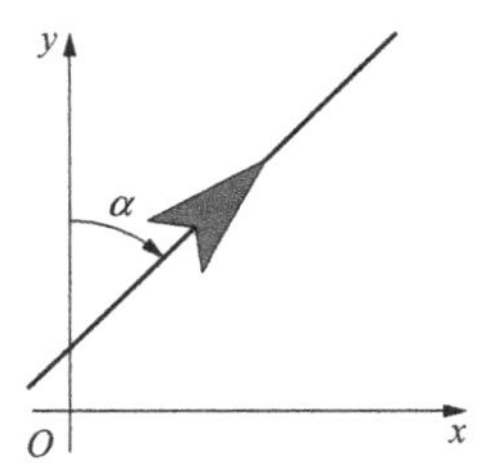

Figure 3.10. *An agent's orientation is defined by the angle α between the y-axis and the agent's trajectory (this angle is given in degrees, and in a clockwise direction)*

In our example, the mosquitoes have a movement behavior consistent with Brownian motion, which is made up of a rotation and a forward movement. The `lt random 360` command rotates the chosen agent to the left (`lt`) by an angle α chosen randomly from the domain $\alpha \in [0; 360[$. Then, the `fd 1` command moves the agent forward by 1 unit.

```
to go-mosquitoes
  ask mosquitoes
  [
    lt random 360
```

```
    fd 1
    bite
  ]
end
```

Many other commands exist, most notably `die`, which instantly kills the agent (removing it from the simulation). We invite the reader to discover these within the relevant documentation when they further experiment with modeling.

3.4.2.4. *Visualization*

A multiagent simulation can produce a multitude of results. It is useful for the modelers to be able to analyze and intelligently synthesize these so as to display them within the interface in the form of monitors, graphs or 2D maps.

3.4.2.4.1. 2D display of the simulated world

Displaying the simulation within a 2D graphical interface is obligatory and cannot be removed. The display can be resized and there is an option to visualize the multi-agent systems (MAS) in pseudo-3D. However, the interface and its use are heavily restricted because of its uniqueness and due to the fact that it does not offer different viewpoints of the simulated world without specifically programming these in. If this were to be the case, special procedures would have to be created to change the *patch* colors as well as the size and color of the *turtles* and *links*, based on their internal states.

NetLogo distinguishes between two different display modes: 1) the first is known as *on tick* mode, which updates the interface on each *tick*; 2) the other is known as *continuous* mode, which updates the interface independently of the model's execution, which can lead to the display refreshing inconsistently. While developing and testing the model, it is advisable to use *on tick* mode, which will allow for a rigorous visualization of the model. The *continuous* mode can then used while exploring a complete, finished model, as it considerably reduces the amount of time needed for the simulation.

3.4.2.4.2. Displaying alphanumeric results

A monitor (*Monitor* in NetLogo's interface) is an alphanumeric section of the interface which displays a variable or the result of an expression (*reporter*). This type of display is very useful for obtaining aggregated results about the *turtles*, *patches* and *links* during a simulation.

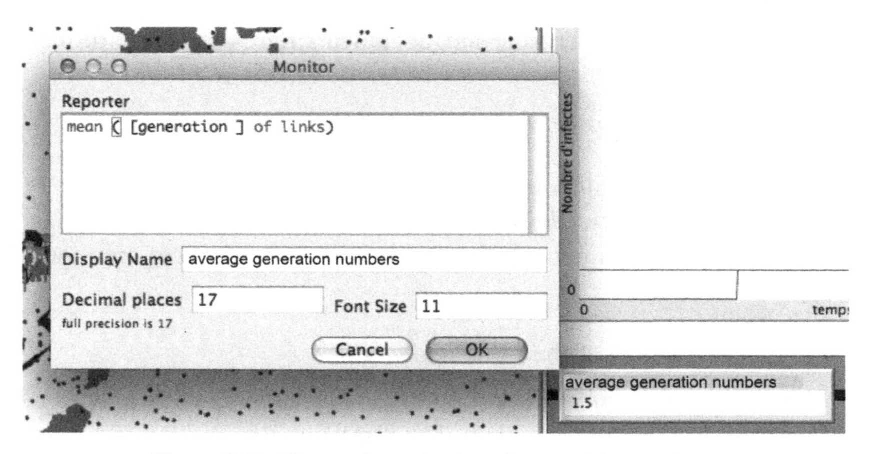

Figure 3.11. *The configuration interface used for monitors*

Figure 3.11 shows a monitor named "average generation number". Via the `mean([generation] of links)` expression, this monitor calculates the average of the values of the `generation` variable that the *link* agents possess, which effectively calculates the average distance between contaminated individuals and individual who was the source of the contamination.

3.4.2.4.3. Displaying results in graphical form

A graph (called a *plot* in NetLogo's interface) is a part of the interface which follows one or more variables that evolve with the progression of the simulation. This type of display resembles the monitor, but with the added factor of time at the expense of precision.

Several graphs may be used within the same model. Each shows one or more series of points (which is known as *pens* in NetLogo) displayed in an orthonormal plane bounded by axes with set coordinates (X min, X max and Y min, Y max).

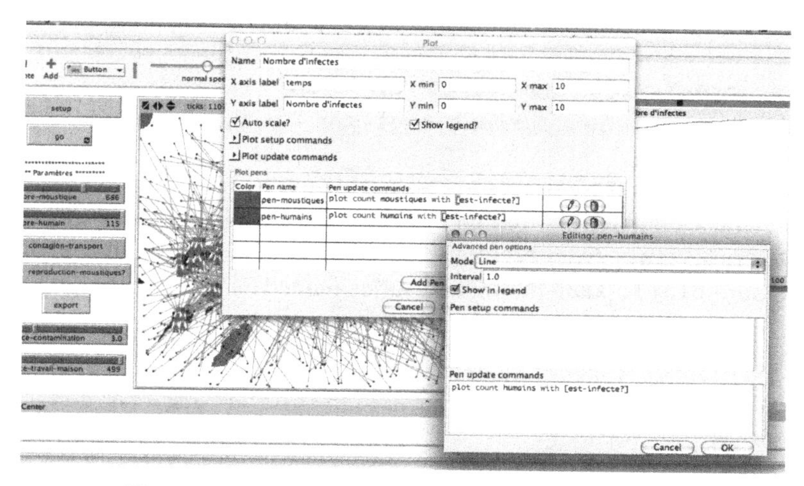

Figure 3.12. *The configuration interface used for graphs*

For each series, the user must define a display mode (line, point or bar), the interval between two values along the *x*-axis, an expression that sets the value of the first point and a second expression that defines the value of each of the subsequent points to be graphed for each *tick* of time.

It is possible to modify a graph with programming code. This feature gives the user many more possibilities than NetLogo's graphical interface. The following primitives are used along with the `do-plot` procedure to redefine the manner in which a graph will update:

– `set-current-plot name_graph` → selects a graph (`name_graph`) to be modified;

– `set-current-plot-pen nane_series` → selects a series (`name_series`) of the previously selected graph that is to be modified;

– `plot y` → add a point to the previously selected series. This point is situated at the *y* coordinate of the previous point to which is added the value of the interval as defined in the configuration interface;

– `plotxy x y` → adds a new point at the x, y coordinates of the previously selected series.

Initially, the `do-plot` procedure selects a graph:

`set-current-plot "number of infected"`
and then, a series: `set-current-plot-pen "pen-mosquitoes"`.

Finally, the `plot count mosquitoes with [isInfected?]` command calculates the number of infected mosquitoes and updates the series. The two previous commands (`set-current-plot-pen` and `plot`) update the second series named as `pen-humans`.

```
to go
   go-patches
   go-mosquitoes
   go-humans
   do-plot ticks; passing to next tick
end
to do-plot
   set-current-plot "number of infected"
   set-current-plot-pen "pen-mosquitoes"
   plot count mosquitoes with [isInfected?]

  set-current-plot-pen "pen-humans"
  plot count humans with [isInfected?]
end
```

In the case of the running example, two series need to be updated on the same graph.

3.5. Agent–agent and agent–environment interactions

3.5.1. *Agent–agent interactions*

One of the advantages of multiagent simulation, notably compared to microsimulation, is that it is possible to model interactions between different agents. In NetLogo, interactions take the form of commands and "questions" (ask commands) that certain agents can make of others. By respecting the principle aim of encapsulation in this manner, the agents are not allowed to directly modify the variables of other agents within the model. So as to do this and as such to implement an interaction, an agent (a) must ask another agent (b) to do something by using the ask primitive that has previously been introduced.

As such, within our example, a random human agent that would destroy all of the mosquitoes would appear in the following form:

```
ask one-of humans
   [
       ask mosquitoes [die]
   ]
```

The one-of command allows for the random selection of a single element of a particular group (in this case, humans). The corresponding program would be translated as follows: ask one of the humans to ask each of the mosquitoes to die.

It should be noted that this question takes the form of an order in the sense that the agent who receives it does not have the possibility to refuse to carry it out or discuss its terms. It is an imperative demand which enters the communications in the form of a message written in object-oriented language.

So as to have a wider scope of expression of the interactions, it may be necessary to reference each of the agents concerned: the asker (a) and the executer (b). NetLogo allows this by using the keywords self and myself. The self term corresponds to the selected agent (who is the executer in our case) and myself corresponds to the agent from the superior level (who is the asker in our case).

In the case of the infection of a human by a mosquito in our model, the mosquitoes are hence asked to carry out the attack procedure:

```
to go-mosquitoes
   ask mosquitoes
    [
    ...
    attack
    ]
end
```

The `attack` procedure is therefore carried out by a mosquito. In an object-focused view, `attack` would be a method belonging only to the mosquito. As such, it can be said that the corresponding code will be carried out from the point of view of the latter. To carry out its attack, the mosquito begins by putting together a list (an *agentset*) of the humans who surround it (at a distance lesser than the `distance-contamination` variable).

```
to attack
   let humansNear humans with [distance myself <
       distance-contamination]
```

In this case, `myself` refers to the mosquito which is currently carrying out the procedure and the `humansNear` group will contain all of the humans at a lesser distance than the `distance-contamination` variable relative to the mosquito in question.

The attack itself then translates to a question posed by the mosquito to all nearby uninfected humans to let it infect them (as long as the mosquito itself is infected, naturally) and will be written as follows:

```
to attack
    ;;context of a mosquito agent
    ask humansNear
    [
      ;;context of a human agent
    if (not [isInfected?] of self) and [isInfected?]
        of myself
    [
```

While this code is being carried out, we will be changing context, passing from the context of the mosquito agent to that of the human agent. This will cause the evolution of the agents that the `self` and `myself` primitives refer to.

In the context of the mosquito agent (before the `ask humansNear` command), `self` refers to the mosquito agent which is currently executing the code and `myself`, which by default should refer to the agent which asked the formerly mentioned mosquito to execute the procedure, actually refers to nothing at all (`nobody`), since the command was called by the model at a upper level.

In the context of the human agent (after the `ask humansNear` command, which asks each of the human agents in the `humansNear` group to execute the subsequent code), `self` refers to the human agent that is currently executing the code and `myself` refers to the mosquito agent which asked it to do so.

To practically illustrate the references detailed above, the human and mosquito agents which both own a Boolean (true/false) `isInfected?` variable allowing us to store whether the agent is infected or not, `[isInfected?] of self` corresponds to the `isInfected?` variable of the human agent (`self` refers to the current context) and `[isInfected?] of myself` corresponds to the `isInfected?` variable of the mosquito agent. Finally, `myself` refers to the context of the upper level.

The `if (not [isInfected?] of self) and [isInfected?] of myself` command can, as such, be translated as follows: "if the currently selected human agent is not infected and the mosquito is infected, then...".

Let us briefly return to the process that puts together the `humansNear` group:

```
to attack
    let humansNear humans with [distance myself <
        distance-contamination]
```

Please note the reference to `myself`. In this situation, the code: `[distance myself < distance-contamination]` is executed in the context of a human agent and `myself` refers to the mosquito agent of the upper level that is currently executing the attack procedure.

3.5.2. *Structuring interactions as part of a social network composed of links*

Originally, NetLogo was more of a platform designed to simulate spatial phenomena, as shown by the numerous examples available in the Models Library. Nonetheless, since social networks were being more and more often used in multiagent simulations to model interactions between individual agents, NetLogo satisfied the demand for this functionality by introducing *links* in its 4.0 version. As shown in Figure 3.1, the *links* take the shape of special agents which link two *turtles* and can be selectively given directionality. When directed, link creation takes on the form of NetLogo's common syntax (`create-link-to`, `creation-<breed>-to`, `create-link-from`), which are commands that link the agent calling for the creation of the link to the agent given as a variable:

```
if any? humans-near with [is-infected?] [
    become-infected
    ask one-of humans-near with [is-infected?]
    [
        create-infection-to myself
        [
                create date ticks
        ]
    ]
]
```

The *infection* species is a special class of *link* (or a *link* type created in the context of this model), `create-infection-to myself` creates a link between the agent executing the function and the agent of the upper level (`myself`), with the direction of the link being specified by the use of `from` or `to` (a *link* is created going toward or away from an agent).

3.5.3. *Adjacency*

When we wish to simulate spatial interactions between entities, such as in the case of a prey-predator model, the notion of adjacency is extremely important: a predator may only eat its prey when immediately adjacent to it. Identifying which entities are adjacent to an agent depends upon the type of topology of the environment (adjacency is not the same on a grid as it is within a network). In the environment defined within NetLogo (a continuous environment coated in a grid made up of *patches*), there are two ways in which adjacency can be calculated. The first solution consists of selecting the subgroup of agents that is at a distance less than a given threshold (e.g. a perception threshold):

```
ask turtles with [distance myself
       < threshold-perception]|.
```

The second solution consists of using, perhaps less precisely, the *patches* which pave the environment upon which exist the *turtles*.

The keyword `here` will allow for the grouping of all the *turtles* which are found on the *patch* which is calling the (`ask turtles-here[...]`) command. Also, the `neighbors` keyword gives access to all the patches adjacent to the current `patch`. Therefore, to access any *turtles* which might be found on adjacent *patches* (and as such, within proximity) all that is necessary is to ask which *turtles* are found on adjacent *patches*, as follows: (`ask turtles-on neighbors`).

The same principle has been kept for the *links* with which it is essentially needed to access some or all of the neighbors linked to a specific agent, and as such `ask one-of link-neighbors` gives access to each of the agents (which are selected in a random order) that are linked to the chosen agent.

Despite the very intuitive implementation of these different functions, identifying the types of functions that can be used or combined across the three main agent types (*turtles*, *patches* and *links*) can be difficult. Once each of these three different approaches has been well identified and understood, NetLogo allows for these functions to be easily combined together.

3.6. Introduction to NetLogo's additional functionalities

As well as the basic model editing and simulation execution tools presented in this chapter, NetLogo provides a collection of additional tools useful for modelers. Additionally, numerous extensions have been created for NetLogo, which serve to extend its language with the aim of integrating new objects into its simulations (such as GIS or networks).

3.6.1. *The Behavior space tool*

Accessible from the *Tools* menu, the *Behavior space* tool allows for the quick setup of experimental test designs to be performed on the model. Global variables and parameters can be defined with all their possible values for their exploration. It then executes an exhaustive experimental design and is able to save any interesting variables or indicators within a .csv file, to be studied using appropriate tools at a later date. Despite the limited capacity of the *Behavior Space*, it is often necessary to use it to launch quick and simple test designs that can help with the detection of any eventual bugs before using more powerful tools whose primary purpose is to study models in great depth (such as *OpenMole*[9]). The study of a model and the usage of the *Behavior Space* are described in the following section.

3.6.2. *Multiplayer (HubNet)*

HubNet is a NetLogo mode dedicated to the management of individual, remote interfaces. This mode is particularly useful for the implementation of serious participatory games where each actor connects, via a local network, to a same simulation within which they play a particular role. HubNet modifies the model based on a particular viewpoint, structured by its own interface which contains a personalized

9 http://www.openmole.org/.

view of the simulation as well as any specific actions available to that player. The user interface is graphically constructed by a instructive interface (*HubNet Client Editor*) but user management is carried out within NetLogo via specific primitives such as `hubnet-send-message`. Participative simulation is further detailed in section 6.5.3.

3.6.3. *Dynamic systems*

While multiagent modeling concerns itself with the individual behaviors of agents, modeling based on dynamic systems is instead focused on the global behaviors of the agent population. The *System Dynamics Modeler* extension (menu *Tools* then *System Dynamics Modeler*) allows for the representation of systems in which there are few entities that effectively represent groups of individuals. Values that are associated to entities evolve thanks to the interactions between these entities. This evolution is commonly represented by a system of ordinary differential equations. Four basic elements allow for the construction of a dynamic system diagram: stocks, variables, flows and links.

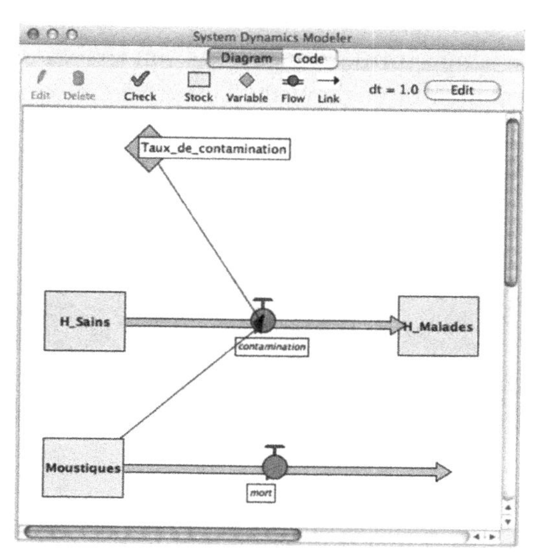

Figure 3.13. *The configuration interface used for modeling dynamic systems*

A stock represents an aggregate, such as a population of healthy humans, a population of contaminated humans or a population of mosquitoes. A flow represents a quantity that passes from one stock to another and of which the volume is controlled by a tap. For example, the flow between the stock of healthy humans and the stock of contaminated humans is a function of the interactions between the stock of healthy humans and the stock of mosquitoes. A variable can represent a constant or an equation that depends on other variables. For example, a variable representing the infection rate is added to the interaction between the stock of healthy humans and the stock of mosquitoes. Finally, a link allows for a value resulting from a stock or a variable to be available (known) to several entities of stocks or variables. As a result, the flow between the two human stocks depends on the stock of mosquitoes. This module, as well as modeling based on equations, is presented in greater detail in section 5.5.

3.6.4. *Introduction to models in 3D environments*

3D, or the use of a 3D space for the movement of agents, allows for the modeler to have access to many improvements with respect to display and interaction (made realistic and immersive, superimposing additional information throughout the simulation, etc.). However, the introduction of 3D into a model does not have as its only goal to make the environment more realistic, it also allows for a more intuitive and immersive study of the model.

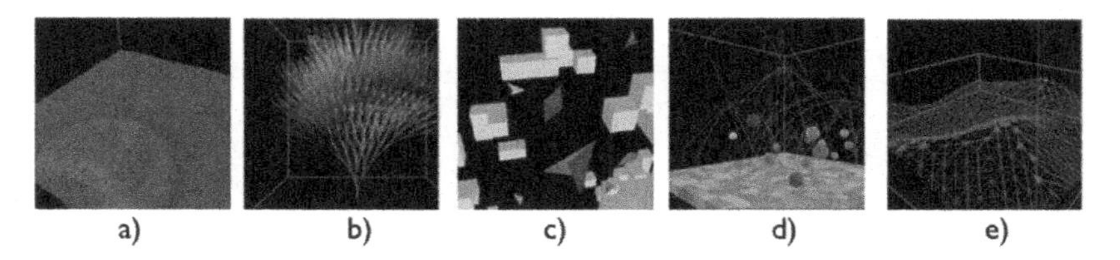

Figure 3.14. *Example of 3D models in NetLogo3D: a) a water drop falling on a solid surface, b) a 3D fractal tree, c) termites, d) a bouncing ball and e) turtles evolving upon a 3D surface. For a color version of the figure, see www.iste.co.uk/banos/netlogo.zip*

NetLogo allows for a 3D world to be easily defined using NetLogo3D (an application bundled with NetLogo). The environment in a 3D world possesses a `width`, a `height` and a `depth`. The *patches* become cubes with an additional coordinate `pzcor`. Now the *turtles* also possess three Cartesian coordinates `xcor`, `ycor` and `zcor` as well as an orientation defined by three variables (`heading`, `pitch` and `roll`). The viewpoint from which the user sees the world corresponds to the location and orientation of the *observer*, which faces an initial point as defined by the `face` or `facexyz` commands. Its position is defined by the `setxyz` command. An agent may move within the 3D world using the `follow`, `follow-me`, `ride` and `ride-me` primitives. It is also possible to change the viewpoint of the simulation by using the `watch` and `watch-me` primitives. Finally, it is possible to import 3D shapes into the environment with the `load-shapes-3d` primitive.

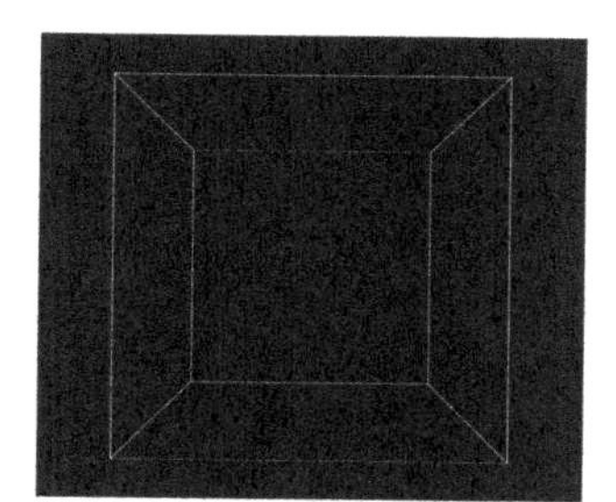

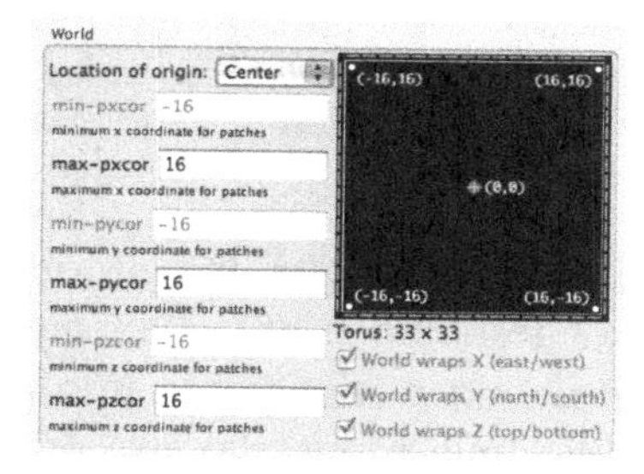

Figure 3.15. *An environment modeled in NetLogo3D*

When NetLogo3D is launched, the world is represented in the shape of a cube. The *Model Settings* add limiting coordinates in the third dimension (`max-pzcor` and `min-pzcor`), which are added to the x and y coordinate information available previously (`max-pxcor`, `min-pxcor`, `max-pycor` and `min-pycor`).

It should be noted that a model written in NetLogo can often be opened with NetLogo3D and will then be displayed on a 2D plane. The opposite is scarcely true, as the 3D primitives and variables are not recognized by NetLogo.

3.6.5. *Geographical information systems*

When the heterogeneous nature of environmental data is an important element affecting the dynamic of a multiagent system, then the use of the GIS extension (`extensions [gis]` at the beginning of the main block of code) is most useful.

Various raster file formats, such as ascii `grid` (.asc and .grd) and vector shapefiles (.shp), can be read with the use of the `gis:load-dataset "name.(shp l asc)"` primitive. The included operations consist of reading the data, defining its coordinate system and defining or executing operations upon this data. It is therefore possible to import a group of values by *patch*, by points, by lines or by polygons.

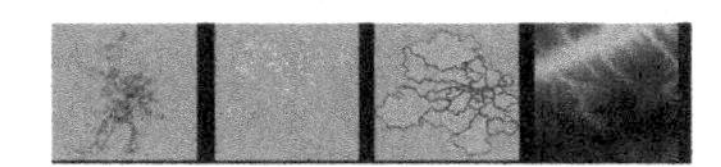

Figure 3.16. *Examples of importing geographical data. For a color version of the figure, see www.iste.co.uk/banos/netlogo.zip*

In a general sense, the information needed to be able to project the values resulting from a GIS layer into NetLogo are the [minimum-x maximum-x minimum-y maximum-y] coordinates of the GIS layer and the [min-pxcor max-pxcor min-pycor max-pycor] coordinates of the NetLogo space. It is possible to use one of the GIS extensions' primitives to transfer these values, as follows:

– in a predefined domain, with:

```
gis:set-transformation gis:envelope-of name_of_the_layer
 [min-pxcor max-pxcor min-pycor max-pycor]
```

– in the entire domain, with:

```
gis:set-world-envelope gis:envelope-of name_of_the_layer
```

A group of primitives can then be used to perform operations of this data such as selection based on a variable's value, the calculation of polygon centroids, the intersection between two entities with `gis:intersects? A B`, or A and B, can be of the *VectorDataset* type, *VectorFeature*, *turtle*, *link*, *patch*, *agentset* or list, or even to assign the values of a variable to *patches* or to *turtles*.

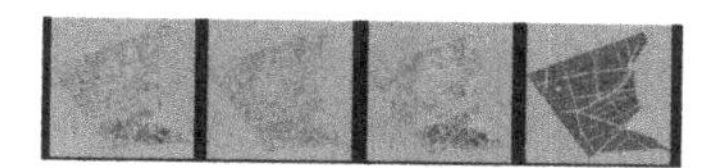

Figure 3.17. *Display of different layers of information. For a color version of the figure, see www.iste.co.uk/banos/netlogo.zip*

Finally, it is also possible to put together .shp data files from the *turtle*, *patch* and *link* data so as to read a work with them in GIS. For example, the `gis:turtle-dataset turtles` primitive returns all the values of the agentset's variables. These are then modified and saved with the use of the `gis:store-dataset` primitive. The following command:

```
gis:store-dataset gis:turtle-dataset turtles "centroid"
```

allows for the *turtles* which happen to be centroids of polygons to be exported within a .shp file. In this manner, NetLogo data can be transformed into a format that can be read by a GIS such as QGIS (previously known as QuantumGIS).

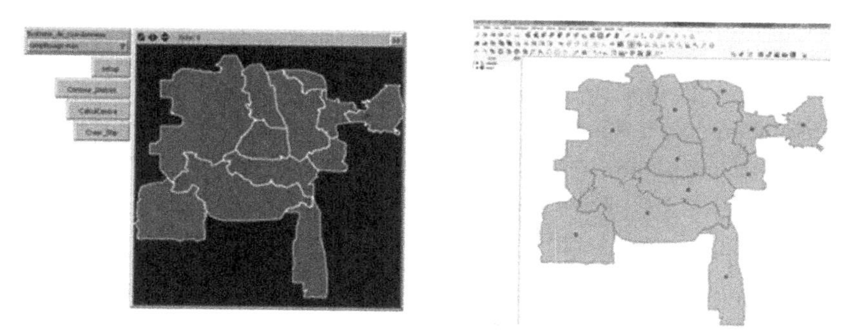

Figure 3.18. *Comparing the display of a shapefile in NetLogo and QGIS*

3.6.6. *Algorithms in graphs*

As mentioned in this section and the previous sections, agents are entities that interact with each other regardless of adjacency, as well as the environment that surrounds them. It is possible to display a representative graph of these interactions, in which agents are represented by vertices and the interactions are shown by edges. Relationships between the various elements may be expressed or implied. For example, if we were modeling a city with roads and intersections, the relationships are clearly stated with weights associated with the edges that can be distances or traffic density (maximum and/or current) which cannot be exceeded. Equally, if the model contained drains and sewers, the limit to be exceeded would be a flow rate assigned as before to the edges. On the other hand, the relationships between a model's entities may be implied and therefore depend on properties associated with a particular agent, which will vary greatly over the course of the simulation. For example, it is possible to model relationships such as those based on affinities between agents, such as musical tastes, belonging to a same company, friendships via social networks, coworkers, etc. Here, again, it is possible to create graphs that are the result of focusing on a particular relationship present during the model's simulation. It is also possible to combine several of these into yet another graph.

Once a graph has been created from the model, it can be useful to extract information from it to better analyze the model. In this situation, the graph has the only purpose of clearly displaying a particular property of the model. In fact, this display of data is very broad, as any data can be displayed on a graph, provided that it makes sense. This ranges from tubular representation to the representation of lists and all unorganized relationships as well as the absence of relationships.

When a graph has been put together and correctly displays the chosen data, it is possible to benefit from a large amount of reading around the study of graphs. The first use of a graph goes back to the 18th Century. Léonhard Euler showed the inhabitants of Königsberg – who had invited him there in 1736 – that it was not possible to cross all of the bridges in the town once and only once. He set down the conditions that a graph must respect for this challenge to be solved. Hence, such a graph is today referred to as an Eulerian graph. His results were published in 1741, but without a proof. It was Hierholzer who eventually published the proof in 1873. The origins and rise of modern graph theory are attributed to Claude Berge, who developed his ideas on the topic in the late 1950s. It was the advances in computational techniques which helped to highlight the utility of graphs for a great number of fields, as automatic computer processing made them a viable tool for data analysis, which was not the case when all graphing had to be done manually. As a result of this, a great number of algorithms were developed to help exploit the numerous properties of graphs, whether on a literal or theoretical level.

Among the algorithms, which immediately appear to be of use for the exploitation of a multiagent model, are the following: Dijkstra, Bellman-Ford and Floyd-Warshall's algorithms, for finding the shortest path; Bellman-Ford's algorithm, for finding the longest; Tarjan's algorithm, for finding the strongly connected components of a graph;), Ford–Fulkerson's algorithm, for calculating the maximum flow in a flow network; the Hungarian algorithm, a combinatorial optimization algorithm; the Traveling Salesman algorithm (if one passes once through each edge) or Eulerian algorithm (passing only once through each vertex), used for pathing and routing problems; and Prim and Kruskal's algorithms, for finding minimum spanning trees in weighted graphs.

Equally, it is possible to use a particular type of graph to display social networks, these are known as small-world networks. They allow us to show relationships between nodes, with very dense areas in some places. They are based on the concept that everyone is linked to all others in some fashion, whether through common likes or dislikes, or any other property of social relations, and that this link is very short. Milgram carried out the first experiment of its kind in the United States (published in 1967 amid high criticism) during which envelopes were handed from person to person, from the sender to the recipient. One of the letters took only 4 days to arrive at destination. Within the same school of thought, mathematicians created a number, the Erds number, which gives the "collaborative distance" between any researcher to the Hungarian mathematician Paul Erdös, measured from co-authorship of scientific papers. For example, if I were to publish a paper with Paul Erdös, I am at a distance of 1 from him, yet if I publish instead with one of his co-authors, I am at a distance of 2, and so on. The same calculation was made to find the average distance between individual Facebook users. Thus, the study of the interactions between actors in a social model can be beneficial for its analysis in a multiagent simulation.

Finally, graphs are excellent at displaying classifications of agents based on their intrinsic or acquired properties. They allow for agent populations with common or similar characteristics to be clearly visible, which, in turn, means that the main groups and subgroups of a simulation can be easily identified, which may not have been possible beforehand, as the creators of the model will not necessarily have been able to predict which groups would emerge as the largest. As well as being able to follow the evolution of a model during its simulation, the capacity for illustrating the emergence of new agent categories is another benefit for a study of a multiagent simulation. As a result of this brief presentation on the uses of graphs in the context of multiagent simulations, it is quite clear that a comprehensive understanding of their functionality is important for the creation and analysis of multiagent models. This is the case at the simulation level, by influencing agent behavior based on the decisions they may make during the course of a simulation. This is also true during analysis, where they can be used to explain the reasoning behind the creation of a simulation, such as a study of the impacts of roadworks on urban journeys or a study of emergent behaviors outside city sports facilities.

3.6.7. *NetLogo dictionary and abbreviated commands*

All of NetLogo's commands are documented on the software's website, in the *NetLogo dictionary*[10]. The site allows most notably to identify which instructions can be used in the context of the *observer* (), of a *turtle* (), of a *patch* () or of a *link* ().

The NetLogo dictionary also introduces an abbreviated notation for the main commands. Both forms of a command (full and abbreviated) are exactly the same in terms of functionality. For example:

– `create-turtles` can be abbreviated to `crt`;

10 http://ccl.northwestern.edu/netlogo/5.0/docs/dictionary.html.

– `create-turtles 10 [ ... ]` is equivalent to `crt 10 [ ... ]`.

3.7. Conclusion

This chapter introduced the basics of the NetLogo language by the use of our running example. While not comprehensive, it gives the reader the basics needed to build their first models. It also allows them to understand our example, as well as the various models supplied with the NetLogo software. Yet, it is only practice that will help the reader to master the language and use it without external help.

Now that the model has been built and tested, and that the modeler has "played" with their model, that is to say that they have changed it by modifying its basic variables, a more in-depth analysis of simulations is necessary (notably, to carry out a sensitivity test). This is the aim that the following chapter has been given, by describing the *Behavior Space* tool that was briefly introduced previously.

4

Agent-based Model Exploration

4.1. Introduction

4.1.1. *Introductory example*

The previous chapters have allowed us to introduce the basics of agent-based model creation with NetLogo. This has resulted in a model such as the one used in our running example. Once the model has been built, the aim is to manipulate it in such a way that new knowledge about the modeled phenomenon can be created. For example, we could look to study the rate of infection resulting from certain parameter values. The use and study of a model is nonetheless as complex as its creation. As such, using our model, we could launch the simulation with standard initial parameters (say 300 humans, 500 mosquitoes, a contamination distance of 5 and a work–home distance of 500), and we would obtain the graph in Figure 4.1(a), indicating no infection beyond the source mosquito, which would lead us to conclude that these parameters lead to no infections. However, upon relaunching the simulation with the exact same values, we might obtain the graph in Figure 4.1(b), with the infection present in almost 100% of individuals after 1,000 iterations.

Such results, typical of stochastic models, invite us to proceed to a more detailed analysis of the situation:

Chapter written by Arnaud BANOS, Philippe CAILLOU, Benoît GAUDOU and Nicolas MARILLEAU.

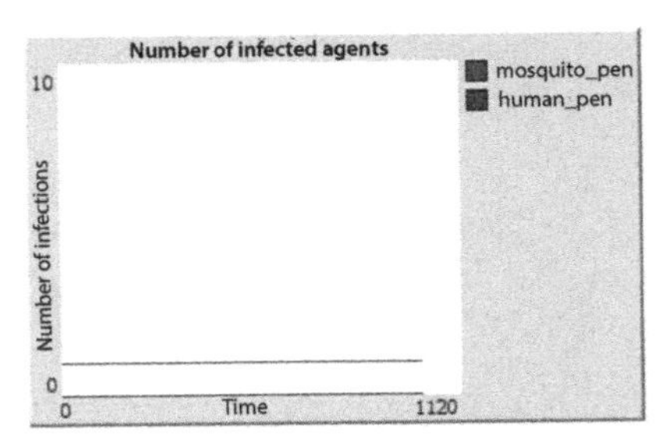

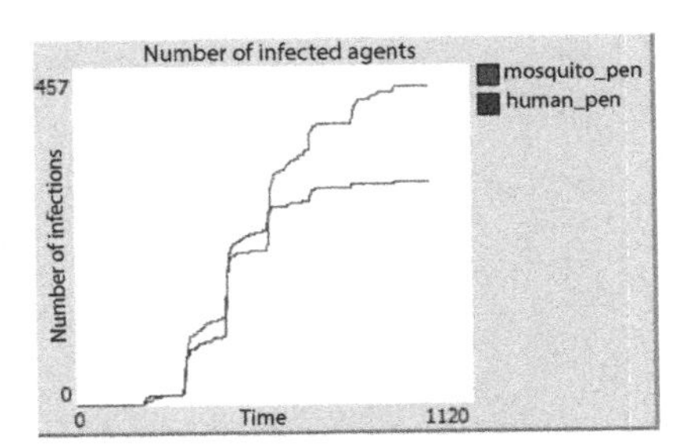

Figure 4.1. *Evolution of the number of humans and mosquitoes infected after 1,000 iterations, during two separate simulations based on the same initial conditions (identical initialization parameters). For a color version of the figure, see www.iste.co.uk/banos/netlogo.zip*

– Where does the infection come from during the simulation? It would be useful to better visualize the simulation by perhaps representing the distribution of infection dates (Figure 4.2 (a), see section 4.2.2) and the infection sites compared to the movements of the source mosquito (Figure 4.5, see section 4.2.3.1)

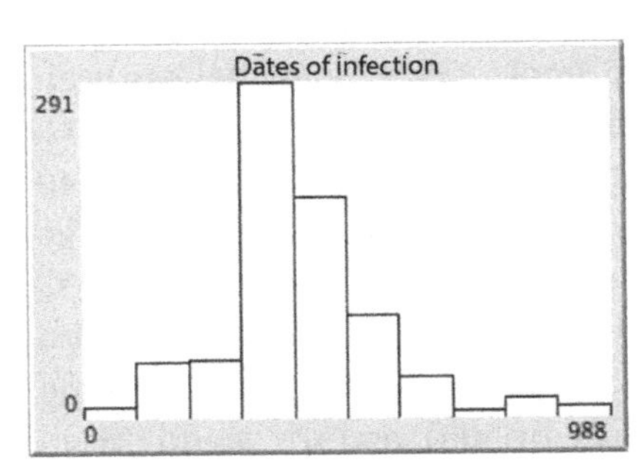

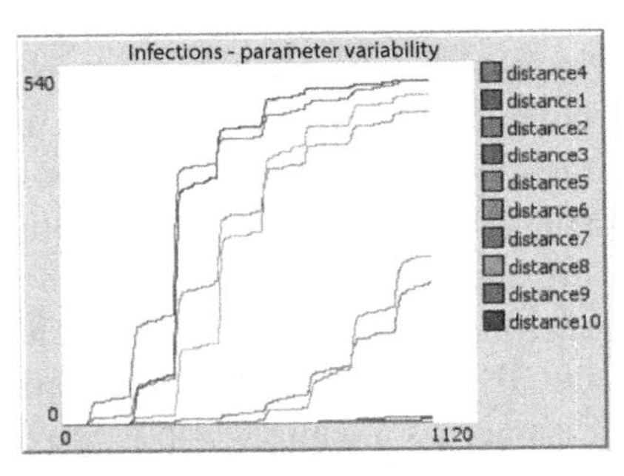

Figure 4.2. *Distribution of the agent infection dates during the course of a simulation (on the left) and the change in infection count across several simulations with different values for one of the model's variables (on the right). For a color version of the figure, see www.iste.co.uk/banos/netlogo.zip*

– How can several simulations be displayed in order for a comparison? Given the different results obtained across several simulations, it is interesting to display a graph that compares different simulations (for example, the infection count across several simulations, Figure 4.2 (b), see section 4.2.6)

– How can the impact of different parameters on the final result be analyzed? We have defined four main parameters, but which has the greatest effect, and which of these have an impact upon the final infection count? Ideally, a large number of simulations would be carried out with different values for the parameters (for example, to analyze the impact of the contamination distance, Figure 4.2 (b), see section 4.3.2 for the definition of exploration and section 4.3.3.1 for a graph). We would also like to be able to say whether or not the impact is statistically significant (see section 4.3.4).

4.1.2. *Objectives*

More generally speaking, creating a simulation model is only the first step to receive useful results. Any data received from running a simulation once will not necessarily be the same if you launch the same simulation again: random phenomena or even simply the order in which certain agents act may have important consequences leading to widely varying results, even based on the same initial conditions. In our running example, the first infected mosquito may remain in a corner without infecting anyone, as his movements are random. Equally, if a human is infected near the start of the simulation, the infection might spread very quickly, as this agent will rapidly transmit it to his/her neighbors as he/she moves around. This instability phenomenon is even more amplified when the parameters are modified. The inherent unpredictability in complex systems renders a systematic exploration of a model very important, which is facilitated by certain functionalities offered by NetLogo, most particularly graphs and the BehaviorSpace.

Exploring a simulation consists of studying the behavior of the model during and after its execution, and in particular, observing variables defined as objectives (such as the number of infected individuals). Three main approaches are detailed as following:

– How does the model behave during a simulation for a given set of parameters? This first exploration step, which will be covered in the following section, is primarily based on numerical indicators and graphs, updated dynamically throughout the simulation.

– How do the different parameters influence the model's behavior? Here, a possibility is to carry out several simulations with different parameter values, whether similar or far apart, thus to study the sensitivity of the model to different parameter changes. By doing this, we carry out an exploration of the parameter space. NetLogo's BehaviorSpace allows for this type of exploration and will be covered in a second section. Analyzing data resulting from the implemented experimental design, with the goal of obtaining results from the sensitivity analysis, mainly requires the use of external tools such as R or Excel. This option will be covered at the end of the second section.

– How can we arrive at one of the simulation's specific objectives? The goal here is to test virtual scenarios, searching for the "best" solution. For example: whom to vaccinate and at which point in time so that an epidemic spreads as slowly as possible? This is a case of objective optimization. This type of approach, typical of what is known as an "inverse problem", can be carried out in NetLogo with the help of the Behavior Search extension (http://behaviorsearch.org/documentation/tutorial.html), or in a more sophisticated manner with the OpenMole platform (http://www.openmole.org/), which allows for distribution of simulations on distributed computing environments. This type of approach will not be studied in this chapter and will instead be covered in its own chapter in Volume 2 [BAN 15].

4.2. Exploring a simulation

4.2.1. *Objectives*

NetLogo's interface is one of its main assets. Simple in use, it offers numerous possibilities for the exploration of models and in particular, the exploration of dynamic graphs which allow the user to follow the behavior of chosen variables during the simulation. The basics of graph creation in NetLogo were presented in Chapter 3. We will now concentrate on the use of these graphs for studying models.

Understanding what is happening during a single simulation requires an initial effort to obtain pertinent data. Knowing which data would be interesting to extract out of a simulation depends on the simulation itself. For example, the interface of a social network simulation will be different from that of a stadium evacuation simulation. We will now present several commonalities and examples which demonstrate the different possible situations.

During a simulation, two different information types that can be studied may be distinguished as follows:

– variables belonging to agents, which may be represented as distributions or scatter plots;

– aggregated variables (such as the average evacuation speed of the number of infected individuals). These values will have a unique value at each tick of time, and are usually represented as time series (evolution of the number of infected agents) or coupled in an xy-plot (the number of humans infected over the number of mosquitoes).

We will now define three graph types which facilitate the analysis of these data categories:

– The study of the distribution of a variable within an agent population with the help of a histogram;

– Following an agents trajectory with an xy-plot;

– The use of a same graph across different simulations to carry out an initial sensibility study with identical or different parameters.

We will also modify the observers main window so as to produce maps, display infection links and follow a specific agent.

4.2.2. *Using a histogram to display distributions*

Objective: displaying the distribution of infection dates (Figure 4.3)

Method: using a histogram whose range of axes is automatically defined.

Histograms are particularly useful for studying the distribution of values against a continuous variable. For example, we will display the distribution of the infection date of each agent, which is stored in the `date` variable of each infection link (see running example). NetLogo can automatically display this with a predetermined discretization.

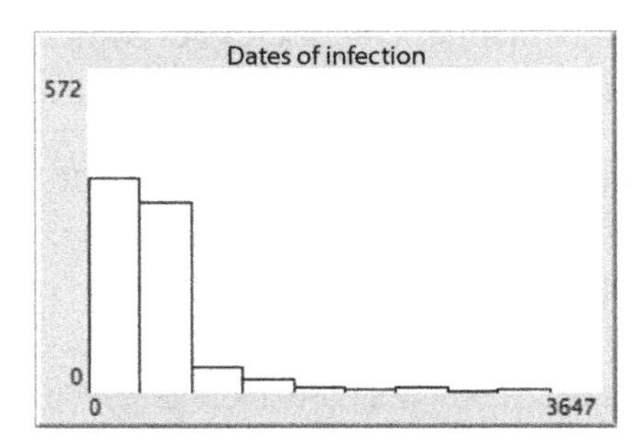

Figure 4.3. *Distribution of the number of infected individuals (along the y-axis) relative to the infection date (along the x-axis)*

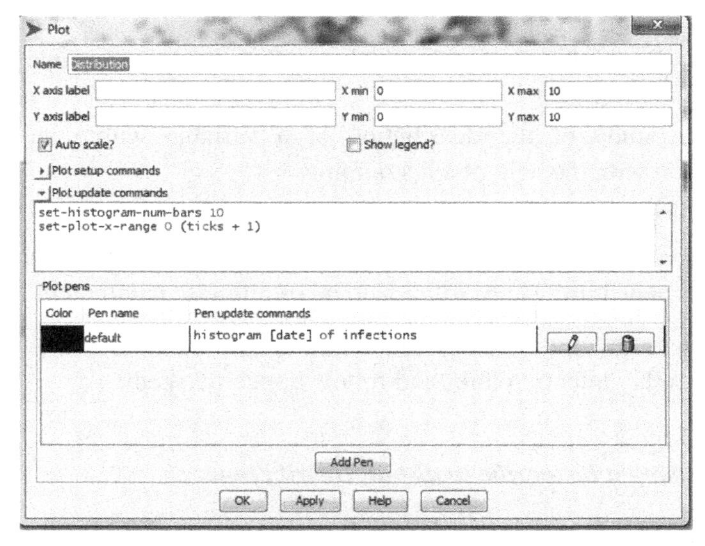

Figure 4.4. *Settings window for the graph displaying the distribution of infections in the form of a histogram*

The commands used to create a histogram are as follows:

– `histogram` allows for the displayed variable to be specified (`date` of each agent link `infection` with `[date] of infections`). This command allows for the creation of a histogram from any numerical list (non-number variables are ignored);

– `set-histogram-num-bars` allows for the number of classes of the histogram to be specified. A default value (10 in this case) must be given, but a slider named after this value could also be created, which would allow for the dynamic modification of the number of classes of the histogram.

4.2.3. *Using an xy-plot*

Objective: displaying the locations of all infection events with a color dependent on the date and trajectory of the first infected mosquitoes (Figure 4.5).

Method: creating an xy-plot, defining a color taken from a color pallet based on a variable, adding pens and naming them automatically.

XY-plots allow for points to be traced and if desired, joined, by setting two coordinates (as opposed to series where the *x*-axis always displays time).

They can be used in many different ways during a simulation:

– to represent the change of a variable relative to another so as to display the evolution of the number of infected humans as compared to the number of infected mosquitoes, for example:

- a particular situation consists of displaying *x* and *y* positional coordinates along the *x*- and *y*-axes, respectively. In this case, the change of position and therefore the trajectory of one or several agents is displayed. However, it is also possible to display the change of average position, such as to show where the current center of infection is situated;

– finally, it is also possible to display the location of particular events, such as infection sites.

4.2.3.1. *Displaying a group of points (individuals/elements)*

A certain number of primitives are used to define the tracing of xy-plots. The `plotxy` primitive allows for a point to be added to the current graph by specifying the *x* and *y* coordinates. For example, in order to display the location of each infection recorded in the `infection` links, the following command can be used to update the graph in Figure 4.5:

```
ask infections
[
  set-plot-pen-color scale-color red date 0 ticks
  plotxy lieuInfectionX lieuInfectionY
]
```

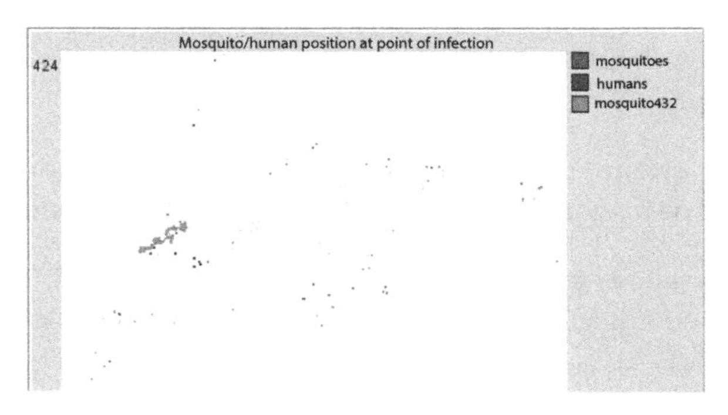

Figure 4.5. *Display of infection sites and of the trajectory of the first infected mosquitoes. The red/blue color of the infection sites is darker for earlier infections. For a color version of the figure, see www.iste.co.uk/banos/netlogo.zip*

The `scale-color` command allows for a color gradient to be easily defined by using a variable to define each level. Here, the `date` variable (infection date, attribute of each `infection` link) is used to display the location with a color (`red`) that is darker for earlier infections. The last two variables allow for the minimum (`0`) and maximum (`ticks`) limits of the scale to be defined.

4.2.3.2. *Displaying one or several trajectories with the help of dynamic pens*

As well as infection sites, we might wish to add the trajectories of the initially infected mosquito or mosquitoes. If we want a separate color for each originally infected mosquito, NetLogo allows for new pens to be dynamically created. In this situation, we can create a new pen for each originally infected `turtle` (with `isInfectionExternal` being true).

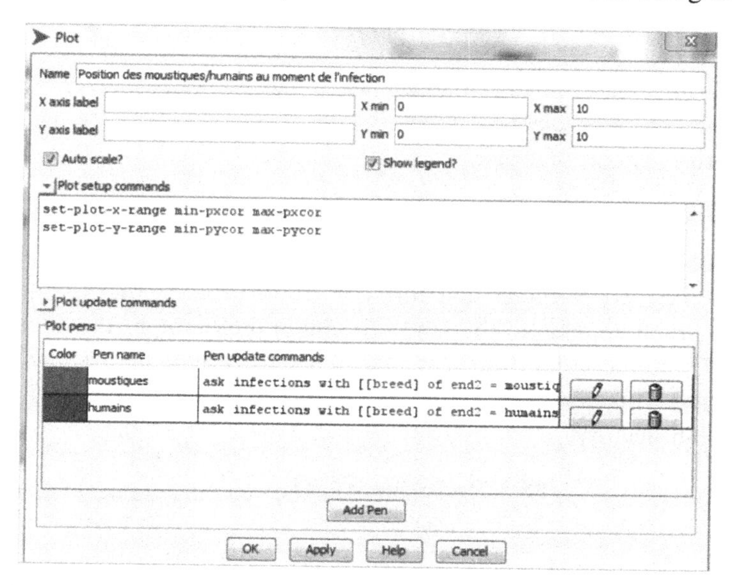

Figure 4.6. *Defining an xy-plot, with a pen for human infections and another for mosquito infections*

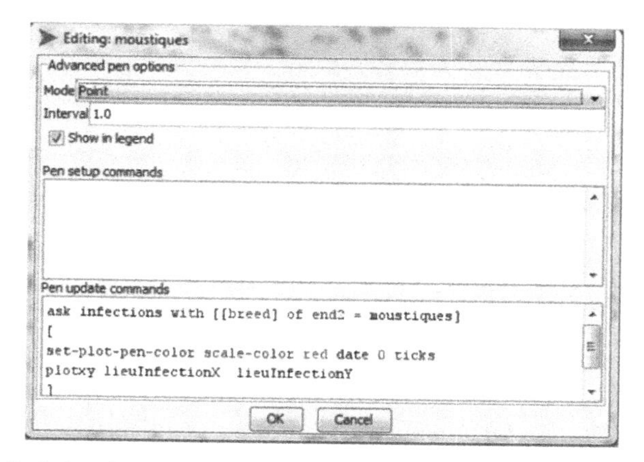

Figure 4.7. *Defining the xy-plots mosquito pen: points are placed at the infection site with a color that is lighter the closer the infection date (`date`) is to the current time of the simulation (`ticks`)*

In the *update* field of the graph, enter:

```
ask turtles with [estInfectionExterieur]
[
  create-temporary-plot-pen word breed who
  set-plot-pen-color green
  plotxy pxcor pycor
]
```

`create-temporary-plot-pen` creates the new pen for each identified agent. The only variable that this command takes is that of the pen name (which appears in the key). To obtain the name of the agent, its (`breed`) and identifier (`who`) are concatenated with the help of the `word` command. This gives us a legible (species) and unique (identifier) name for each trajectory.

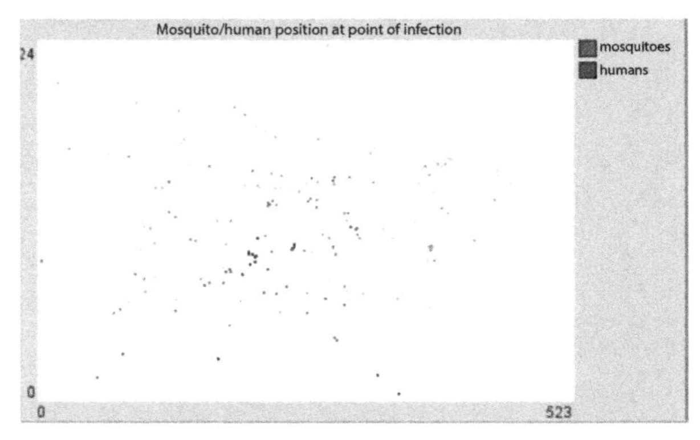

Figure 4.8. *Displaying infection sites with a color gradient dependent on the infection date. For a color version of the figure, see www.iste.co.uk/banos/netlogo.zip*

As this is a new pen, we cannot write this command in the pen update field (*Pen update command*) but instead it must be written in the graph update field (*Plot update command*). Another solution would be to place this command directly within the model's code, while specifying which graph is used with a similar command to the following:

```
set-current-plot "Position of mosquitoes and humans at
moment of infection"
```

4.2.3.3. *Following the infection source mosquito with watch-me*

Given the large number of displayed agents, it may be useful to focus on a single agent. The `watch-me` command allows for an agent to be focused upon (the initially infected agent, for example). A simple implementation of this is to create a *switch* named `Follow_Source-Agent?`, and then to call a simple procedure that uses this Boolean value within the `Go` procedure.

```
to follow-source-agent
 if FollowSource-Agent? and source-agent-follow? = 0
 [
  ask turtles with [isInfectionExternal]
  [
    watch-me
  ] set source-agent-follow? 1
 ]
 if not FollowSource-Agent? and source-agent-follow? = 1
   [
   reset-perspective
   set source-agent-follow? 0
   ]
end
```

The highly permissive character of the NetLogo language should be noted here, as it allows for a high-level primitive (`reset-perspective`) to be called by an agent. This permissivity offers great flexibility but is not always free from ambiguities and requires a certain formality. Equally, calling the `follow-source-agent` procedure from within the `Go` procedure, while practical, means that it is called at each tick. Resorting to a global variable (`source-agent-follow?`) allows for its use to be limited by introducing an intermediate test: the agent is only focused upon if the switch is activated and if the agent in question is not already being followed. We will see an alternative approach later, which separates the call function from the central `Go` procedure.

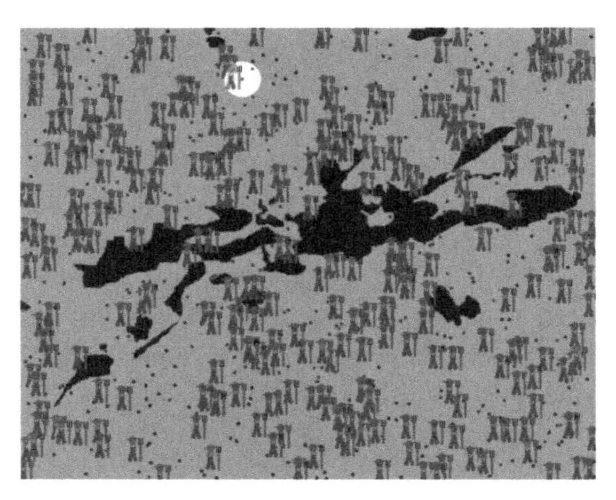

Figure 4.9. *Result of using the watch-me command which allows for an agent to be followed. For a color version of the figure, see www.iste.co.uk/banos/netlogo.zip*

4.2.4. *Mapping with the help of patches*

Objective: cartographic display of spatial variables (Figure 4.10).

Method: constructing a smoothed thematic map with the help of the *`diffuse` and `scale-color`* primitives.

Mapping spatial variables is particularly useful in the case of spatial models such as the one developed here. NetLogo does not have any predefined tools in this field, but certain included primitives offer remarkable possibilities, notably when the base patch entities are exploited. Nonetheless, there remains a delicate issue with the interaction with the user. The user must be able to create their maps at any moment, without interrupting the simulation, and without excessive computation time. This is all the more true with a larger number of patches: in our example, there are 222,700, a value which can be obtained by entering `show count patches` in the observer field.

Unlike the approach detailed in the previous example, the principal idea here is to only activate this cartographic option at the user's request, at the press of a button (`Map`) and with the help of a scrollable menu (Chooser) which facilitates them to choose the variable to be mapped : "Number of infected humans" or "Number of infected mosquitoes"

Nevertheless, two important bridges must be crossed before arriving at proper cartographic representation. The first step consists of creating the spatial variable at the correct locations. While attempting to exploit the possibilities offered by the patches, it is during this stage that the new nb-infections-humans and nb-infections-mosquitoes must be stored:

```
patches-own[
locationHome?
nb-infections-humans
nb-infections-mosquitoes
]
```

The second step consists of updating these two variables throughout the simulation. In order to accomplish this, the principal process that influences the calculation of these variables is used, which is the Sting procedure in our case. At the moment when an interaction between a mosquito and a human takes place, the virus can be effectively transmitted from the mosquito to the human, or the other way round. In both cases, a record of this "transaction" is kept by incrementally increasing the variable of the corresponding patch (nb-infections-humans in the first case and nb-infections-mosquitoes in the second):

```
ask patch-here [
set nb-infections-humans
nb-infections-humans + 1
]
```

Once this variable is updated, it becomes possible to map it with the use of two of NetLogo's primitives: diffuse and scale-color. The former (diffuse) allows for the smoothing of the variable in question by taking the value of each of a patch's neighboring patches. The amount of smoothing depends not only on the numerical variable (here, `0.5`), but also on the number of iterations of the procedure (`repeat 20`). The `scale-color` procedure, already discussed earlier, allows for the simple creation of a color gradient once the lower (`min-VC`) and higher (`max-VC`) limits have been defined. For increased legibility, it is possible to turn off the graphical display of the agents present (humans and mosquitoes but also links):

```
to map
 if MappedVariable = "Number of infected humans"
 [
  ask turtles [ht]
  ask links [hide-link]
  ask patches [set pcolor black]
  repeat 20 [diffuse nb-infections-humans 0.5]
  let min-VC min [nb-infections-humans] of patches
  let max-VC max [nb-infections-humans] of patches
  ask patches with [nb-infections-humans > 0]
  [set pcolor scale-color red nb-infections-humains
   min-VC max-VC]
 ]
 if MappedVariable = "Number of infected mosquitoes"
   [
    ask turtles [ht]
    ask links [hide-link]
    ask patches [set pcolor black]
    repeat 20 [diffuse nb-infections-mosquitoes 0.5]
    let min-VC min [nb-infections-mosquitoes] of patches
    let max-VC max [nb-infections-mosquitoes] of patches
    ask patches with [nb-infections-mosquitoes > 0]
    [set pcolor scale-color green nb-infections-
    mosquitoes min-VC max-VC]
   ]
   if MappedVariable = "Land use"
   [
    ask turtles [st]
    ask links [show-link]
```

```
    ask patches [set pcolor black]
    ask patches with [not locationHome?] [set pcolor
      white]
    ask patches with [locationHome?] [set pcolor gray]
  ]
end
```

The maps obtained (Figure 4.10) allow for the spatial distribution of the mosquito–human and human–mosquito transmissions to be visualized.

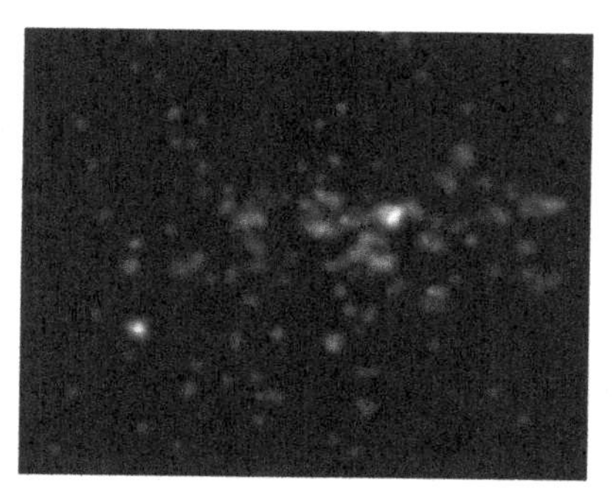

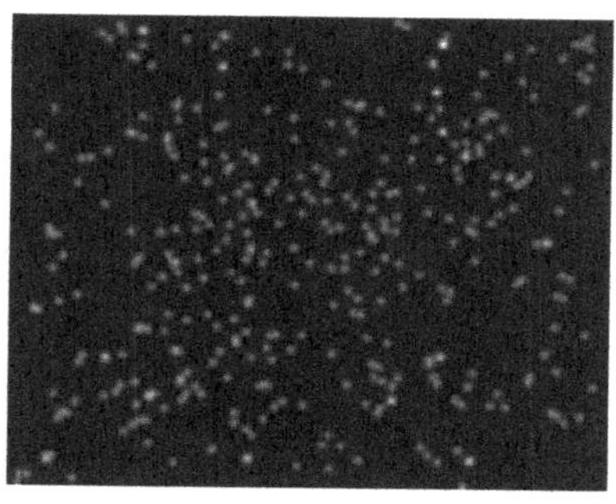

Figure 4.10. *Spatial distribution of the mosquito–human and human–mosquito transmissions. For a color version of the figure, see www.iste.co.uk/banos/netlogo.zip*

4.2.5. *Display of the mosquito/human interaction network*

The model is based on dynamic interactions between humans and mosquitoes. Due to this, it is useful to visualize the underlying interaction network. In order not to penalize the execution of the model by displaying an ever-increasing number of links, we may use a `Show_Links?` switch, which will activate and deactivate the display.

The `show-hide_links` procedure, called from within the Go function, allows for the display of the dynamically created interaction network. The `scale-color` procedure is once again very useful for differentiating objects. In this case, it takes the infection date as a variable: the later the infection, the lighter the link color.

```
to show-hide_links
ifelse Show_Links? and any? links
[
 let min-date min [date] of
 links let max-date max [date] of links
 ask links
 [
   set hidden? false
   if min-date != max-date [set color scale-color green
   date min-date max-date]
   ]]
[ask links [set hidden? true]]
end
```

The link primitives (*links*) allow for the simple manipulation of the graph. As such, the `my-in-links` and `my-out-links` functions called by the `human` agents would allow for the subgraphs of the mosquito–human infections and the human–mosquito infections to be displayed separately and respectively. A dynamic coupling with the GraphStream software (http://graphstream-project.org/) would allow for real-time calculations of the graph indicators, describing the structures displayed within NetLogo more precisely.

4.2.6. *Use of graphs across several simulations*

Objective: following the infection count across several simulations (Figure 4.15).

Method : creating a graph that does not reset in between simulations.

Graphs allow us to follow the state of a simulation at a particular instant (distributions) or its evolution across time (series). It may also be interesting to follow a variable across several simulations, or to compare its evolution between several simulations.

The definition of "persistent" graphs differs from that of standard graphs in the following two ways:

– the simulation must not clear the graph when it relaunches;

– the definition of a temporary graph must take into account that the pens must pass through the origin again, without drawing a line between the last point and the origin.

To accomplish the first objective, the commonly used `clear-all` function must not be used, as it automatically calls the `clear-plots` function, which clears all graphs.

A function alternative to `setup` must be created which includes all the elements of the basic function except for the function that clears all graphs:

```
to clean
  clear-ticks
  clear-turtles
  clear-patches
  clear-drawing
  clear-globals
  load-map
  init-mosquito
  init-human
  create-epidemic
  reset-ticks
end
```

We can link this function to an alternative button to the standard `Setup` (Figure 4.11).

Once this has been carried out, certain graph types can already be persistently used, such as the xy-plot displaying the infection age and the trajectory of the original host mosquitoes defined in the previous section (Figure 4.12). In this case, we can visualize the trajectories of the mosquitoes as well as the infection locations and dates across three simulations.

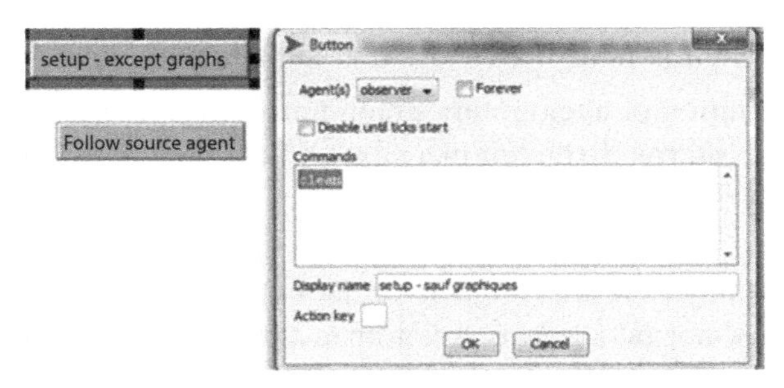

Figure 4.11. *Defining a button which calls the clean function, as opposed to the setup function, which allows for the simulation to be reset without clearing the graphs*

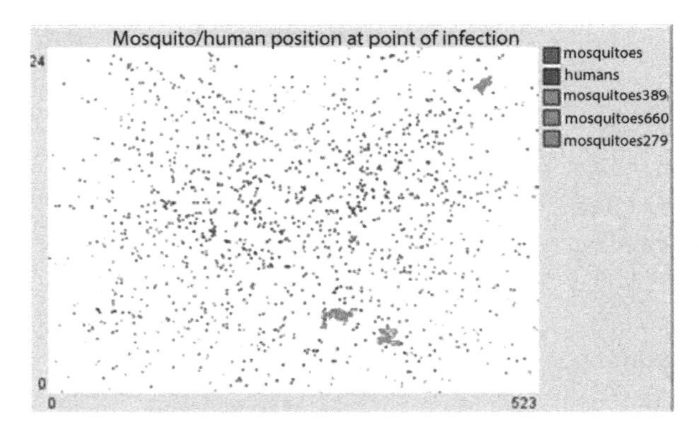

Figure 4.12. *xy-plot of the infection locations and mosquito trajectories across three successive simulations, which notably allows for the random locations of origin of the source mosquitoes. For a color version of the figure, see www.iste.co.uk/banos/netlogo.zip*

Numerous graphs are not, however, able to be used across different simulations. For example, a series representing the number of infected mosquitoes and humans leads to the following result (Figure 4.13). In effect, in a basic series graph, the *x*-axis is incrementally increased at each period. Also, when passing to the next simulation, the pen remains active and NetLogo therefore links the last value of the previous simulation to the first value of the new simulation.

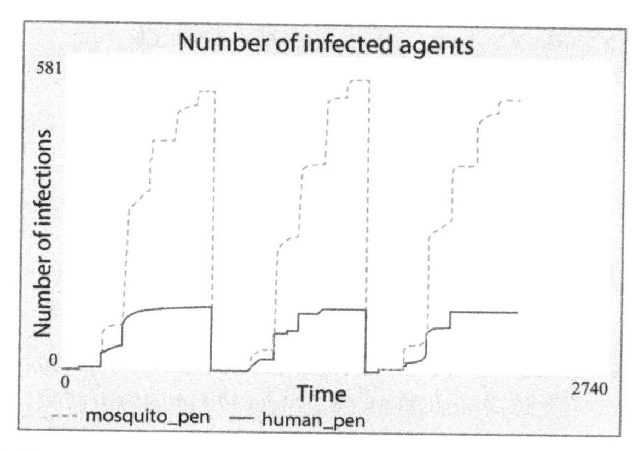

Figure 4.13. *Series graph used across three simulations: the simulation data is combined without returning to the origin for each new simulation*

One solution for defining a graph in series consists of:

– using an xy-plot with the *x*-axis manually defined as representing time (`ticks`);

– deactivating the pen (`plot-pen-up`) while moving to a new simulation, that is to say when `ticks` is equal to `0`.

The pen update command hence becomes (Figure 4.14):

```
if ticks = 0
[
        plot-pen-up
]
plotxy ticks count infections
plot-pen-down
```

This type of graph allows us to easily compare the same variable across several simulations (in our case, with the same parameters so as to carry out an initial stability test of the variable with said parameters) (Figure 4.15).

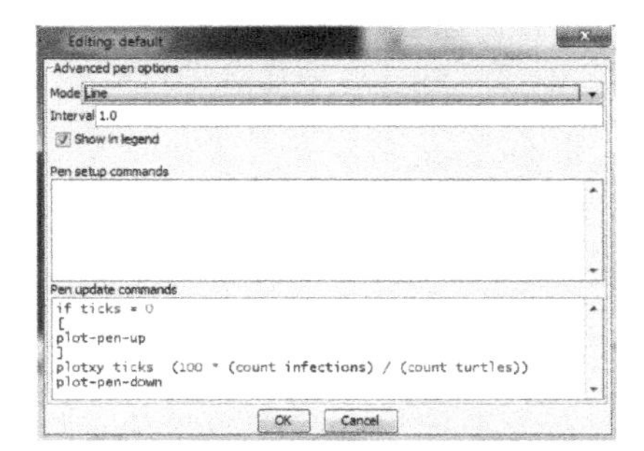

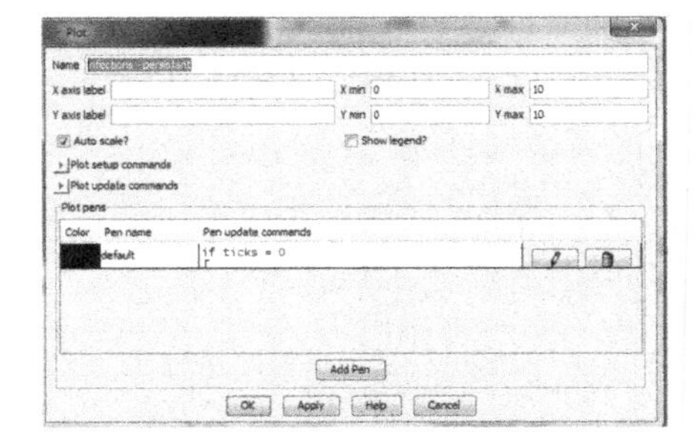

Figure 4.14. *Defining a new graph representing the infection count across several simulations, and defining the pen for this persistent series graph*

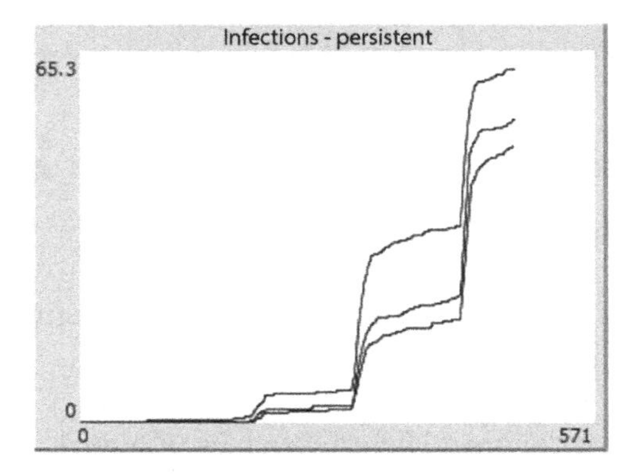

Figure 4.15. *Following the infection count across three successive simulations with identical parameters*

4.3. Exploring several simulations

4.3.1. *Introduction*

The persistent graphs studied in the previous section allow for the user to form an initial idea as to the behavior of the model across several simulations. Nonetheless, this does not allow for a more systematic and detailed study of the variable stability or the models parameter space. For this, NetLogo's BehaviorSpace allows for a large number of simulations to be launched by specifying the parameter values and the desired number of simulations (replications) to be launched for each combination of values.

This tool is particularly useful for:

– studying the stability of the results obtained with the current parameter values. This type of analysis may be carried out by analyzing the standard deviation of the results obtained across several replications;

– studying the impact of each variation of a parameter's value around the current solution (local sensitivity) so as to identify the most influential parameters;

– exploring the spread of possible results for each of the acceptable parameter values (exploring the parameter space). This gives an impression of the results attainable by the simulation based on the main possible configurations.

The BehaviorSpace allows for simple experiment designs to be defined (complete designs), to run these (this can be optionally done in parallel, on several cores), and to export the data resulting from these experiments in CSV files. The goal is usually not to analyze these within NetLogo, as its processing features are rather limited.

4.3.2. *Exploring the parameter space: the BehaviorSpace, step by step*

The BehaviorSpace tool is found in the *Tools* menu. It allows for different experiment plans to be defined (experiments, see Figure 4.16). Each experiment plan defines the values taken by the parameters, the number of times that the simulation is replicated for each combination of parameters, the exit variables and the stop conditions, etc.

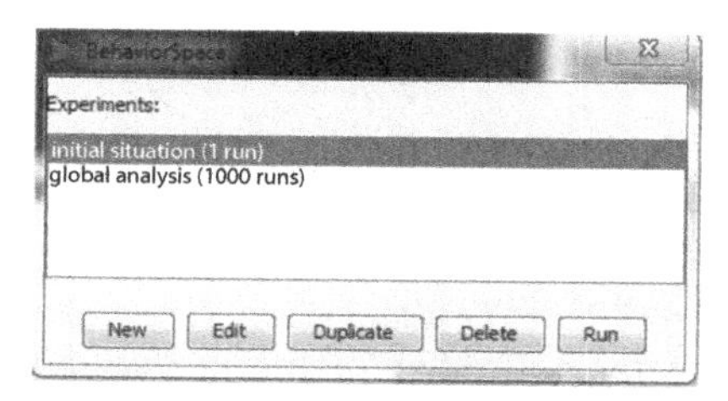

Figure 4.16. *The BehaviorSpace's startup window, giving access to the list of already defined experiment plans, allowing for their modification (*Edit*), their duplication (*Duplicate*), their deletion (*Delete*), their execution (*Run*) or for the creation of another (*New*)*

By default, the experiment plan is defined as the current situation: a single execution with the parameters fixed to their current values and with no stop conditions (see Figure 4.17).

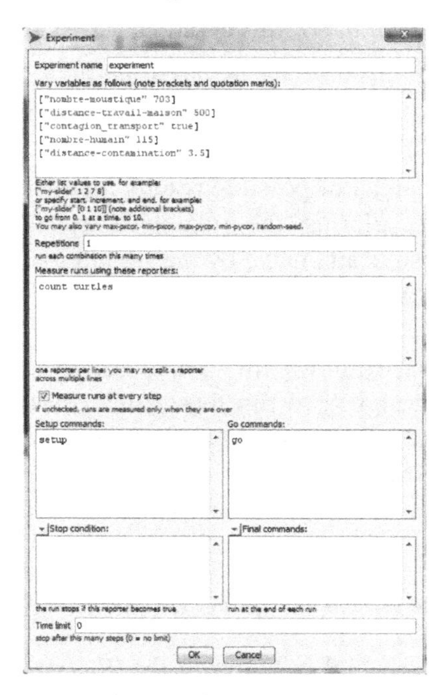

Figure 4.17. *Experiment plan with the current parameter values and a single execution by default*

We will define an experiment plan whose goal is to analyze what influences the number of humans infected after 1,000 ticks of time (Figure 4.18):

– *observed variables*: number of humans infected at the end of the execution, proportion of infected humans, number of mosquitoes and proportion of infected mosquitoes;

– *variable parameters*: number of initial humans and mosquitoes, contamination distance and home–work distance.

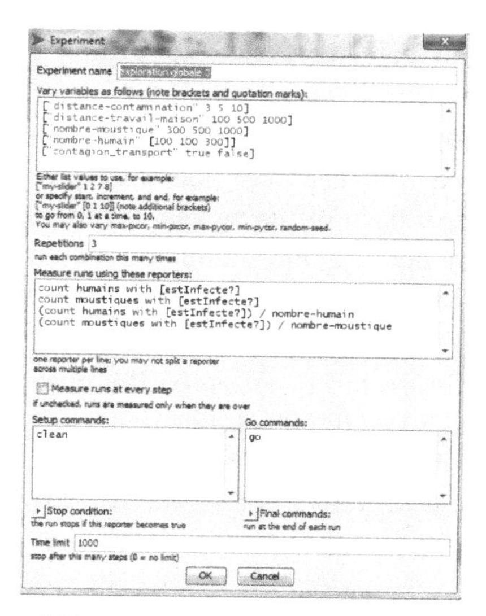

Figure 4.18. *Defining an experiment plan to globally explore the parameter space*

We begin by defining a new experiment plan (*New*). The different options to be defined are:

– *Experiment name*: the name of the experiment which will allow for easy identification and which will determine the default name of savefiles. Example: global exploration.

– *Vary variables as follows*: determines the values which will be taken by the parameters. Each line corresponds to a variable. After having specified the name of the variable in between quotation marks, we can specify the values taken by the parameters in two different ways:

- by directly stating which values will be taken by the variable, for e.g. `[‘‘number-mosquito’’ 300 500 1000]` which indicates that the possible values for `number-mosquito` are 300, 500 and 1,000, or `[‘‘contagion_transport’’ true false]` to indicate that `contagion_transport` can take the values `true` and `false`;

- by specifying an initial value, an increment and a final value for the variable, in the form `[‘‘name-variable [initial increment final]]`. For example, `[‘‘number-human’’ [100 100 300]]` indicates that `number-human` will take the values 100, 200 and

300 (which is, in this case, equivalent to writing [''number-human'' 100 200 300]).

– *Repetitions*: the number of times (replications) that each configuration will be executed. For identical parameter values, the observed variable may have different values (due to the stochasticity present within the model) and the simulation may be executed several times for each combination of chosen values so as to obtain more precise results.

– *Measure runs using these reporters*: the observed values which will be exported into a savefile. Each line defines an exported value. It may be a global variable (of the type `date-first-infection`) or more commonly a sum: e.g. `count humans with [isInfected?]` which returns the number of infected humans.

– *Measure runs at every step*: if this box is ticked, the previously defined observed values will be recorded at each simulation step. Otherwise, only the final value will be recorded.

– *Setup commands*: the commands to be executed at the start of each simulation. Usually, this will be the `setup` command, but other commands may also be included, if desired. A command different to `setup` may be used if we specifically require a certain graph or global variable to be conserved throughout the exploration (see following section on advanced analysis).

– *Go commands*: the command to be executed at each simulation step, usually go.

– *Stop conditions*: a stop condition if we desire for the simulation to end before the specified time limit (or if no limit is given). For example, if we wanted only to analyze the date of the first human infection, the stop condition could be defined as: `any? humans with [isInfected?]` and to export the infection date by adding `ticks` in the following variables.

– *Final commands*: potential commands to be executed when the stop condition or the time limit are reached. It is possible to export plots or to save the state of the world as new files, for example.

– *Time limit*: the maximum number of steps that the simulation may reach.

The BehaviorSpace will carry out all the possible combinations between the parameters defined in the list. The number of defined simulations can as such increase exponentially: four parameters with five values each already represent 5 x 5 x 5 x 5 = 625 possible combinations. With 10 parameters and 10 values per parameter, we reach 1010 combinations, which means that 10 million simulations must be carried out for a complete study.

The order in which the parameters are listed determines the order in which the simulations will be executed. Let us take the example of two parameters with two and three values, respectively, and a single execution per configuration:

```
[“contagion_transport” true false]

[“number-human” 100 200 300]
```

The six simulations will be successively executed as follows: (100; true), (200; true), (300; true), (100; false), (200; false), (300; false).

Once the experiment plan has been defined, we can execute it by selecting it in the experiment list and clicking on *Run*. In this case, we can choose the execution options (Figure 4.19):

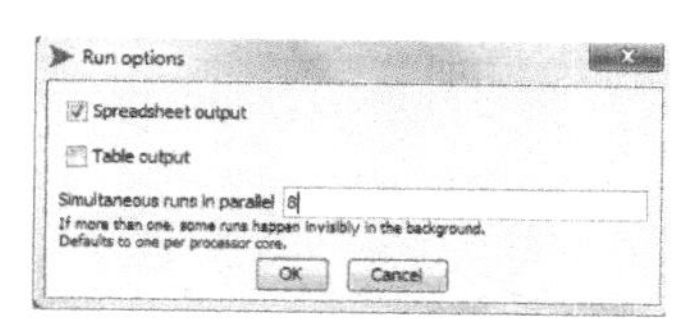

Figure 4.19. *Choice of options for launching an experiment plan within the BehaviorSpace*

Spreadsheet output and *Table output* allow for the file export format to be chosen:

– *Spreadsheet* will generate a spreadsheet with a single line per simulation step (so a single line if only the final value is exported), and one column per variable – simulation couple. If the plan includes 6 simulation runs and 4 observed variables, the spreadsheet will be composed of $6 \times 4 = 24$ columns (as well as the column with headings). An example is given in Figure 4.21. This layout is adapted when all the intermediate steps are recorded (*Measure runs at every step* ticked within the experiment plan options window).

– *Table* will generate a file with one line per simulation–iteration couple (so as many lines as there are simulations if only the final value is recorded, and $n*m$ lines if n simulations are executed with m recorded iterations). Each column will correspond to a variable. One example is given in Figure 4.20. This layout is made for the analysis of data from a large number of simulations.

A	B	C	D	E	F	G	H	I	J
BehaviorSpace results (NetLogo 5.1.0)									
landuseV4cp6.nlogo									
exploration globale									
08/08/2014 10:28:27 175 +0200									
min-pxcor	max-pxcor	min-pycor	max-pycor						
0	423	0	424						
[run number]	nombre-moustique	distance-travail-maison	contagion_transport	nombre-humain	distance-contamination	[step]	count humains with [estInfecte?]	count moustiques with [estInfecte?]	(count humains with [estInfecte?]) / nombr
4	100	100	true	100	3	1000	0	0	0
2	100	100	true	100	1	1000	0	0	0
3	100	100	true	100	1	1000	0	1	0
5	100	100	true	100	3	1000	0	1	0
6	100	100	true	100	3	1000	1	1	0.01
1	100	100	true	100	1	1000	6	1	0.06
8	100	100	true	100	10	1000	0	1	0
7	100	100	true	100	10	1000	19	10	0.19
9	100	100	true	100	10	1000	33	26	0.33
10	100	100	true	200	1	1000	0	1	0
11	100	100	true	200	1	1000	0	1	0
12	100	100	true	200	1	1000	1	1	0.0050
13	100	100	true	200	3	1000	0	0	0
14	100	100	true	200	3	1000	0	1	0
15	100	100	true	200	3	1000	0	1	0
16	100	100	true	200	10	1000	0	1	0
17	100	100	true	200	10	1000	1	2	0.0050

Figure 4.20. *Example of a CSV table (imported into OpenOffice) obtained from the BehaviorSpace with the Table output box ticked*

A	B	C	D	E	F	G	H
BehaviorSpace results (NetLogo 5.1.0)							
landuseV4cp6.nlogo							
exploration globale							
08/08/2014 16:17:38 669 +0200							
min-pxcor	max-pxcor	min-pycor	max-pycor				
0	423	0	424				
[run number]	1	1	1	1	2	2	2
nombre-moustique	100				100		
distance-travail-maison	100				100		
contagion_transport	true				true		
nombre-humain	100				100		
distance-contamination	1				1		
[steps]	1000	1000	1000	1000	1000	1000	1000
[initial & final values]	count humains with [estInfecte?]	count moustiques with [estInfecte?]	(count humains with	(count moustiques with	count humains with [estInfecte?]	count moustiques with [estInfecte?]	(count humains with [estInfecte?]) / nom
	0	1	0	0.01	1	1	0.01

Figure 4.21. *Example of a CSV table (imported into OpenOffice) obtained from the BehaviorSpace with the Spreadsheet output box ticked*

Simultaneous runs in parallel: number of simulations which will be run at the same time. NetLogo is able to run several simulations at once to speed up the analysis, as long as the computer's processor contains several cores (choosing a value higher than the number of cores would slow down the execution instead of speeding it up). The default value is equal to the number of cores. This option is tempting but has several consequences:

– Using all of a processor's cores makes any other use of the computer during the execution of the experiment plan very difficult as all of the processing power is being used by NetLogo. At least one or two cores should be left free so that continued use of the computer is possible.

– As the number of parallel simulations increases, so does the memory used by NetLogo.

– Only one simulation can access the graphical display, which means that if several simulations are running alongside each other, they will not be able to be observed or displayed in graphs (see the use of graphs with the BehaviorSpace in the following section).

– If any global variable is conserved in between simulations, their value will depend on which core they are being run on (see the following section).

– The order of the lines of exported data will be randomly arranged if simulations are running in parallel, especially if variables are being exported at each iteration.

Once the options and filenames have been chosen, the simulations will be successively executed (and occasionally in parallel depending on the chosen options). In order to speed up the processing, it is possible to turn off the main view updates *update view update* and/or the graph and monitor updates *(update plots and monitors)*. If the user has chosen to record each iteration's variables, a graph displaying these variables within the current simulation will automatically be generated (see Figure 4.22).

4.3.3. *Analyzing data within NetLogo (advanced use of BehaviorSpace)*

Basic use of the BehaviorSpace allows for data tables to be easily obtained, which can then be analyzed with external tools (Excel, R, etc.). Nonetheless, it is possible to obtain an initial display of data within the simulation, of which we will present certain uses for carrying out a data analysis of the results within NetLogo.

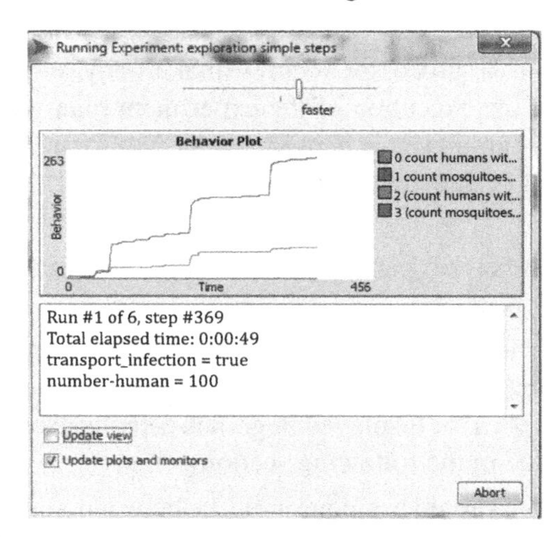

Figure 4.22. *Monitor window for the BehaviorSpace execution, with the number of completed and total simulations, as well as information about the current simulation and interface updating options. For a color version of the figure, see www.iste.co.uk/banos/netlogo.zip*

4.3.3.1. *Use of graphs with BehaviorSpace*

4.3.3.1.1. Constraints specific to BehaviorSpace

In the previous section, we studied the use of a graph across several simulations. It is possible to use the same principle and to improve it with the BehaviorSpace. As such, existing persistent graphs will work with the BehaviorSpace, and will allow for series graphs or xy-plots to be viewed across several simulations. The use of persistent graphs with the BehaviorSpace does, however, have two constraints:

– Just as a new initialization button calling the `clean` function was needed, the standard setup function (which usually calls the `clear-all` and therefore `clear-all-plots` functions) must be replaced by a new function such as `clean` so as to initialize simulations within the experiment plan.

– Only one simulation can access the interface at any given point in time; so if several simulations are being run in parallel (on several cores), only one of them will be displayed upon the graphs.

4.3.3.1.2. Transferring BehaviorSpace parameters onto a graph

In order to visualize the impact of a parameter on a variable, the BehaviorSpace allows for a large number of simulations to be run while varying one or several parameters, and for the results of each simulation to be displayed on persistent graphs. In order to obtain a more legible and complete result, it is possible to add the value of each pen's parameter as a tag, which gives a graph similar to the following one.

Even so, this adds additional constraints relative to the simple persistent graph previously defined:

– It is unfortunately impossible to ask the BehaviorSpace or the user what the name of the variable currently being analyzed is, therefore the graph's update function must be modified.

– Although a pen is defined by its name, this will depend on its value in this case, which means that the pen must be dynamically created and this can only occur at the beginning. The graph will therefore initially not have any pens, and the pen will be added when the graph next updates.

– The type of pen must also be defined, with the use of the `set-plot-pen-mode` command, which allows for the type of graph to be created by the pen (it corresponds to a choice taken from the scrollable *mode* menu in the advanced pen configuration window):

1) `set-plot-pen-mode 0` will cause the pen to trace lines (series graphs or connected xy-plots), see Figure 4.23;

2) `set-plot-pen-mode 1` will create a histogram;

3) `set-plot-pen-mode 2` will draw points (such as for xy-plots, see following example).

– The name of the pen to be created or chosen may be the name of the parameter followed by its chosen value, created by using the concatenation function: `word : word "distance" distance-contamination`.

– Verifying the existence of a pen (once it has been created) can be done with `plot-pen-exists?`.

– A pen's color can be chosen from a color pallet by using `scale-color`. In order to better differentiate pens and if one is certain that the number of pencils will remain low, NetLogo's included color list (`base-colors`), which offers 14 basic colors, may be used. To receive a reference and to choose the color, the BehaviorSpace run number may be used with the `behaviorspace-run-number` variable.

The `update` function of the graph may be written as follows:

```
ifelse plot-pen-exists? word "distance"
  distance-contamination
[
  set-current-plot-pen word "distance"
    distance-contamination
]
[
ifelse (behaviorspace-run-number < 14)
[
  create-temporary-plot-pen word "distance"
    distance-contamination
  set-plot-pen-color item behaviorspace-run-number
    base-colors
]
[
  set-plot-pen-color wrap-color behaviorspace-run-number
]
]
set-plot-pen-mode 0
if ticks = 0
[
plot-pen-up ] plotxy ticks (100 * (count infections) /
  (count turtles))
plot-pen-down
```

This function allows for the display of the number of infections against the value of the `distance-contamination` parameter (Figure 4.23).

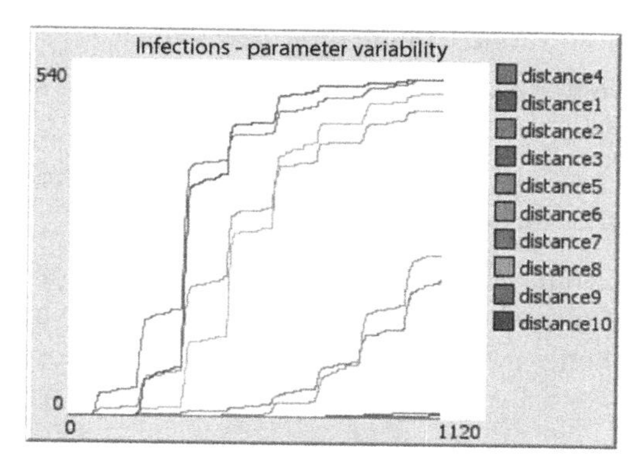

Figure 4.23. *Infection count obtained across several infections by using a pen with the value of its* `distance-contamination` *parameter for each simulation. For a color version of the figure, see www.iste.co.uk/banos/netlogo.zip*

4.3.3.2. *Analyzing data with BehaviorSpace*

In order to delve further within data analysis, data manipulation and aggregation across several simulations is necessary. NetLogo is not suitable for this type of analysis, and it would perhaps be advisable to use an external software such as R (see the next section) or Excel. It is nonetheless possible to carry out certain analyses directly within NetLogo so as to illustrate their potentials and limitations.

The aim is to carry out:

– a representation of the average infection count obtained across the previous simulations, which approximately equates to the standard deviation (Figure 4.24);

– a sensitivity analysis to view the part of the variance represented by each variable. This analysis allows us to see which variables have the largest impact on the final result, the infection count (Figure 4.27).

In order to achieve this aim, the following must be done:

– creating global variables which will record the values of the variable to be analyzed within each simulation;

– updating these variables with their new values;

– making sure these values are not cleared when the simulations are reset.

4.3.3.2.1. Graph of the average and standard deviation

This type of graph allows for the evolution of the average and the stability of a result, whether for fixed parameters or not, to be seen in a more synthetic manner than a graph superimposing all of the simulations.

For example, Figure 4.24 is obtained after 81 simulations following an exploration of the parameter space (4 parameters with 3 values each). The graph is illegible and gives little useful information (other than the fact that the result is unpredictable…). Representing the average and standard deviation allows for the data to be synthesized: the average is clearly increasing by jumps per day (transports). The standard deviation, and thus the instability, becomes particularly high from the fourth day onward, but remains stable at a very high level afterward.

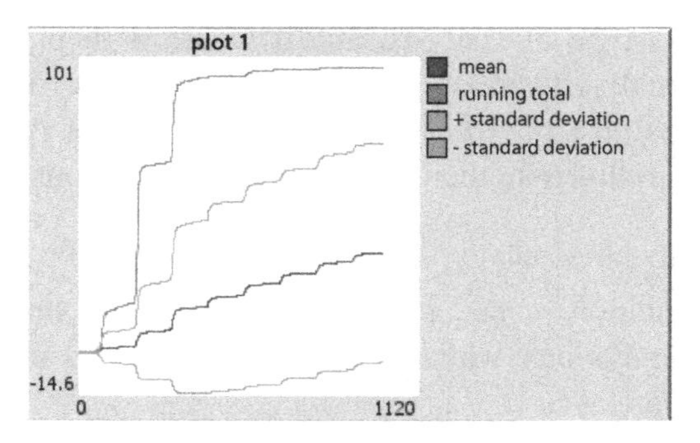

Figure 4.24. *On the left, the infection counts obtained over 81 simulations with different parameters. On the right, a representation of the average (in purple) plus or minus the standard deviation (in blue) of the previous simulations, as well as of the current one (in red). For a color version of the figure, see www.iste.co.uk/banos/netlogo.zip*

Results such as those shown in Figure 4.25, obtained after 10 simulations with identical parameters, demonstrate great stability after the fourth day (as every entity is infected), while the first three days remain highly unpredictable (with a large standard deviation).

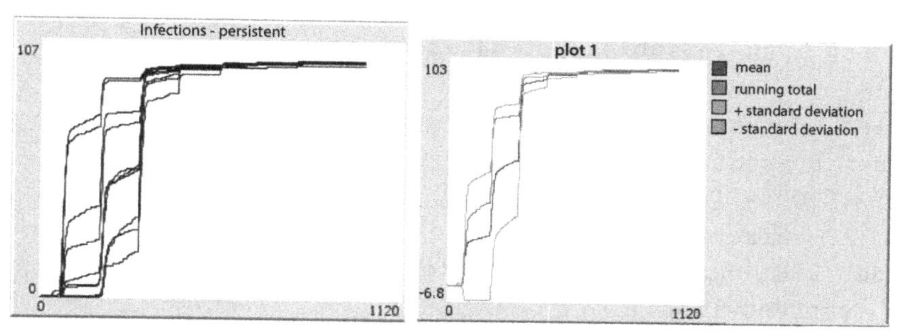

Figure 4.25. *Results of 10 simulations with identical parameters and a high transmission distance. For a color version of the figure, see www.iste.co.uk/banos/netlogo.zip*

4.3.3.2.2. Creating global variables to record the values of the variable to be analyzed within each simulation

In the section at the beginning of the NetLogo code, where species are declared, the global variable which will stock the variable values must be added:

```
globals [list-variable]
```

Then, the following initialization is added to the `setup` function (and not to the `clean` function, as this initialization must only be carried out once):

```
set list-variable [[]]
```

4.3.3.2.3. Updating these variables with the new values

The values can be added to the list both within the NetLogo code and within the `update` function of the graph. The advantage of using the `update` function is that it will not be called during usage of the BehaviorSpace where plots are not being updated, which will reduce the memory use and calculation time. The plots `update` function is therefore:

```
while [(length list-variable) < (ticks + 1)]
 [
  set list-variable lput [] list-variable
 ]
 let current-list item ticks list-variable
 set current-list lput
    (100 * (count infections) / (count turtles))
      current-list
 set list-variable replace-item ticks list-variable
   current-list
```

`list-variable` is a list of lists containing the value taken by the variable for each tick of the previous simulations. If 10 simulations with a length of 50 ticks are carried out, then `list-variable` will contain 50 lists of 10 elements.

The first section of the code serves to add an empty list if the current tick has not been reached during previous simulations.

The second section finds the list corresponding to the current tick, adds the target variable (the infection count) to it and replaces the old list by the updated `current-list` version.

4.3.3.2.4. Defining graph and pen updates

Once the value has been saved within `list-variable`, all that is needed is to define the pens which will display the average plus and minus the standard deviation, and potentially the current simulation (Figure 4.26).

In order to calculate the average and standard deviation, NetLogo has the `mean` and `standard-deviation` functions allowing for these values to be obtained from a list.

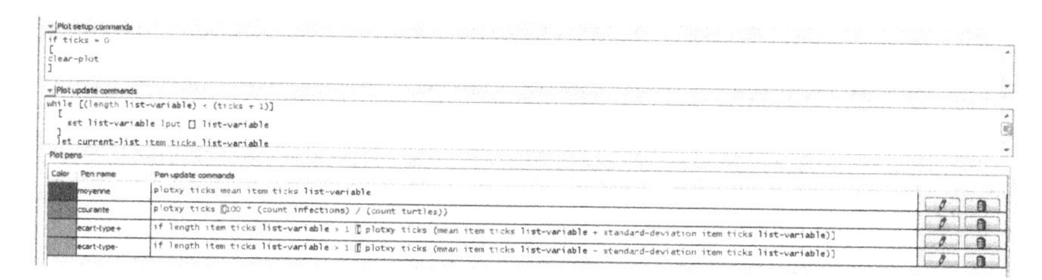

Figure 4.26. *Defining the average and standard deviation pens of the graph*

The `mean` pen will therefore be defined by:

```
plotxy ticks mean item ticks list-variable
```

For standard deviation, it is necessary to verify that the number of values is greater than or equal to 2 in order to avoid the `standard-deviation` function returning an error message:

```
if length item ticks list-variable > 1
[
      plotxy ticks (mean item ticks list-variable +
            standard-deviation item ticks list-variable)
]
```

4.3.3.2.5. Making sure these values are not cleared when the simulations are reset

One final important element to take into account when global variables are being used to store values across several simulations: these global variables must not be cleared when the simulation is reset. This problem is identical to that with graph reinitialization when defining persistent graphs.

The `clear-all` function that is usually used calls the `clear-globals` function, which clears all global variables. We have seen in the previous section that a new initialization function `clean` has to be defined, which does not call `clear-all`, but instead calls all of its elements barring `clear-plots`. Two solutions are possible for conserving global variables:

– not calling `clear-globals`, but then care must be taken to clear the global variables which are not to be kept;

– using `let` to keep the desired global variables: since local variables are not cleared by `clear-globals`, we can make the `clean` function keep the values of `list-variable`, for example:

```
let list-variable-temp list-variable
clear-globals
let list-variable list-variable-temp
```

4.3.3.3. *Analyzing variance: presentation*

Going even deeper within data analysis, we can wish to understand where the variability of received results arises from. For example, let us return to the 81 executions needed for a complete exploration of the parameter space for a model with three values for four parameters, which led to the infection count graph in Figure 4.24. These graphs show that results can vary considerably depending on the parameter values, and it is thus important to correctly calibrate these parameters if we want to obtain realistic results. However, searching for the correct parameter values is complicated and costly (when it is even possible), and it might be interesting to know which parameters have the greatest impact upon the result. If certain parameters have no impact, it is hardly important to precisely define them, and more attention should instead be put toward refining those with a greater importance.

To determine the weight of each parameter on the result (and thus to perform a sensibility analysis based on the variations of a parameter), a possible method is a variance analysis [FAI 13, SAL 09].

We will now break up the variance of a variable x, based on three parameters i, j and k, with n observations of x, written as x_{ijk} (to simplify the notation, the parameter k indicates the kth simulation for each of the i and j parameters). This analysis can be generalized to any number of parameters. The variance (square of the standard deviation calculated above) summarizes the deviations from the mean of the variable:

$$V(x) = \frac{1}{(n-1)} \sum_{ijk} (x_{ijk} - \overline{x_{...}})^2$$

where $\overline{x_{...}}$ and $\overline{x}$ both represent the observed global mean of x: $\overline{x_{...}} = \overline{x} = \frac{1}{n} \sum_{ijk} x_{ijk}$.

As $n-1$ is constant for all variables, we can consider only the sum of squares (SS) for charts/analysis:

$$SS_{total} = \sum_{ijk} (x_{ijk} - \overline{x_{...}})^2$$

These deviations correspond to the instability and unpredictability of the variable under study. It is possible to break down these deviations. For example, for the first parameter, two extreme cases would be:

– if this parameter is responsible for all the changes in the x variable, this would indicate that if the value of this parameter is fixed, so would be x. For a value of i, x will always be identical and therefore equal to the means of x for this value of i: $x_{ijk} = \overline{x_{i..}}$, with $\overline{x_{i..}} = \frac{1}{n_j n_k} \sum_{jk} x_{ijk}$. Here, $SS_{total} = \sum_{ijk} (\overline{x_{i..}} - \overline{x_{...}})^2 = n_j.n_k \sum_i (\overline{x_{i..}} - \overline{x_{...}})^2$, which means that the deviations correspond to the deviations between the partial means of the parameter and the global variable. The variability within classes is as such nil for the parameter, and the variability between classes is at maximum;

– if no parameters in a sufficiently large sample size have any impact on the final result, the mean of each parameter value will be equal to that of the global variable: $\overline{x_{i..}} = \overline{x_{...}}$. This will also be true for each parameter couple: $\overline{x_{ij.}} = \overline{x_{...}}$ In this case, the previously calculated value, which is the variability between classes, will be nil. Any and all variability will depend on the remainders: any variations of x which are not contained in the means: $SS_{total} = SS_{residual} = \sum_{ijk} (x_{ijk} - \overline{x_{ij.}})^2$. The residual SSs will measure what results from inherent randomness and from non-measured parameters. The higher this value, the less predictable the model is, if only the tested parameter values are known.

The general case is situated in between these two extremes.

When only one parameter, i, exists (and there remain n_k observations for each value of i), the variability (SS_{total}) can be broken down between the variability between classes ($SS_{variable}$) and the residuals (variability within classes, $SS_{residual}$)

$$SS_{total} = SS_{variable} + SS_{residual}$$

$$\sum_{ik} (x_{ik} - \overline{x})^2 = n_k \sum_{i} (\overline{x_{i.}} - \overline{x})^2 + \sum_{ik} (x_{ik} - \overline{x_{i.}})^2$$

For example, if the number of humans takes the values 100, 200 and 300, the variability from the number of humans (nh) will be:

$$SS_{nh} = n_k(\overline{x_{nh=100}} - \overline{x})^2 + n_k(\overline{x_{nh=200}} - \overline{x})^2 + n_k(\overline{x_{nh=300}} - \overline{x})^2$$

For a larger number of parameters, the effect of interactions between parameters must be added: the interaction SSs measure the impact of independent parameters. For example, this may be useful if both the number of humans and mosquitoes must be high for the infection to be significant (as opposed to only one of the values being large).

$$SS_{total} = SS_{variable} + SS_{interaction} + SS_{residual}$$

The variable SSs (the variability between intermediate and global means described previously) are easily calculated and will be analyzed within NetLogo. For the interaction SSs, see section 4.3.4.

4.3.3.4. *Graph of the variance analysis*

The graph obtained (Figure 4.27) represents the evolution of the percentage of total variance attributed to each variable (which is identical to the part of the SS_{total}).

To carry out the variance analysis, the variable values must be stored as with the previous graph, and the values of each parameter must be known for each simulation that is run (so as to be able to calculate the partial means depending on the parameter values).

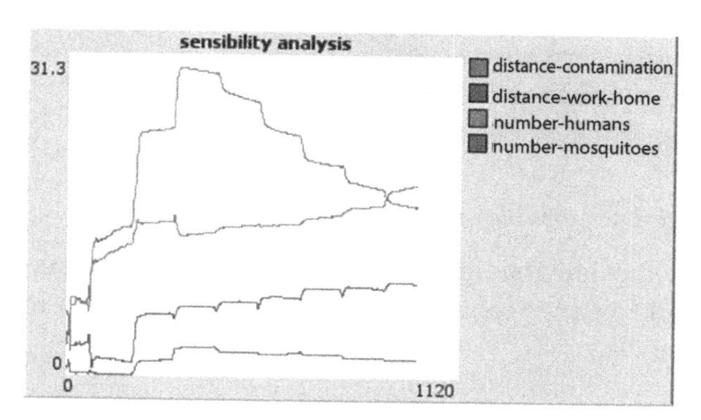

Figure 4.27. *Breaking down the infection count variance from the exploration of a 4 parameter space*

The process this graph follows can be summarized in several steps:

– creation of global variables for storing parameter names and values;

– storing of global variables in between simulations;

– recording of the parameter values at each period;

– calculation of parameter variance;

– display of these values on the corresponding pen.

4.3.3.4.1. In the NetLogo code

Creation of global variable for storing parameter names and values

As with the previous graph, we will use global variables to store the names of the studied parameters as well as their lists of values. We will also continue to use the `list-variable` variable which we defined previously so as to keep the chosen variable's list of values (here, the infection count).

```
globals [list-variable list-parameter-values
  list-parameters]
```

These variables are initialized within the setup as follows:

```
set list-variable [[]]
```

```
set list-parameter-values [[]]
set list-parameters ["distance-contamination"
"distance-work-home"]
```

Storing of global variables in between simulations

As with the previous graph, we use the `clean` function (which does not call `clear-global`) to store the variable values in between simulations.

4.3.3.4.2. In the BehaviorSpace experiment setup options

Defining the list of parameters to be followed within the BehaviorSpace

Due to `list-parameters` being defined as a global variable, it is possible to choose and analyze different parameters in each experiment (the same method can be used for the variable to be analyzed, which here is still the global infection count).

The `list-parameters` variable is therefore defined within the *setup* of the experiment plan (Figure 4.28).

```
set list-parameters
 ["distance-contamination"
 "distance-work-home"
 "number-human"
 "number-mosquito"]
clean
```

4.3.3.4.3. In the graph setup options

Recording the parameter value at each tick

The graph's `setup` function will be used to record the parameter values for the current simulation. The code will be split into two parts.

First, the function will check that the variable containing the parameter values (`list-parameter-values`) contains at least as many lists as there are values (a list per parameter is required). If this is not the case, empty lists are added:

```
while [(length list-parameter-values) < (length
   list-parameters)]
 [
    set list-parameter-values lput [] list-parameter-
      values
 ]
```

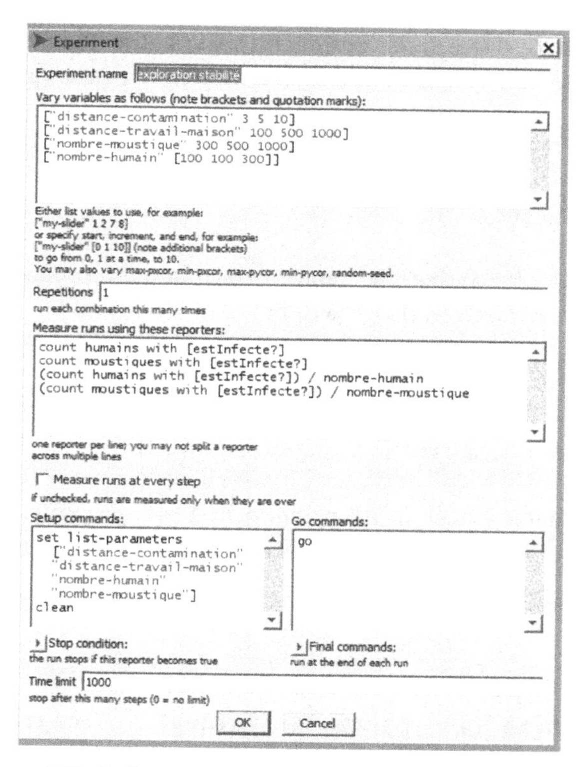

Figure 4.28. *Defining an experiment plan allowing for a sensitivity analysis of the infection count*

Then, the function will go through the parameter list defined in `parameters-list`. We are now interested in the *i*th parameter corresponding to the *i*th list of `list-parameter-values`.

We cannot add a new value corresponding to the parameter value of the current simulation to this list without running into one of

NetLogo's limitations: we have the variable name (it is the *i*th element of `list-parameters` copied into `current-parameter`), but there is no simple way to obtain its value from its name.

We will therefore use NetLogo's `Run` function, which allows for an instruction to be directly passed from a text to a command line. It is impossible to create a local variable with this command, as it would be instantly deleted; instead, this command will be directly executed so as to update `list-parameter-values`, by adding the new value:

```
Run (word "set list-parameter-values replace-item i
list-parameter-values lput " current-parameter "
  current-list")
```

If `current-parameter` is equal to "`distance-contamination`", the command given to NetLogo will be:

```
set list-parameter-values replace-item i list-parameter-
  values
lput distance-contamination current-list
```

The command places in *i*th position in `list-parameter-values` the `current-list` list to which `distance-contamination` is added.

```
if ticks = 0
[
clear-plot
while [(length list-parameter-values) < (length
  list-parameters)]
[
 set list-parameter-values lput [] list-parameter-values
]
let i 0
while [i < length list-parameters]
[
  let current-parameter item i list-parameters
  let current-list item i list-parameter-values
  Run (word "set list-parameter-values replace-item i
```

```
    list-parameter-values lput" current-parameter "
      current-list")
  set i i + 1 ] ]
```

Calculating parameter variance and display of values

The graph's `update` function will carry out the calculations and display them for each of the parameters:

```
let i 0
let current-list item ticks list-variable
if length current-list > 1
[
let total-pop length current-list
let global-mean mean current-list
let total-variance variance current-list
if total-variance > 0
[
while [i < length list-parameters]
[
  let parameter-values item i list-parameter-values
```

The aim is to calculate, for each parameter, the parts of $SS_{variable}$: $\sum n_{i.}(\overline{x_{i.}} - \overline{x})^2/SS_{total}$

With $n_{i.}$, the number of simulations carried out with the value of the *i* parameter is $\overline{x_{i.}} = \sum_{jk} x_{ijk}/n_{i.}$

and $SS_{total} = (n-1) * V(x)$

Independent from the current parameter are the following:

– `Current-list` corresponds to the list of variable values for the current tick during previous simulations (the x_{ijk});

– `Total-pop` corresponds to the total number of simulations that have been carried out (n);

– `Global-mean` corresponds to the global mean ($\overline{x}$);

– `Total-variance` corresponds to the global variance ($V(x)$).

Therefore, we need to calculate $\overline{x_{i.}}$, as well as $n_{i.}$, the population size and the mean of the x_{ijk} – all simulations using the same parameter value.

During the loop, we are interested in the *i*th parameter, and `parameter-values` will correspond to the values of this parameter during previous simulations:

```
if (length current-list) < (length parameter-values)
[
set parameter-values sublist parameter-values
   (length parameter-values - length current-list)
       (length parameter-values)
]
```

If the list of values is smaller than the list of parameter values, the last parameter values of the list are used.

```
let unique-values []
let unique-means []
let unique-size []
```

To explain the importance of these three variables, let us say that we have carried out six simulations, with the two parameters `number-human` and `number-mosquito` set to the following values:

- `Number-human [100 200 100 200 100 200];`
- `Number-mosquito [100 100 500 500 1000 1000].`

Let us also state that the infection counts for the current tick (the x_{ijk} values contained in `current-list`) are the following: `[2 2 2 10 10 10]`.

For the first parameter (i=0), `parameter-values` will therefore be `[100 200 100 200 100 200]`.

We will attempt to find the means of x_{ijk} for the two values taken by parameter-values, 100 and 200. In order to do this, we use:

– `Unique-values` to store the different values taken by the parameter. At the end, `unique-values = [100 200];`

– `Unique-means` to store the sum of the x_{ijk} corresponding to each unique value (which we will divide by the number of elements to find the mean). At the end, `unique-means=[2+2+10 1+10+10]=[14 21];`

– `Unique-size` to store the number of simulations corresponding to each unique value. At the end, `unique-size=[3 3]`.

```
(foreach current-list parameter-values
```

For each `current-list` / `Parameter-values` couple, `?1` will be the current x_{ijk}, with ?2 being the current parameter value

```
[
let index position ?2 unique-values
```

`index` is the position of `?2` in the already identified parameter values.

If the value does not yet exist, it will be added:

```
ifelse index = false
[
set unique-size lput 1 unique-size
set unique-values lput ?2 unique-values
set unique-means lput ?1 unique-means
]
```

Otherwise, the mean and size lists are updated by the current value:

```
[
set unique-means replace-item index unique-means
(?1 + item index unique-means)
set unique-size replace-item index unique-size
(1 + item index unique-size)
]
])
```

Then, the SS is calculated. In order to do this, the variance is updated for each mean – size couple:

```
let var-part 0
  (foreach unique-means unique-size
  [
  set var-part (var-part + ?2 * (?1 / ?2 -
     global-mean) ^ 2)
])
```

Finally, we divide by the population (so as to obtain the parameter variance) and by the total variance (to obtain the proportion of the total variance):

```
set var-part var-part / (total-pop - 1) * 100 /
  total-variance
```

The result can then be displayed, by creating the appropriate pen if it does not yet exist:

```
ifelse plot-pen-exists? item i list-parameters
[
set-current-plot-pen item i list-parameters
]
[
create-temporary-plot-pen item i list-parameters
set-plot-pen-color item i base-colors
]
plotxy ticks var-part
set i i + 1
```

The graph's complete `update` function is thus:

```
let i 0
let current-list item ticks list-variable
if length current-list > 1
[
let total-pop length current-list
```

```
let global-mean mean current-list
let total-variance variance current-list
if total-variance > 0
[
while [i < length list-parameters]
[
 let parameter-values item i list-parameter-values
 if (length current-list) < (length parameter-values)
 [
 set parameter-values sublist parameter-values
    (length parameter-values - length current-list)
       (length parameter-values)
 ]

 let unique-values []
 let unique-means []
 let unique-size []
 (foreach current-list parameter-values
 [
 let index position ?2 unique-values
 ifelse index = false
 [
 set unique-size lput 1 unique-size
 set unique-values lput ?2 unique-values
 set unique-means lput ?1 unique-means
 ]
 [
 set unique-means replace-item index unique-means
 (?1 + item index unique-means)
 set unique-size replace-item index unique-size
 (1 + item index unique-size)
 ]
])
let var-part 0
  (foreach unique-means unique-size
  [
  set var-part (var-part + ?2 * (?1 / ?2 -
```

```
    global-mean) 2)
])

set var-part var-part / (total-pop - 1) * 100 /
total-variance ifelse plot-pen-exists? item i
list-parameters [ set-current-plot-pen item
i list-parameters ] [ create-temporary-plot-pen
item i list-parameters set-plot-pen-color
item i base-colors ] plotxy ticks var-part set
i i + 1 ] ] ]
```

The graph obtained (Figure 4.27) allows for the part of the variance that each variable is causing to be clearly seen. The contamination distance appears to be the variable with the greatest effect during the first few days. Slowly, however, its importance diminishes and the total human population becomes more important. The work–home distance and the number of mosquitoes seem to have a much lesser impact.

The use of this graph/analysis has several limitations which must be noted:

– These results do not take into account the interactions between variables. A more complete variance analysis would allow for a larger part of the total variance to be explained by analyzing the impact of couple variables (the impact of a simultaneous increase of two factors).

– The calculations undertaken here do not allow us to say whether the results obtained are of any significance. Hypothesis tests must instead be added, similar to those we will use with the R software in the following section.

– From a technical point of view, this graph and the previous graph require a large number of calculations and a great deal of memory space to store the value history. They therefore slow down the exploration of the mode incredibly (and do not allow for running parallel simulations). As such, they should only be used as a first approach before carrying a more detailed (and faster) analysis with external tools.

4.3.4. *Data analysis beyond NetLogo: the example of R*

The files obtained from the BehaviorSpace may be analyzed with external tools. For example, the R freeware (http://www.r-project.org/) can be used to carry out simple or complex statistical analyses.

Based on the file from the previous analysis (three different values for four parameters, with one execution per combination), obtained in the form of a table, we will carry out a variance analysis in order to test whether the results are significant or not (see section 4.3.3.3 for a description of a variance analysis). The type of results obtained at the end of the procedure is as follows:

```
Df Sum Sq Mean Sq F value   Pr(>F)
distance.contamination  1 1.389 1.3893 15.407
       0.000212 ***
distance.travail.maison 1 0.703 0.7029  7.795
      0.006873 **
number.mosquito         1 0.095 0.0950  1.053 0.308539
number.human            1 1.712 1.7124 18.989
      4.78e-05 ***
```

4.3.4.1. *Preliminary stage: modifying the CSV file*

The file obtained from NetLogo is a CSV file (see Figure 4.20) which needs to be modified so that it may be imported by R.

By opening the file with a text editor (such as NotePad++ on Windows), we will modify the file in two ways:

1) *Removing the first lines which are not needed for the analysis*

The first 6 lines are deleted (all those before the variable list):

Deleted lines:

```
"BehaviorSpace results (NetLogo 5.1.0)"
"landuseV5a.nlogo"
"stability analysis"
```

```
"08/11/2014 18:00:06:646 +0200"
"min-pxcor","max-pxcor","min-pycor","max-pycor"
"0","523","0","424"
```

Lines kept:

```
"[run number]","distance-contamination",
   "distance-work-home",
"number-mosquito","number-human","[step]",
"count humans with [isInfected?]",
"count mosquitoes with [isInfected?]",
"(count humans with [isInfected?]) / number-human",
"(count mosquitoes with [isInfected?]) /
   number-mosquito"
"1","3","100","300","100","1000","6","8","0.06",
   "0.026...67"
"2","3","100","300","200","1000","30","24","0.15","0.08"
```

2) *Removing the inverted commas*

NetLogo adds inverted commas (") all over the place, including around numerical values. Therefore, a Search/Replace operation must be carried out to replace all occurrences of " by a blank space so as to remove them.

Once these modifications have been made, the file can be used with R.

4.3.4.2. *Analysis with R*

Once the current directory has been defined, the file can be imported into R:

```
> dataexf=read.table("landuse.csv",header=T,sep=",
   ",dec=".")
```

We can now check that the values and columns correspond correctly by displaying a data synthesis:

```
> summary(dataexf)
X.run.number. distance.contamination distance.work.home
number.mosquito number.human X.step.
Min.   : 1    Min.   : 3    Min.    : 100.0
Min.   : 300  Min.   :100   Min.    : 1000
1st Qu.: 21  1st Qu.: 3    1st Qu.: 100.0
1st Qu.: 300  1st Qu.:100   1st Qu.:1000
Median : 41  Median : 5    Median : 500.0
Median : 500  Median :200     Median : 1000
Mean   : 41   Mean   : 6    Mean    : 533.3
Mean   : 600  Mean   :200   Mean    :1000
3rd Qu.: 61  3rd Qu.:10    3rd Qu.:1000.0
3rd Qu.: 1000 3rd Qu.: 300  3rd Qu.:1000
Max.   : 81   Max.   : 10   Max.    :1000.0
Max.   : 1000 Max.   : 300  Max.    :1000

count.humans.with..isInfected..
count.mosquitoes.with..isInfected..
X.count.humans.with..isInfected......number.human
 Min.   :  0.00                  Min.   :  1.0
0    :25
 1st Qu.:  0.00                  1st Qu.:  1.0
1    :14
 Median : 52.00                  Median : 64.0
0.01    : 2
 Mean   : 98.96                  Mean   :198.2
0.06    : 2
 3rd Qu.:199.00                  3rd Qu.:290.0
0.78    : 2
 Max.   :300.00                  Max.   :973.0
0.98    : 2

(Other):34
X.count.mosquitos..with..isInfected......
       number.mosquitos
 0.0010                 : 9
 0.003333333333333335: 9
```

```
0.0020              : 8
0.128               : 2
0.58                : 2
0.918               : 2
(Other)             : 49
```

If we want to carry out operations between columns (in a faster manner than with NetLogo), or if we have forgotten to calculate the target variable (like in this situation, where we only have the total of mosquitoes and the total of infected humans), we can use R's functionalities to perform calculations on matrices. Here, we will replace column 6 (which contained the final tick, 1000) by the infection count and then rename the column:

```
> dataexf[,6]<-(dataexf[,7]+dataexf[,8])/(dataexf[,4]+
  dataexf[,5])
> colnames(dataexf)[6]<-"infections"
```

We check that the values are coherent:

```
> dataexf[,6]
 [1] 0.0350000000 0.1080000000 0.0016666667 0.0016666667
0.1157142857 0.1650000000 0.0018181818 0.1725000000
0.1246153846 0.0025000000
[11] 0.1980000000 0.1350000000 0.0066666667 0.4414285714
0.2375000000 0.0009090909 0.0008333333 0.8446153846
0.0100000000  0.0020000000
[21] 0.3466666667 0.0016666667 0.1442857143 0.0012500000
0.0009090909 0.6875000000 0.0492307692 0.0850000000
0.0240000000  0.0016666667
[31] 0.0016666667 0.4128571429 0.5462500000 0.0254545455
0.3675000000 0.1138461538 0.5375000000 0.3240000000
0.7816666667 0.1216666667
[41] 0.8357142857 0.0012500000 0.0009090909 0.7766666667
0.2900000000 0.5825000000 0.6960000000 0.9266666667
0.6466666667 0.8628571429
[51] 0.0012500000 0.0009090909 0.7558333333 0.9538461538
0.0025000000 0.0080000000 0.0016666667 0.3333333333
0.3385714286 0.7462500000
```

```
[61] 0.0009090909 0.6466666667 0.7430769231 0.0025000000
0.0020000000 0.9833333333 0.0016666667 0.9500000000
0.9837500000 0.8545454545
[71] 0.9316666667 0.9792307692 0.0025000000 0.9760000000
0.9650000000 0.0016666667 0.9414285714 0.9787500000
0.0009090909 0.0008333333
[81] 0.9769230769
> summary(dataexf[,6])
     Min.   1st Qu.    Median      Mean   3rd Qu.      Max.
0.0008333 0.0020000 0.1443000 0.3440000 0.7431000 0.9838000
>
```

We can then launch the variance analysis in a single line:

```
> aovexf<-aov(infections~distance.contamination
*distance.work.home*number.mosquito
*number.human,data=dataexf)
```

Then we display a synthesis of results:

```
> summary(aovex)
                  Df Sum Sq Mean Sq F value Pr(>F)
distance.contamination 1 1.389 1.3893 15.407 0.000212 ***
distance.work.home 1 0.703 0.7029 7.795 0.006873 **
number.mosquito 1 0.095 0.0950 1.053 0.308539
number.human 1 1.712 1.7124 18.989 4.78e-05 ***
distance.contamination:distance.work.home
1 0.012 0.0118 0.130 0.719290
distance.contamination:number.mosquito
1 0.043 0.0431 0.478 0.491639
distance.work.home:number.mosquito 1
0.176 0.1765 1.957 0.166583 d
istance.contamination:number.human 1
0.653 0.6531 7.242 0.009044 **
distance.work.home:number.human
1 0.104 0.1040 1.154 0.286717
number.mosquito:number.human
1 0.066 0.0660 0.732 0.395395
distance.contamination:distance.work.home:number.mosquito
1 0.305 0.3053 3.386 0.070328
```

```
distance.contamination:distance.work.home:number.human
1 0.144 0.1440 1.597 0.210906
distance.contamination:number.mosquito:number.human
1 0.051 0.0512 0.568 0.453742
distance.work.home:number.mosquito:number.human
1 0.000 0.0001 0.001 0.973626
distance.contamination:distance.work.home:number.mosquito
  :number.human
1 0.022 0.0221 0.245 0.622349
Residuals            65 5.861 0.0902 ---
Signif. codes: 0 *** 0.001 ** 0.01 * 0.05 . 0.1 1
```

The third column (Sum Sq) corresponds to the sums of the squares of the deviations (*SS*), such as those which we calculated with NetLogo in the previous part (the 4 first lines).

We can also obtain each variable relative part by dividing each SS by the total of the deviations (this also gives us the part of the variance):

```
> round(summary(aovex)[[1]][2]/
        sum(summary(aovex)[[1]][2])*100,2)
              zSum Sq
distance.contamination 12.25
distance.work.home 6.20
number.mosquito 0.84
number.human 15.10
distance.contamination:distance.work.home 0.10
distance.contamination:number.mosquito 0.38
distance.work.home:number.mosquito 1.56
distance.contamination:number.human 5.76
distance.work.home:number.human 0.92
number.mosquito:number.human 0.58
distance.contamination:distance.work.home
  :number.mosquito 2.69
distance.contamination:distance.work.home
  :number.human 1.27
distance.contamination:number.mosquito
  :number.human 0.45
```

```
distance.work.home:number.mosquito:number.human 0.00
distance.contamination:distance.work.home
  :number.mosquito:number.human 0.19
Residuals
```

We can confirm the results obtained from NetLogo in the previous section: the parameters with the greatest impacts are clearly number-human (15% of the total variance) and distance-contamination (12% of the total variance).

The complete analysis done with R offers us numerous additional information relative to our NetLogo graph:

– We also have the weight of paired factors now: the combined impact of `distance-contamination` and `number-human` also appears to be rather important (5.7% of the variance).

– The residual part (`Residuals`) is particularly interesting: it corresponds to the variance which is not explained by the deviations between partial means and the global mean, that is to say, all the deviations obtained with identical parameters. This is the variance which is due to other parameters or random phenomena present in the model (in our case, mosquito movement and, more importantly, the location of the original infected mosquito). We can see that our four parameters only justify 48% of the total variance. The model is therefore very unstable even with fixed parameters.

– Another piece of useful information received in the R analysis is the statistical test carried out for each parameter ((`F value`, `Pr(>F)`). The columns correspond to a Fisher's test which tests the following hypothesis: "the parameter has no impact upon the variable" (if we assume a linear impact). The indicated probability is the probability that this statement is true. There is therefore 0.02% probability that, with the obtained results, the `distance-contamination` parameter has no impact on the `count-infection` variable. The stars (`*** ** *`) synthesize this value. This value gives the analysis a statistical justification (the impact of `distance-contamination` is statistically significant within our model). Nonetheless, care must be taken so as not to misinterpret this value: a parameter without a star (*) (where Pr>10%) does not mean that the parameter has no impact, but instead that no conclusion can be made using the obtained results.

4.4. Conclusion

The exploration of NetLogo models is greatly facilitated, both by the graphical, dynamic and reactive interface and by the BehaviorSpace, an integrated tool which allows for experiment plans to be carried out simply and intuitively. Coupled with NetLogo graphs, or with an external data analysis software such as R, this tool offers robust and statistically founded analysis perspectives for any NetLogo model.

Several important and more advanced aspects of model exploration with NetLogo have nonetheless not been covered here and will be specifically focused upon in Volume 2 [BAN 15].

First, these need to be done with automatic calibration of models, as well as optimization, which requires the maximization/minimization of an objective function, which might allow for a configuration that minimizes the final infection count to be found. This process requires a large number of calculations and is thus not included within the BehaviorSpace, but can nonetheless be used in NetLogo with the help of the BehaviorSearch extension (http://behaviorsearch.org/documentation/tutorial.html), or in a more sophisticated manner with the OpenMole platform ([REU 13] http://www.openmole.org/), which allows for the distribution of simulations on distributed computing environments.

Second, this has to be done with the direct integration of R's or GraphStream's analysis functions into the NetLogo code, via the use of existing plug-ins, so as to directly obtain the statistical indicators (R) or graphs (R, GraphStream) necessary for the evaluation of the model within NetLogo.

Finally, this has to be done with the use of more advanced statistical tools such as clustering algorithms, with or without interaction with the NetLogo model, allowing for the analysis of homogeneous groups of individuals or of parameter groups which produce homogeneous results from an exploration of their parameter space.

5

Dynamical Systems with NetLogo

5.1. Introduction

Numerous scientific fields are involved in the study of real-world phenomena based on theoretical models. These can have many different roles, going from describing problems, so as to understand them better, to predicting how they will evolve. This last aspect requires the representation of the phenomenon's dynamics, which allows for the chosen model's evolution over time to be followed. In order to accomplish this, the problem can be presented at different scales. Roughly speaking, it can be said that there are two main scales: the microscopic scale, which is centered on the modeling of individuals, and the macroscopic scale, which relies on mathematical theories proposed in the context of dynamic systems.

In this chapter, this dual notion is developed upon with particular focus given to system dynamics. In order to support our aims, we will study the spread of panic in a crowd.

Crowd behavior has been studied since the mid-20th Century by sociologists [BON 03]. It is only recently that physicians, mathematicians and computer scientists have considered the subject. The problems studied, as well as the tools used to do so, have

Chapter written by Nathalie CORSON and Damien OLIVIER.

changed, by reducing qualitative aspects and instead favoring models and attempting to turn them into methods of study, prediction and exploratory research. This is all the more true considering recent catastrophes, such as those in 2006, during the yearly pilgrimage to Mecca, or in 2010, during the Love Parade in Duisburg, that have shown the importance of a better understanding of the collective phenomena which develop within crowds.

The latter two are composed of groups of individuals with interacting heterogeneous behaviors. They also contain organizations (groups, families, etc.) which act upon the same individuals.

This describes a complex system that, as with all complex systems, possesses properties of robustness and resilience when faced with internal or external events. Emergent phenomena may also occur. Nonetheless, even if a crowd is a resilient system, it can deviate from its course, especially when a panic event occurs; a phenomenon which constitutes the specific issue discussed within the chapter.

Our aim is therefore to reflect upon this collective phenomenon as well as to suggest a research process. NetLogo is a perfectly adapted tool for this context.

Once the panic propagation has been modeled into ordinary differential equations (ODEs), the equational model is implemented with NetLogo's `System Dynamics Modeler` module. The results will then be compared with those obtained with classical analysis methods so as to evaluate the accuracy of this tool.

Finally, we will consider how aggregate and agent-based modeling can be compared.

5.2. Aggregate model versus agent-based model

Questioning different forms of modeling naturally leads to attempting to define the scientific notion of a model. A model is composed of a simplified representation of a studied reference system. It must specifically allow for the functioning of the system to be understood and thus allow for questions about it to be answered. This representation is constructed with a language. The differences between aggregate modeling and agent-based modeling are related not only to the languages used but also to their possibilities, since they capture the various elements of the problem and depend on domain ontology and the epistemological beliefs of each scientific field. While models were previously linguistic and descriptive or mathematical and rigid, since the introduction of computational tools, new forms that allow for a simplified system to be followed over time have been created [COQ 96].

The models presented in the previous chapters are computer models, whereas those discussed in this chapter are mathematical. The latter offer a strong formalism, based on expression rigor and structural consistence at the expense of flexibility and expressivity. Conversely, computer models are heavily descriptive and offer a high level of flexibility but have problems with generalization.

Agent-based modeling focuses on a particular level of organization, the individual. The simulation of a group of individuals leads to the emergence of collective behaviors. The focus is no longer on the population but instead on the individual. It is for this reason that such models are placed in the "bottom-up" category, due to the fact that they are defined based on their constituents and because their simulation allows for the behavior of the "higher level" to be studied, that is to say that of the system as a whole. The study of an individual's or a group's behavior is then possible. This scale has certain disadvantages, however, as it sometimes leads to very complicated models whose global behavior is difficult to analyze and document. It is a modeling method that is well adapted to the study of complex systems, as long as we are interested in the system dynamics created from the interaction of the entities within it. Stochastical elements can easily be introduced. Agent-based models often allow for the effects of spatialization to be taken into account, but can struggle with quantitative aspects or with generalization and predictability. Calculation time constraints often also have to be taken into account.

Aggregate modeling allows for the evolution of specific variables to be compared against a parameter often time. It describes the evolution of populations of individuals with specific characteristics, and not the evolution of the individuals themselves. Their evolution over time is usually considered to be continuous, which translates itself mathematically into one or a system of ODEs (ODE). This approach aggregates a set of interacting elements that make up a system whose characteristics are the emergent result of the global dynamic. Stability, structure, order and equilibrium are usually an average, resulting from a large number of interactions. Behind the "regularities" is hidden the disorder which created them. ODEs provide an remarkable tool for the study of such systems and their progress over time. They most particularly allow for the study of sensitivity to initial conditions, as well as to equilibrium conditions. However, certain limitations can appear when it comes to taking account of spatial or temporal dimensions or the heterogeneity of the system's components.

As well as the mathematical formality that is so well adapted for this type of modeling, there exists a number of algorithmic formalities as well as graphical display methods of agent-based modeling (StarLogo [RES 97], Unified Modeling Language (UML), Agent Modeling Language (AML) (Chapter 2)) or even graphical display methods of aggregate modeling, such as Forrester diagrams, which are integrated within NetLogo's `System Dynamics Modeler` module that we will present later.

5.3. Aggregate representation of the spread of panic

By "aggregate representation" of the spread of panic, we are referring to the representation of this issue with a dynamic system. This consists of describing such a system using measurable quantities whose evolution will be followed over time. The variables which represent these quantities are known as state variables. In this section, we will introduce these variables and their respective evolutions in the specific context of the spread of panic [BON 03].

In this section, we base our model on a real event described by the U.S. Press [US 83a, US 83b], which occurred in 1883 on Brooklyn Bridge. This bridge crosses the East River and links the Manhattan and

Brooklyn neighborhoods of New York. On the 24th of May 1883, the bridge was inaugurated, which elicited a lot of interest from the local population. On the 30th of May, at about 4 pm, there were more than 1,600 individuals crossing the bridge at the same time. People were wandering around and looking at passing boats. A group of men then decided to cross the bridge as quickly as possible, each placing his hands on the shoulders of the person preceding him. People began pushing each other, and according to several accounts, someone shouted that the bridge was collapsing. The confusion of cries led several individuals to believe that the bridge was really collapsing, despite the best efforts of the authorities that were present. The panic then spread across the entire bridge as a result of behavioral contamination, and the resulting scramble for safety led many individuals to find themselves crushed against security grating. The death toll reached a total of 12, with many others injured, and it took a year for the population to be completely reassured that the bridge was safe, the result of Phineas T. Barnum making 21 elephants cross it.

The threat of a perceived danger can cause a variety of different reactions within a crowd, linked to each individual's emotions. This observation naturally leads to the concept of separating individuals into different categories or compartments corresponding to their emotional state, whereupon they can be counted. Depending upon the evolution of the situation, the environment and themselves, the state of an individual will vary. This is represented by a change of compartment. Furthermore, there are imitation processes within crowds which are similar to behavioral contamination phenomena. We will therefore observe the variation of the population within each compartment, as well as the dynamics of the spread of panic through the crowd.

This type of compartmental modeling which we are using is already widely used in epidemiology for the study of the spread of an illness where each individual is considered to possibly be healthy but susceptible of being infected (S), already infected (I) or immunized (R). This model, known as SIR, was put forward by Kermack and McKendrick in 1972 [KER 39, KER 91].

In order to study this process, we will consider that a phenomenon likely of creating a panic reaction has occurred. Following this event, we count the number of calm, scared and panicked individuals[1]. This results in three compartments to which each individual can belong being clearly defined. We also suppose that the phenomenon is sustained (possibly self-sustained, remembered, etc.) and that this might cause fear in other initially calm individuals. However, the panic state can only be reached by individuals that are already scared as a result of an amplification process caused by other panicked individuals. The modification of the panicked individuals' emotional states can be linked to temporal factors of stimulus disappearance, forgetfulness, etc.

In the case of our problem, we define three compartments: non-panicked people (NPP), people susceptible to panic (PSP) and panicked people (PP) [PRO 05, PRO 07]. Thus, calm individuals are placed within the NPP compartment. The number of individuals within this compartment is recorded as x. Scared individuals are placed within the PSP compartment. The number of individuals within this compartment is recorded as y. Finally, panicked individuals are placed within the PP compartment. The number of individuals within this compartment is recorded as z.

From the initial spread of N individuals in each of the three compartments, passing in between compartments can be done in different ways:

– An α_1 proportion of calm individuals can become scared. We mention this transition rate as α_1 (Figure 5.1: NPP $\xrightarrow{\alpha_1}$ PSP).

– Scared individuals can become calm, with a transition rate of α_2 (Figure 5.1: PSP $\xrightarrow{\alpha_2}$ NPP).

– Panicked individuals can pass into the group of scared individuals, with a transition rate of β_2 (Figure 5.1: PP $\xrightarrow{\beta_2}$ PSP), or into the group of calm individuals, with a transition rate of λ_2 (Figure 5.1: PP $\xrightarrow{\lambda_2}$ NPP).

1 The range of possible emotions is much wider [DAM 94, FRI 86, LUM 04, SCH 99a, SCH 99b, WAT 92] but for simplicity's sake, we focus here on only three of them.

– Scared individuals might, as a result of contact with panicked individuals, become panicked themselves, with a "contamination" rate of $\beta_1 \times z$, proportional to the number of panicked individuals in the population (Figure 5.1: PSP $\xrightarrow{\beta_1 z}$ PP).

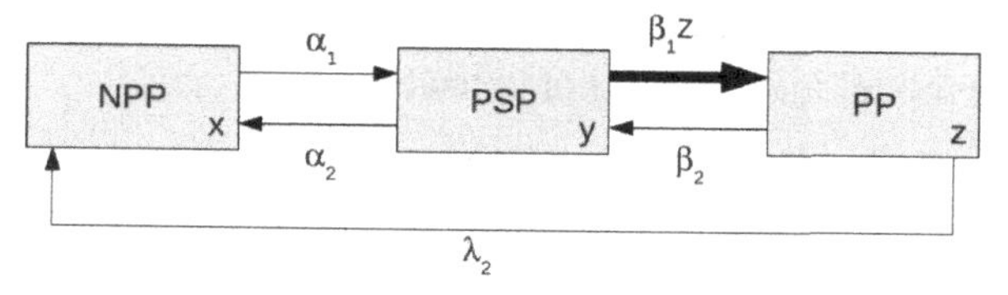

Figure 5.1. *Compartmental model of panic propagation. The individuals of the NPP class are calm, those of the PSP class are afraid, whereas those in the PP class are panicked. Only the passing from the PSP to the PP class occurs by behavioral contamination (bold arrow)*

Following this, the problem is first represented by NetLogo with a Forrester diagram, and then by a system of ODEs. The former allows for the model to be graphically constructed in terms of stocks (compartments) and flows. NetLogo translates this representation into equations and performs calculations so as to obtain certain numerical results. The equations obtained from NetLogo's translation of the Forrester diagram are the same as those put together by more commonly used dynamic system problem modeling tools.

5.3.1. *Representing dynamic systems with NetLogo*

The study of dynamic systems owes much to J.W. Forrester who put forward a modeling method known as DYNAMO [FOR 61, FOR 68, FOR 69], since largely adopted by STELLAR and by NetLogo's `System Dynamics Modeler` module. The approach is systematic and based on interaction and feedback loop concepts; it forms part of the broader scope of the study of complex systems.

5.3.1.1. *Method: Forrester diagram*

At the methodological level, it is necessary to state which elements belong to the environment and the system as well as its eventual decomposition. This allows for the entering (input) and exiting (output) elements to be identified. The system dynamics govern the change of inputs to outputs. It is also at this level that positive and negative feedback loops must be identified. Negative feedback loops have a stabilizing effect as they reduce the phenomenon, whereas positive feedback loops amplify it. This conceptualization stage identifies whether the model is influential or causal.

The following step consists of formalizing the model by specifying the stock variables[2] which characterize the model at any time t. Their values vary depending on the flows which feed or empty the stocks. The flows therefore consist of transport channels of matter or energy. They are conservative and are controlled by taps which regulate the flow depending upon the forces acting upon the system. Finally, the auxiliary variables can be either constant, or the result of an equation which can itself depend upon other variables. They offer the possibility of introducing nonlinearity. These informations are represented within the model by links which act as information routes. They also allow for stocks, flows and auxiliary variables to be connected and for these interactions to be represented as a result.

5.3.1.2. *Tool: `System Dynamics Modeler - NetLogo`*

Modeling a dynamic system with NetLogo consists of creating a Forrester diagram. This is possible due to the `System Dynamics Modeler` module, which can be found in the `Tools` menu (Ctrl+Shift+D). When this module is opened, a second window appears, containing the `Diagram` and `Code` tabs. The `Diagram` tab allows for the diagram's basic elements and relationships to be created, which we will present as we progress (see Figure 5.3). The diagram is then translated into NetLogo code which can be read but not directly edited from within the `Code` tab.

2 The terminology is vast, so a stock can also be referred to as a level, an accumulation compartment or a state.

Thus, the new window is used for creating the model, whereas the primary interface, with the `Interface`, `Info` and `Code` tabs, is used for the simulation of the model.

To begin, it is customary to create a button which will initialize the model.

In order to do this, we create a `Button` within the main interface, named as `Setup`, which takes the following command, as shown by Figure 5.2:

```
clear-all system-dynamics-setup
```

Once created, this `Button` appears in red as the procedure (`system-dynamics-setup`) has not yet been defined.

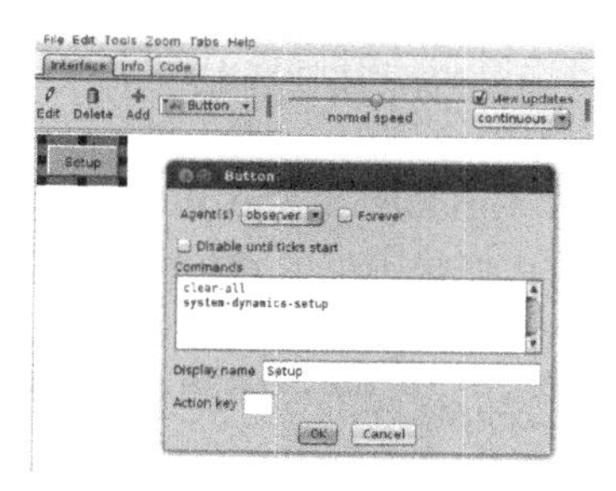

Figure 5.2. *Creating the* **`Setup`** *initialization button*

Let us now return to our case study and follow the previously defined methodology. The following should be defined first (see Figure 5.3):

1) the state variables, named as `stocks` in NetLogo terminology;

2) the connecting flows between `stocks`, named as `flows`;

3) the information channels (`links`) which manipulate auxiliary variables or other parameters (`variables`) which act upon the evolution of the model.

Figure 5.3. *The tools of NetLogo's* `System Dynamics Modeler` *module*

We have already defined three emotional states which determine the size of the `stocks`:

– the `stock` represented by x is the number of calm individuals, belonging to the NPP compartment;

– the `stock` represented by y is the number of scared individuals, belonging to the PSP compartment;

– the `stock` represented by z is the number of panicked individuals, belonging to the PP compartment.

The creation of these `stocks` has two steps (Figure 5.4):

1) Creating the stock in the `Diagram` tab, where the stock is assigned a name (here `Name: x`) and given an initial value (here `Initial value: xInit`). It is also given a number as an initial value, but the use of a global variable allows for the user to modify it more easily through use of the `Interface`. Because we are dealing with population sizes, the setting which allows for negative values (`Allow negative values`) must be unticked.

2) Defining a global variable in the interface, using an `Input` of `type: Number`. It is also possible to replace the `Input` by a `Slider` depending on the user's preference. The aim is to be able to easily modify the initial conditions of the stocks from the primary interface, when necessary.

This procedure must be repeated for each of the three studied variables: `x`, `y`, `z`.

In order to make the simulation interface more understandable, it is possible to add `Notes`.

Figure 5.5 shows the result of repeating this procedure for each of our variables.

Figure 5.1, showing a representation of the compartmental model, illustrates the fact that the dynamics of the studied model are influenced by five parameters: α_1, α_2, β_1, β_2 and λ_2.

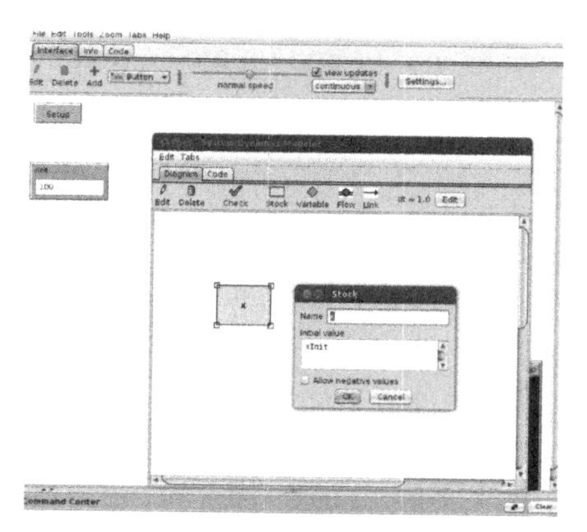

Figure 5.4. *Creating the x compartment (`stock`) in the `System Dynamics Modeler`*

We will create five corresponding `Variables` in the `Diagram` interface: `alpha1`, `alpha2`, `beta1`, `beta2` and `lambda2` to which we will give the respective `Expressions`: `ValueAlpha1`, `ValueAlpha2`, `ValueBeta1`, `ValueBeta2` and `ValueLambda2`.

These `Expressions` correspond to global variables which must be created in the form of `Inputs` (of `Number` type) or `Sliders` in the primary interface so that the user may modify them easily.

Figure 5.6 presents the creation of these variables.

The `flows` show the size and directions of the flows in between `Stocks: x, y` and `z`. As shown in Figure 5.9, we therefore create five `Flows` which take these emotional state changes into account (`xToy`, `yToz`, etc.).

For example, passing from the NPP class to the PSP class – so from the x `stock` to the$y$ `stock` – is controlled by a transition rate `alpha1` and depends on the x `Stock`. In the `Diagram` tab, the expression which calculates this flow is therefore: `x` $\times$ `alpha1` (see Figure 5.7). Furthermore, the `yToz Flow` has the particularity of happening as a result of contamination in between individuals in the PP (`z`) class and those in the PSP (`y`) class. This flow therefore depends on the encounters between individuals from the `y` and `z Stocks` (these encounters are written as y × z) and on the contamination rate β_1 (and therefore on the beta1 Variable). This is written as: y × z × beta1 (see Figure 5.8).

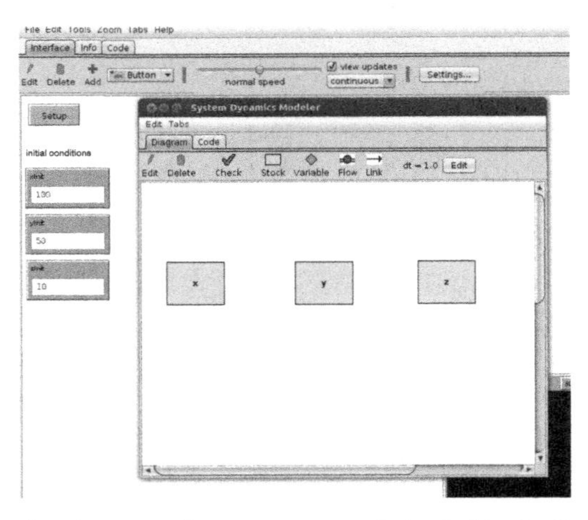

Figure 5.5. *Creating the x, y and z compartments (stocks) in the System Dynamics Modeler, and creating the Inputs that can be used to assign initial values to each of these variables, as well as adding a Note: Initial conditions on the interface so as to make it easier and clearer to use*

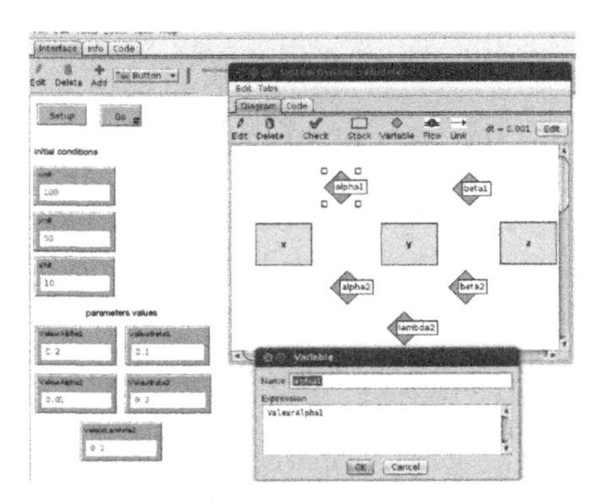

Figure 5.6. *Creating the five Variables: alpha1, alpha2, beta1, beta2 and lambda2 to which we give the respective Expressions: ValueAlpha1, ValueAlpha2, ValueBeta1, ValueBeta2 and ValueLambda2, which are global variables controlled by Inputs within the interface*

Figure 5.9 shows the Flows, which describe the shifts between compartments.

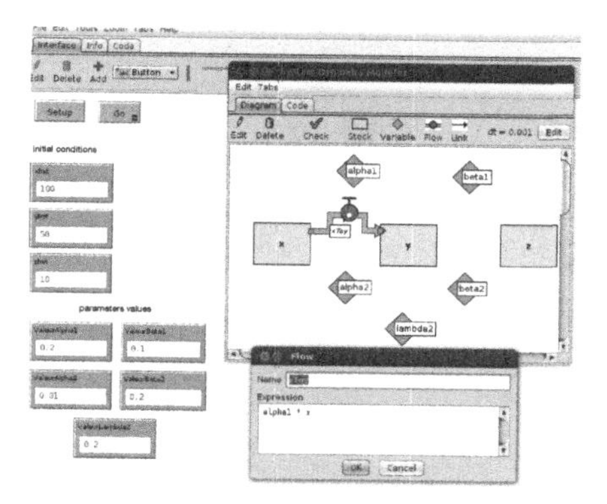

Figure 5.7. *`Flow` describing movement from the* x *`Stock` to the* y *`Stock`*

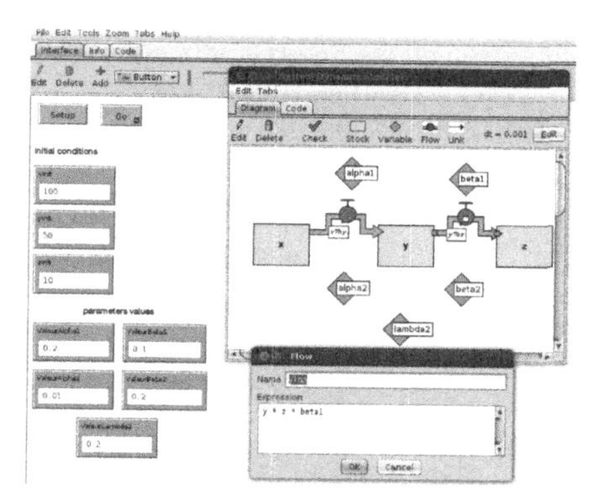

Figure 5.8. *`Flow` describing movement from the* y *`Stock` to the* z *`Stock`*

Finally, we associate `links` to each of the five `Variables` and the `Flows` that they impact (see Figure 5.10).

In order to be able to launch the simulation, we create a button within the primary interface, which we will call `name:` Go, and whose `Command` is:

```
system-dynamics-go
```

as shown by Figure 5.11. Furthermore, for the simulation to run across several steps of time, the Forever box should be ticked.

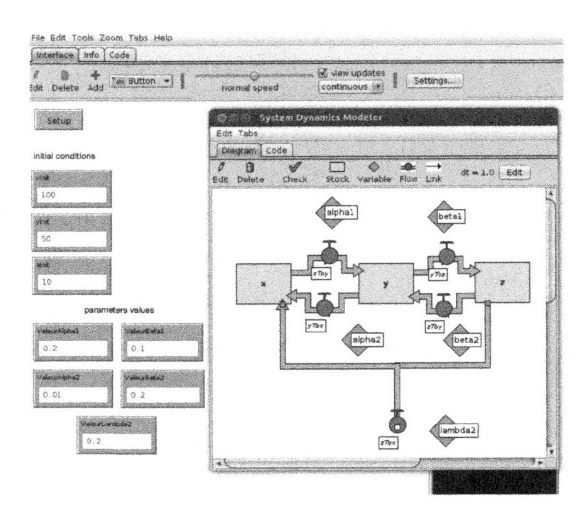

Figure 5.9. *`Diagram` with all the `Flows` representing the movements from each compartment to the others*

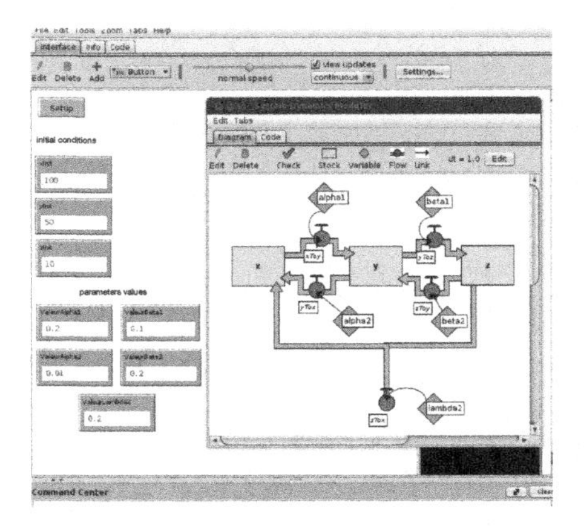

Figure 5.10. *`Diagram` with all `Flows` and `Links` representing the movements from each compartment to the others*

The diagram created is then directly translated into NetLogo code. NetLogo's main interface is henceforth used to manage the simulation and its display.

Before discussing the possible simulations and outputs resulting from such a model, the next section will show that it is possible to build a system of ODEs equivalent to the diagram created here.

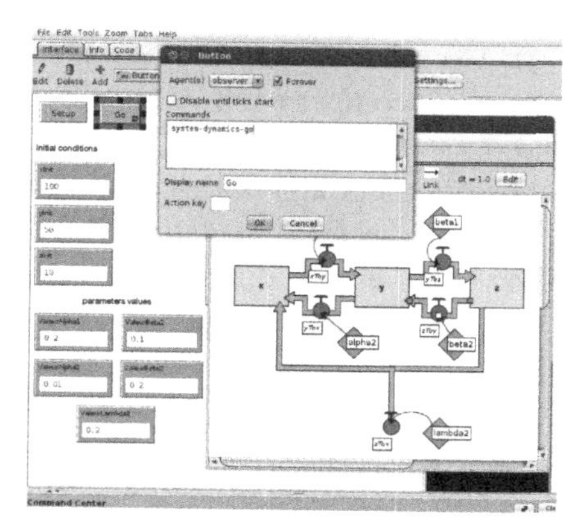

Figure 5.11. *Creating the* `Go` *button*

5.3.2. *Constructing a dynamical system model by a system of ODEs*

As previously indicated, it is also possible to model the problem with a system of ODEs. We will presently explain how this model should be created. As a reminder, a system of ODEs is a dynamic system which describes the evolution of variables over time using equations. In the case we are discussing, these variables are x, y and z and represent the number of individuals in the NPP, PSP and PP compartments, respectively. The inputs and outputs of each compartment are the addition of individuals entering and the subtraction of individuals leaving, respectively.

The variation of NPP's x population for a given step of time (dt) is characterized by the derivative of this x value compared to time, written as $\frac{dx}{dt}$. For each compartment, this variation is a result of the entry and exit of individuals. Following a disturbance, a proportion (α_1) of calm individuals become afraid and no longer belong to the NPP compartment but instead are part of the PSP compartment. Thus, this transition can be seen within the system as a subtraction of individuals from the NPP compartment ($-\alpha_1 x$) and an addition of these to the PSP compartment ($+\alpha_1 x$). A proportion of individuals (α_2) of the PSP compartment become calm again. This change of state is seen as a transition ($-\alpha_2 y$) of PSP individuals to the NPP

compartment ($+\alpha_2 y$). The same applies for the restoration of panicked individuals from the PP compartment to a calm state. The PP population diminishes by$-\lambda_2 z$, whereas the NPP increases by $+\lambda_2 z$. Finally, the contamination effect appears in the form of the nonlinear term $\beta_1 yz$, which increases the PP population and reduces that of the PSP. It highlights the fact that the contamination rate is proportional, with a coefficient of β_1, to the number of panicked individuals (z).

Therefore, the system of differential equations that describes the spread of panic through a group of N individuals is as follows:

$$\begin{cases} \dfrac{dx}{dt} = -\alpha_1 x + \alpha_2 y + \lambda_2 z \\ \dfrac{dy}{dt} = +\alpha_1 x - \alpha_2 y + \beta_2 z - \beta_1 yz \\ \dfrac{dz}{dt} = +\beta_1 yz - \beta_2 z - \lambda_2 z \end{cases}$$

We have now defined our problem by translating it into an equational model composed of three ODEs, which describe the relationships between variables and their derivatives. The system discussed is *autonomous* as time does not explicitly appear within the equation terms. Furthermore, it is *nonlinear* as it contains the term $\beta_1 zy$ that is not represented by a straight line, and is said to be of *first order* because it shows the first derivative of each variable.

We consider that the system is isolated, that is to say there are no births or deaths, and that the total population (N) therefore remains constant. As a result:

$$x + y + z = N$$

Equally:

$$x \leq N,\ y \leq N,\ z \leq N$$

Since our values represent population sizes, we are only interested in positive values for x, y and z; therefore:

$$x \geq 0,\ y \geq 0,\ z \geq 0$$

Furthermore, since the total population is constant, all individuals that leave a compartment must enter another, which gives us:

$$\frac{dx}{dt} + \frac{dy}{dt} + \frac{dz}{dt} = 0$$

We presented two different formats for defining dynamic systems: the former was graphical, generating an algorithm, and the latter was equational. Nonetheless, these two forms present many similarities. Indeed, the code generated by NetLogo within the `Code` tab of the `System Dynamic Modeler` module is as follows (this is an extract). Note that we have grayed out all lines which control the variations that impact the NPP (x) compartment:

```
to system-dynamics-go

;; NetLogo saves global variables within local variables
;; so as to avoid side effects. ;; In gray: everything which
affects the NPP compartment.

let local-alpha1 alpha1 let local-alpha2 alpha2 let
local-beta1  beta1 let local-beta2 beta2 let local-lambda2
lambda2 let local-xToy xToy ;; Movement from the x compartment
to y let local-yToz yToz let local-yTox yTox ;; Movement
from the y compartment to x let local-zToy zToy let
local-zTox zTox ;; Movement from the z compartment to x

;; Updating the x stock variables for the NPP compartment.
;; Using copies of variables to solve the ;; problem of
dependency within equations.

let new-x ( x - local-xToy + local-yTox + local-zTox
) let new-y ( y + local-xToy - local-yToz - local-yTox +
local-zToy)
let new-z ( z + local-yToz - local-zToy - local-zTox )
```

```
;; Updating the global variables from local variables.

set x new-x set y new-y set z new-z

;; Time advances by a single unit.

tick-advance dt end

;; Flow of individuals between x and y to-report
xToy report ( alpha1 * x ) * dt end

;; Flow of individuals between y and z to-report yToz report
( y * z * beta1 ) * dt end

;; Flow of individuals between y and x to-report
yTox report ( alpha2 * x ) * dt end

;; Flow of individuals between z and y to-report zToy report
( beta2 * z ) * dt end

;; Flow of individuals between z and x to-report
zTox report ( lambda2 * z ) * dt end
```

Let us remind ourselves that the equational system is given by:

$$\begin{cases} \dfrac{dx}{dt} = -\alpha_1 x + \alpha_2 y + \lambda_2 z \\ \dfrac{dy}{dt} = +\alpha_1 x - \alpha_2 y + \beta_2 z - \beta_1 yz \\ \dfrac{dz}{dt} = +\beta_1 yz - \beta_2 z - \lambda_2 z \end{cases}$$

Thus, we can see that the same information is contained in both representations.

To analytically solve a system of ODEs, we must find the functions $x(t)$, $y(t)$ and $z(t)$ that will satisfy all the systems equations. These solutions constitute the trajectories of the system's variables. It is, however, rarely possible to solve this analytically and the solution must be found by using numerical methods, perhaps complimented by theoretical studies relating to the existence of solutions and their nature, for example.

The use of NetLogo's `System Dynamics Modeler` module has several advantages. It can be used without any prior knowledge of mathematical tools relating to the modeling of dynamic systems. Furthermore, it allows for a simple and quick manipulation of the initial conditions and parameters. Equally, as previously specified, since it is rarely possible to solve such a system analytically, we will use numerical integration methods in order to obtain approximate trajectories (see the following section) and the use of NetLogo does not require the implementation of these methods, which are present within the model. Therefore, displaying these trajectories is easy.

Without modification, however, the possibilities offered by this module are relatively limited and the calculation time needed to obtain the trajectories is significant.

Moreover, only the equational representation allows for a theoretical study.

We will now present several numerical and theoretical tools that can be used to study our problem.

5.3.3. *Study of the dynamic system*

5.3.3.1. *Numerical study*

Let us consider the following ODE:

$$\frac{dy}{dt} = f(y, t), \text{with } y(t_0) = y_0 \qquad [5.1]$$

Numerically solving this equation consists of using an iterative algorithm that gives the values of $y(t)$ starting from y_0 at time t_0. This amounts to numerically integrating the differential equation.

5.3.3.1.1. Numerical integration of a system of ODEs: methods

In 1768, Leonhard Euler put forward the first numerical method for integrating differential equations. It was based on the finite expression of the derivative:

$$\frac{dy}{dt} = \lim_{h \to 0} \frac{y(t+h) - y(t)}{h}$$

If we take h to be a sufficiently small step of time:

$$y(t+h) = y(t) + h\frac{dy}{dt} + o(t), o(t) \text{ representing the error} \quad [5.2]$$

By substituting [5.1] into [5.2]:

$$y(t+h) = y(t) + hf(y,t) + o(t)$$

Considering a step h that is strictly positive and y_i, which is the approximate value of y at time $t_i = t_0 + ih$, and if $o(h)$ is ignored, then we obtain a concise formulation of the Eulerian method:

$$y_0 = y(t_0)$$
$$y_{i+1} = y_i + hf(t_i, y_i), i > 0$$

The general idea, as shown in Figure 5.12, is to approach a point $(t_0, y(t_0))$ with an unknown function by its tangent, which can then be determined. We then apply this process at each step. The constructed function is continuous and refined in stages.

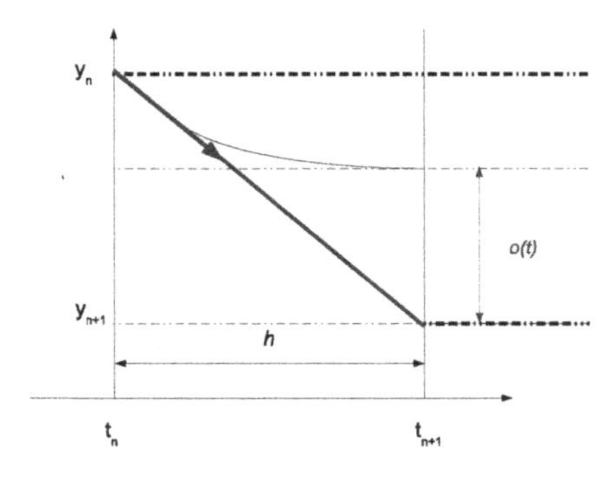

Figure 5.12. *Eulerian method*

NetLogo allows us to illustrate how this process functions. The exact solution to the ODE $\frac{dy}{dt} = y$ with the initial condition of $y(0) = 1$ is $y(t) = e^t$. This result can be obtained using turtles, or with the Eulerian method, and we can therefore observe the effect of the step h. This corresponds to the following commented code:

```
turtles-own [x y] ;; Position of
the turtle of the representation of the globals plane
[exact-turtle approached-turtle step scale-on-x scale-on-y]

to setup ca set step 0.05 ;; no calculation for the exact
function set scale-on-x 2 / (max-pxcor) ;; x-axis set
scale-on-y (exp 2) / (max-pycor ) ;; y-axis setup-axes
setup-exact end

to setup-axes ask patches ;; We trace the vertical and
horizontal axes [ ;; in white. if (pxcor = 0 or pycor = 0)
[set pcolor white] ] end

to setup-exact ;; Creation and initialization of the turtle
create-turtles 1 ;; which represents the exact solution
[ set  exact-turtle self ;; We save its identity set color
gray set  pen-size 2 set x 0 ;; We initialize its position
at x = 0 set y  exp x ;; We calculate y setxy x / scale-on-x
y / scale-on-y  ;; We position it within pen-down
;; the NetLogo world ] end

to setup-approached create-turtles 1 ;; Creation and
initialization of the turtle [ ;; which represent the
approached solution set  approached-turtle self
;; We save its identity set color light gray set  pen-size 1
set x 0 set y 1 ;; We initialize its position at x = 0
and y = 1 setxy x / scale-on-x y / scale-on-y
;; Translation  into pen-down
;; the NetLogo world ] end

to maj-y-exact ;; The exact solution function of the ODEs
set y exp x ;; y = ex end

to trace-exact ;; Calculation of a point of the exact
solution  set x x + pas ;; The curve will be constructed
```

```
point by point  set y exp x setxy x / scale-on-x
y / scale-on-y ;; Translation into end
;; the NetLogo world

to trace-approached ;; We trace the line segment set x
x + h ;; We calculate the new value of x set y (1 + h) * y
;; We  calculate the new value of y ;; We move the turtle
in a straight line ;; from its old position to the new one
facexy x / scale-on-x y / scale-on-y jump
distancexy (x / scale-on-x) (y / scale-on-y) end

to go-exact ;; Turtle representing the exact solution ask
exact-turtle ;; traces the curve point by point [ ;; until
the  predefined limit is reached
while [ x + pas <= 2 ] [ exact-trace ] ]
end

to go-approached ;; Turtle representing the approached
solution  setup-approached ;; traces the line segments
ask approached-turtle ;; until the predefined limit
[ while [ x + h <= 2 ] [ approached-trace ] die
;; We kill the turtle so as to be able to begin a new
approximation if needed. ] end
```

The configuration of the NetLogo `world` is illustrated in Figure 5.13. The essential parameters are `location of origin: Custom`, `max-pxcor 400`, `min-pxcor -10`, `max-pycor 300`, `min-pycor -10` and `Patch size 2`. We also need to associate a `setup` `Button` within the interface to a procedure of the same name, a `exact curve Button` to the `go-exact` procedure and an `approached curve Button` to the `go-approched` procedure. A `Slider` that allows us to define the value of `h` to any number between 0.001 and 1 also needs to be added. The Eulerian method can then be observed in the proposed example, along with the influence of the `h` step upon the approximated value (see Figure 5.14).

Numerous other approximation methods have since been developed, based on the discretization of the study interval into a certain number of steps. Depending on the type of formula used to approach solutions, we can distinguish numerical methods with one or several steps, which can be express or implied.

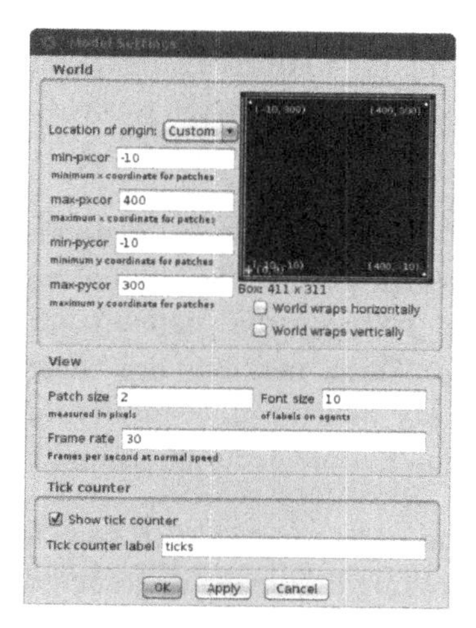

Figure 5.13. *Configuration of the* `NetLogo World`

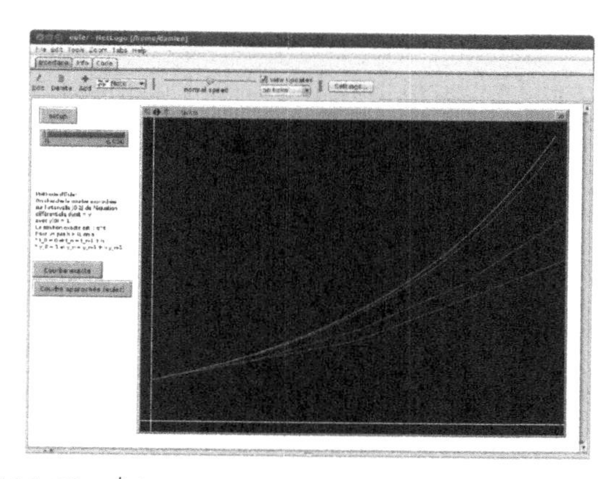

Figure 5.14. *The* e^t *function (in white) and the approximations (in gray) obtained for* $h = 1$, $h = 0.5$ *and* $h = 0.05$. *For a color version of the figure, see www.iste.co.uk/banos/netlogo.zip*

Several criteria are used to measure the performance of numerical methods: the consistency of a method indicates that the theoretical error, present as the solution is approached, tends toward 0 at every step. Stability shows a capacity for controlling the buildup of rounding errors. Together they insure convergence, that is to say the ability to make the global error tend to 0.

Among the most commonly used methods for approximative numerical analysis of solutions of differential equations, we find the methods developed in 1901 by the mathematicians Carl Runge and Martin Wilhelm Kutta. These methods are based on the principle of iteration, which is to say that the first approximation of a solution is used to calculate a second, more accurate estimation, and so on.

Runge–Kutta's first-order method (RK1) is equivalent to the Eulerian method for solving first-order differential equations.

Runge–Kutta's second-order method (RK2), or the mid-point method, is a variation of the Eulerian method (see Figure 5.15). It consists of estimating the derivative at the mid-point of the integration step and recalculating the complete integration step from this estimation.

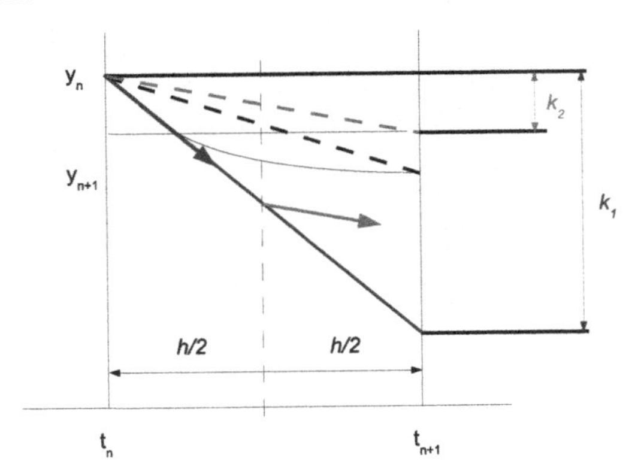

Figure 5.15. *Estimating the mid-point derivative for the current interval*

In Figure 5.15, we have the following:

$$\begin{cases} k_1 = hf(t_n, y_n) \\ k_2 = hf(t_n + h/2, y_n + k_1/2) \\ y_{n+1} = y_n + k_2 \end{cases}$$

Runge–Kutta fourth-order method (RK4) is shown by Figure 5.16. It consists of using the mean of four estimations, which makes it more accurate than the previous methods. In fact, this integration method allows for fourth-order precision by recalculating the derivative four times: once at the start point, twice at mid-points and once at an estimated end point. In Figure 5.16, the following is shown:

$$\begin{cases} k_1 = hf(t_n, y(tn)) \\ k_2 = hf(t_n + h/2, y_n + k_1/2) \\ k_3 = hf(t_n + h/2, y_n + k_2/2) \\ k_4 = hf(t_n + h, y_n + k_3) \\ y_{n+1} = y_n + k_1/6 + k_2/3 + k_3/3 + k_4/6 \end{cases}$$

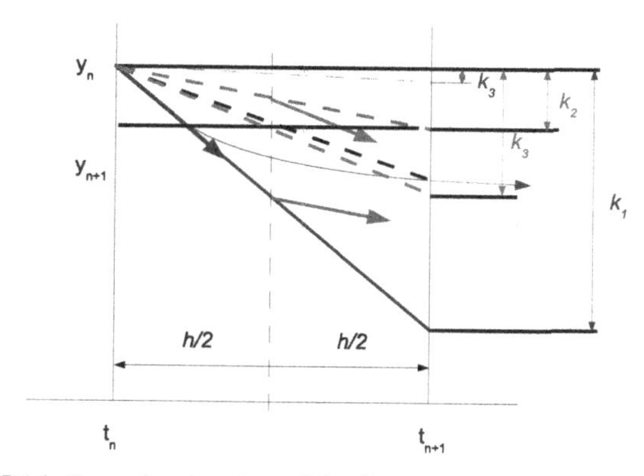

Figure 5.16. *Second estimation of the derivative at the mid-point of the interval and estimation of the derivative at the end point of this interval*

The extent of an error within a method corresponds to the difference between the approximation calculated by the method and the analytical solution. The integration step (h) used gives the order of the error. In fact, for a step method, the error will be of the order of h^2, whereas for a method with 4 steps, it will be of the order of $(h^2)^4$. Consequentially, for a single-step method to obtain the equal level of precision as a four-step method, it is necessary to choose an integration step of the order of 10^4 times greater than that if the four-step method were to be used.

The integration step used for the numerical simulations performed by the `System Dynamics Modeler` module is modifiable from within the interface, as shown in Figure 5.17. Usually, it varies from 10^{-5} for systems which require great precision to 10^{-2} for more simplistic systems.

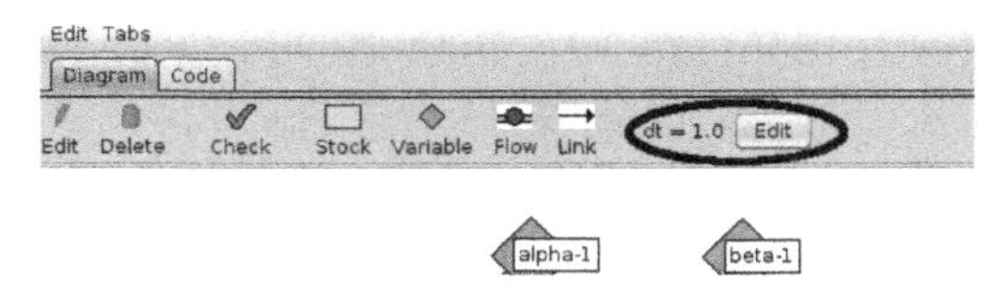

Figure 5.17. *The integration step used for the numerical Eulerian method in NetLogo's `System Dynamics Modeler` module is easily modified by the user in the `Diagram` window*

5.3.3.1.2. Numerical integration of an ODE system: application within a panic model

In order to numerically integrate the dynamic system that the module created from the Forrester diagram, NetLogo uses the *system-dynamics* procedure, which implicitly calls the Eulerian method.

As a result, as long as all of the parameter and initial condition values are known, it is possible to numerically integrate the system so as to observe its paths, that is to say the successive values taken by each of the variables over time.

This integration method is automatically used by NetLogo and therefore there is no need to code it in.

Indeed, in the `Code` tab of the `Diagram` window of the `System Dynamics Modeler`, the following code can be seen:

```
to system-dynamics-do-plot if plot-pen-exists? "x"
[ set-current-plot-pen "x" plotxy ticks
x ] if plot-pen-exists? "y" [ set-current-plot-pen
"y" plotxy ticks y ] if plot-pen-exists?
"z" [ set-current-plot-pen "z"
plotxy ticks z ] end
```

There are three required steps for the display of results of numerical simulations on the main interface:

– adding the `Command` : `system-dynamics-do-plot` in the `Setup` button (see Figure 5.18);

– adding the `Command` : in the `Go` button (see Figure 5.18);

– adding a `Plot` to the interface, for which the axis names and path colors must be defined [5.19].

Please note that it is also possible to create `Monitors` within the `Interface`, which can display the value of `Stocks` as the time passes (see Figure 5.20).

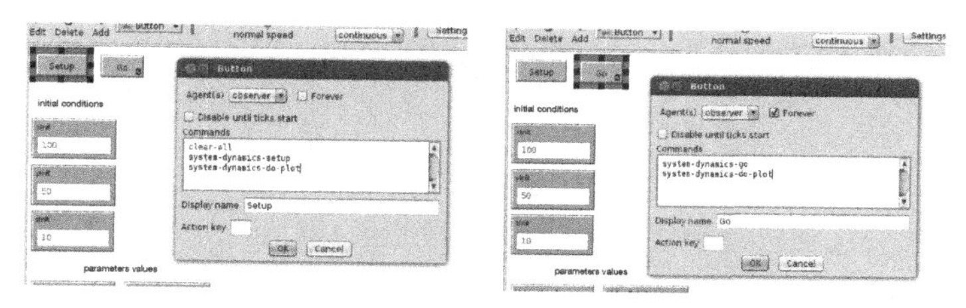

Figure 5.18. *Adding the* `Command :` `system-dynamics-do-plot` *in the* `Setup` *and* `Go` *buttons*

Moreover, knowing the precision limitations of the Eulerian method, it is also possible to use the RK4 method. This method is not available directly within NetLogo but there is an extension available here [CHA 13], within which the RK4 method is coded in the NetLogo language.

The numerical study of a system of ODEs can be done using numerous tools that cover the study areas that interest us. The first important result is the observation of temporal series that give the evolution of each of the variables over time.

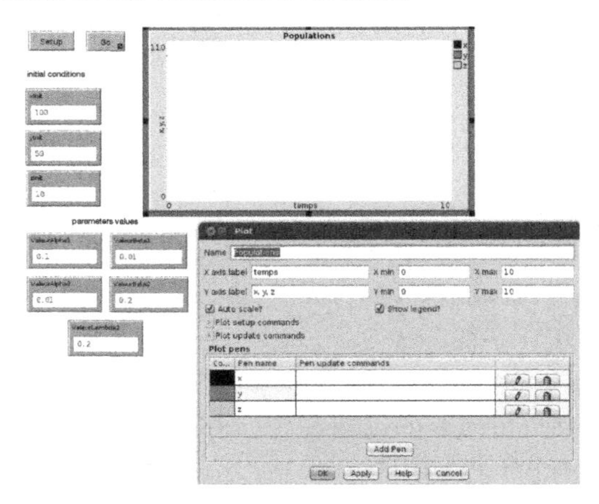

Figure 5.19. *Creating a `Plot` that will display the paths calculated by the numerical integration method*

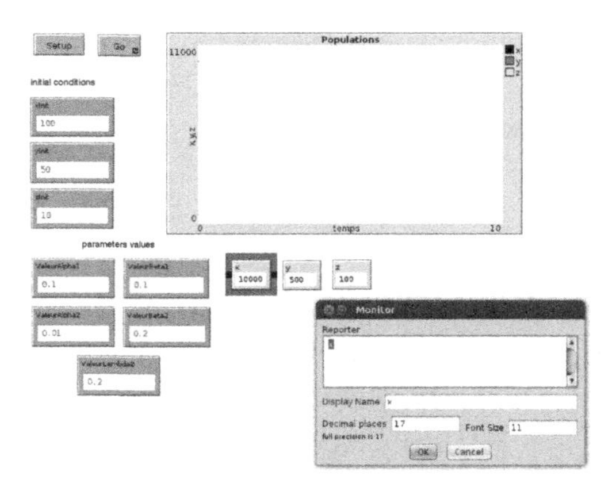

Figure 5.20. *Creating `Monitors` that will display the values of the x, y and z `Stocks` throughout the simulation*

It is also possible to study the evolution of the variables relative to each other. NetLogo is, in fact, able to display these paths. We can therefore observe the evolution of the number of panicked individuals compared to the number of scared individuals.

If we concern ourselves with the influence of the parameter values or initial conditions on the dynamic of the system, it is possible to modify these values in order to observe the result of these modifications on its behavior.

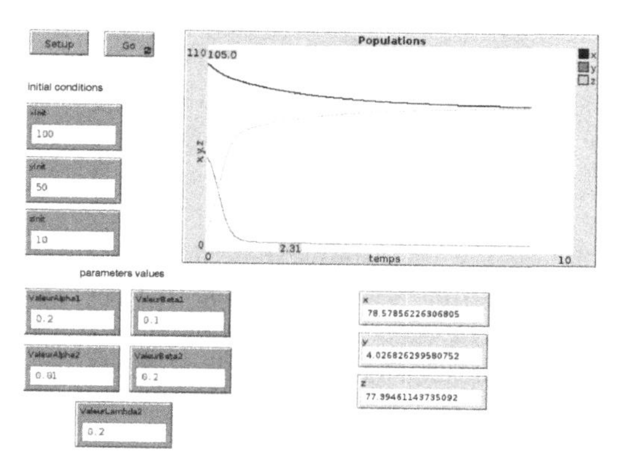

Figure 5.21. *Evolution of the number of calm (x), scared (y) and panic-stricken (z) individuals over time for fixed parameter values and initial conditions*

5.3.3.2. *Theoretical study*

Once such a model has been constructed, beyond numerical integration that allows for an rough idea of the system paths, it is useful to carry out a theoretical study. We will only list a few of the steps that make up the study of such a system, without entering into the specifics of mathematical study.

Thus, a first step consists of proving that there exists at least one solution to the system.

We should remember that a SOLUTION of a system of three differential equations is a set of three derived variables $x(t)$, $y(t)$ and $z(t)$, which satisfy the system for a given interval. When these functions are traced, $(t, x(t))$, $(t, y(t))$ and $(t, z(t))$ then give *trajectories* of the solution, and the set of all possible $x(t)$, $y(t)$ and $z(t)$ values for any time t in the defined interval is called the *phase portrait* of the differential equation.

Let us now suppose that we know the system's initial state, that is to say that we know the number of calm (x), scared (y) and panicked (z) individuals at time $t = 0$. Let us write these initial conditions as x_0, y_0, z_0. In this situation, the system of differential equations (with these initial conditions) is known as the *Cauchy problem*.

Cauchy's problem has a characteristic that makes it unique. For any given initial condition, it will give a single unique solution to the differential system.

The next step consists of proving that these solutions are positive. Indeed, due to the fact that we are dealing with the evolution of the number of individuals in each compartment, it is important to make sure that these quantities are positive. It is also important to show that a solution is bounded.

We will not explain the details of this theoretical existence study, uniqueness, positivity or the bounding of solutions here.

Among the elements used for the study of differential equation systems, we find the search for equilibrium points.

The EQUILIBRIUM POINTS of a model correspond to the values of x, y and z for which x, y and z remain constant over time. Let x_e, y_e and z_e represent these equilibrium values. This means that if we begin with x_e calm individuals (in the NPP compartment), y_e scared individuals (in the PSP compartment) and z_e panicked individual (in the PP compartment), the number of individuals in each of the x, y and z states will remain constant over time and the numerical simulation of these values will give lines parallel to the x-axis with zero gradient, as shown in Figure 5.22. These points therefore correspond to the solutions of $\frac{dx}{dt} = \frac{dy}{dt} = \frac{dz}{dt} = 0$.

Thus, the system [5.1] has the following equilibrium points:

– a trivial equilibrium point which indicates that without an initial population and since the system does not have any external input, the values of x, y and z will remain constant and nil;

– an equilibrium point without panicked individuals. In the absence of panic, there are therefore a number of calm individuals and a number of scared individuals such that these values remain constant and no individual becomes panicked. This point has the following coordinates:

$$\left(N - \frac{\beta_2 + \lambda_2}{\beta_1} - \frac{\beta_1\alpha_1 N - (\alpha_1 + \alpha_2)(\beta_2 + \lambda_2)}{\beta_1(\alpha_1 + \lambda_2)}, \frac{\beta_2 + \lambda_2}{\beta_1}\right.$$
$$\left.\frac{\beta_1\alpha_1 N - (\alpha_1 + \alpha_2)(\beta_2 + \lambda_2)}{\beta_1(\alpha_1 + \lambda_2)}\right)$$

– an *endemic* equilibrium point. For these values of x, y and z, the number of individuals in each of the compartments remains constant and the panic phenomenon therefore remains present.

Figure 5.22 presents the evolution of the system when the initial conditions correspond to the equilibrium point.

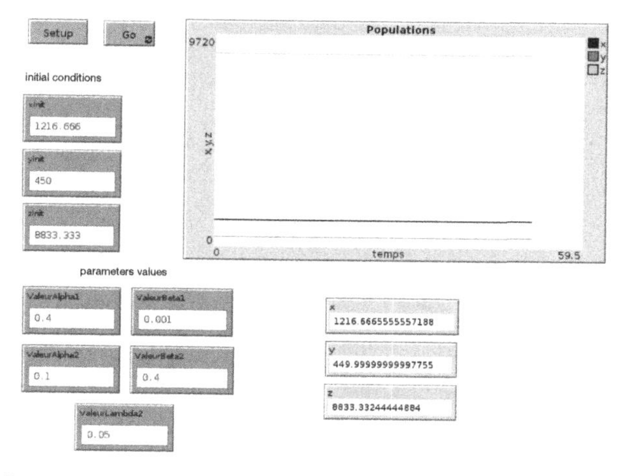

Figure 5.22. *Evolution over time of the number (x) of individuals in the NPP compartment (in black), the number (y) of individuals in the PSP compartment (in gray) and the number (z) of individuals in the PP compartment (in light gray), with the initial conditions corresponding to the equilibrium point where $x_0 = x_e$, $y_0 = y_e$ and $z_0 = z_e$, corresponding to the endemic equilibrium for the following fixed parameter values: $\alpha_1 = 0.4$, $\alpha_2 = 0.1$, $\beta_1 = 0.001$, $\beta_2 = 0.4$ and $\lambda_2 = 0.05$*

Let us suppose that the initial conditions (the values of x, y and z) are close to the values of x_e, y_e and z_e corresponding to the non-trivial equilibrium point without panic. Then, if after a certain amount of time, the number of panicked individuals tends toward 0 and the number of calm and scared individuals tend toward x_e and y_e, respectively, then this equilibrium without panic is locally stable. Finally, if the values of x, y and z tend toward the equilibrium values, no matter what the initial conditions are, then the equilibrium point is globally stable.

There are theoretical methods that allow for the stability of equilibrium points to be determined, but we will not discuss these here. Figures 5.23, 5.24 and 5.25 show the evolutions of the system while starting further away from the equilibrium point.

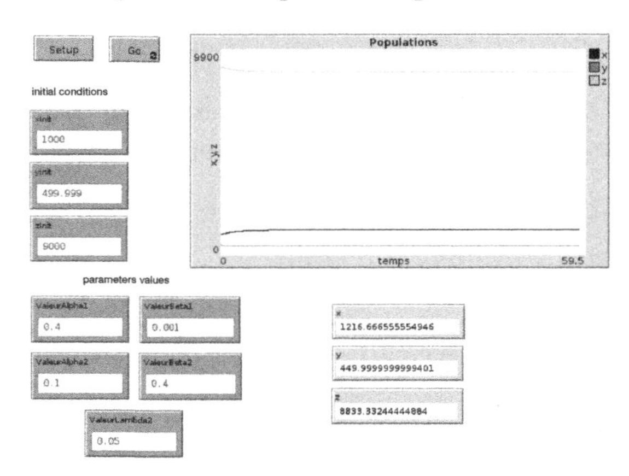

Figure 5.23. *Evolution over time of the number (x) of individuals in the NPP compartment (in black), the number (y) of individuals in the PSP compartment (in gray) and the number (z) of individuals in the PP compartment (in light gray), with the initial conditions close to the equilibrium point. It can be seen that the paths quickly tend toward the equilibrium values observed on the graph in Figure 5.22*

Moreover, it is possible to calculate a coefficient (R_0), named as the basic reproduction number, which depends on the model's parameters. This coefficient, often used in epidemiology, allows for the number of secondary infections, that is to say the number of individuals infected by a single infected individual. This R_0 gives the conditions for which the panic dies out or spreads. Essentially, this amounts to finding the parameter conditions that result in a globally stable equilibrium point without panic:

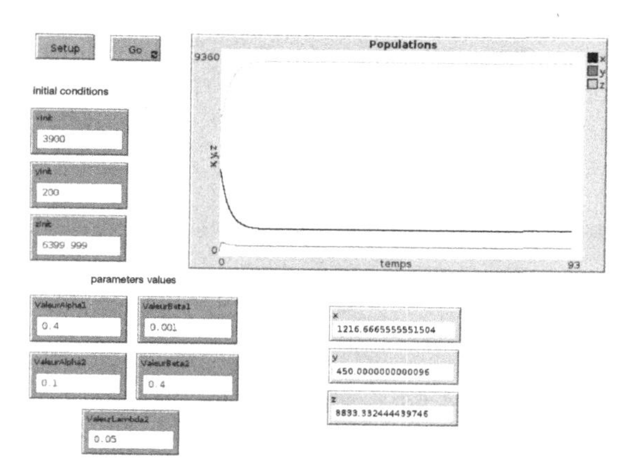

Figure 5.24. *Evolution over time of the number (x) of individuals in the NPP compartment (in black), the number (y) of individuals in the PSP compartment (in gray) and the number (z) of individuals in the PP compartment (in light gray), with the initial conditions further away from the equilibrium point. It can be seen that the paths quickly tend toward the equilibrium values observed on the graph in Figure 5.22*

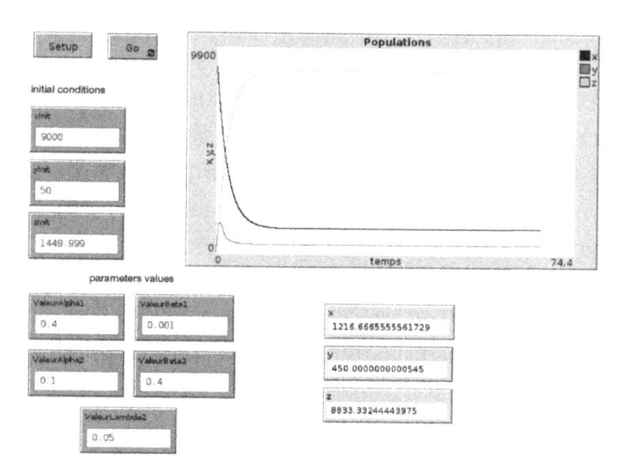

Figure 5.25. *Evolution over time of the number (x) of individuals in the NPP compartment (in black), the number (y) of individuals in the PSP compartment (in gray) and the number (z) of individuals in the PP compartment (in light gray), with the initial conditions very far away from the equilibrium point. It can be seen that the paths quickly tend toward the equilibrium values observed on the graph in Figure 5.22*

– if $R_0 < 1$, then any panicked individual invokes panic in an average of less than one other individual. This means that panic will tend to die out;

– if $R_0 > 1$, then any panicked individual invokes panic in an average of more than one other individual. This means that panic will tend to spread.

5.4. Agent-based panic propagation model

It is possible to construct an agent-based model that corresponds to the aggregate model proposed previously.

An agent-based model takes all individual agents into account, as well as any potential heterogeneity criteria. This type of model is well covered within this publication and we suggest that the other chapters should be studied for further information.

Nonetheless, we wish to highlight the fact that the model presented in equational form can also be represented as an agent-based model, as will be shown with an extremely simple model based on agents with changing states.

With the panic problem, we can, for example, consider mobility, personality or social criteria. The richness of the model then depends on what we wish to study, but the law of parsimony must be remembered. In our case, we will simply observe the propagation phenomenon and its global behaviors such as persistence and extinction.

In order to come as close to the aggregate model that was presented in the previous sections as possible, we will consider the agents who:

– do not move;

– have a global oversight of the environment;

– can be panicked (PP), are susceptible to panic (PSP) or are calm (NPP). This sets the state of a given individual.

This individual can then change state depending on the automatic transition controller labeled with probabilities.

a_1 therefore represents the probability that a single calm agent (NPP) becomes susceptible to panic (PSP), and as a result, we can take the α_1 rate of the aggregate model and apply it to an agent. In the same fashion, b_2, a_2 and l_2 are probabilities that correspond to the β_2, α_2 and λ_2 rate, respectively.

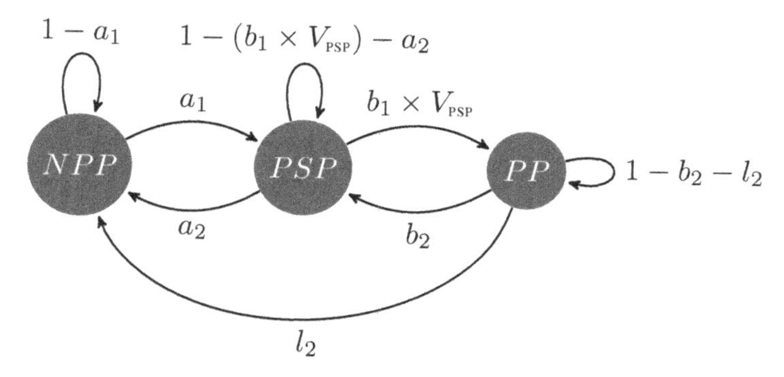

Figure 5.26. *Automatic controller of an agent's state labeled with probabilities*

Passing from the PSP to the PP state occurs by contamination, and it is therefore dependent on the surroundings of each PSP agent; the higher the number of PP agents surrounding a PSP agent, the higher the likelihood for it to pass into a PP state. This contamination can be modeled, either from the spatial location of agents by searching for the number of PP agents within a given distance, or from an average, given by V_{PSP} in Figure 5.26 in both cases. Insofar as we do not take mobility into account, the spatial spread of agents is not essential and we will therefore use the second option.

Let us consider a population of N agents composed of x NPP agents, y PSP agents and z PP agents. For a given distance, there are agents with $0, 1, 2, 3 \ldots$ neighbors. Let us set N_k as the number of agents with k neighbors, which gives us the following $P(k)$ distribution:

$$P(k) = \frac{N_k}{N}$$

which gives an average contact value for each individual:

$$< k > = \sum_k k \times P(k)$$

If we now attempt to calculate V_{PSP}, the average number of PP neighbors to a panicked PSP agent:

$$V_{\text{PSP}} = < k > \times \frac{z}{N} \text{ with } z \text{ agents from } PP$$

If we consider β_1, the transition rate used in our aggregate model, the number of PSP agents contaminated by PP agents for each step of time is:

$$\frac{\beta_1}{N} \times y \times z = b_1 \frac{< k >}{N} \times y \times z$$

Therefore, the probability b_1 that a PSP agent is contaminated by a PP agent is:

$$b_1 = \frac{\beta_1}{< k >}$$

We suggest that the reader should develop this agent-based model of the problem that we are studying in this chapter, in order to compare the results with those obtained with the aggregate model.

5.5. Dynamic system version of our running example model

Let us remind ourselves of the running example model presented throughout the past chapters. This model deals with the geographical spread of an epidemic transmitted from mosquitoes to human. We will now set out the modeling hypotheses, as this is currently useful.

We are dealing with four distinct populations:

- healthy mosquitoes (hM);
- infected mosquitoes (iM);
- healthy humans (hH);
- infected humans (iH).

Population evolution and the passing from one population to another are governed by the following:

– human demographics are not taken into account;

– mosquito births are taken into account (`birth-rate`) but their mortality is not, and all born mosquitoes are healthy, no matter the state of the parent;

– healthy mosquitoes become infected upon biting an infected human, with the following rate: `infection-rate-HtoM`;

– infection is passed to the human population only from the bites of infected mosquitoes: `infection-rate-MtoH`.

Following these rules, it is possible to construct the diagram in Figure 5.27.

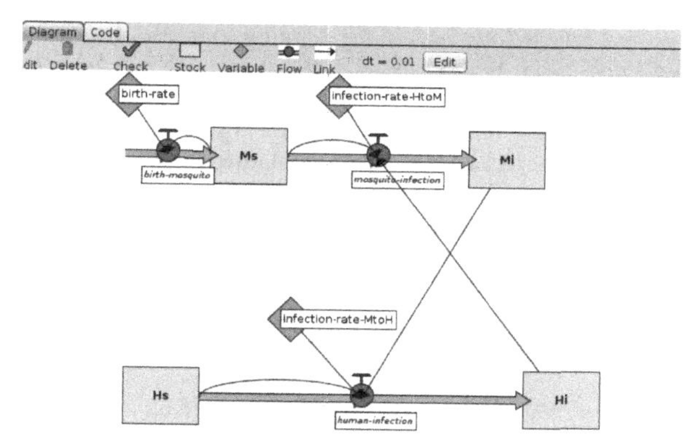

Figure 5.27. *NetLogo representation of the running example*

It can also be described as the following dynamic system:

$$\begin{cases} \dfrac{dMs}{dt} = \texttt{BirthRate}(Ms + Mi) - \texttt{InfectionRateHtoM}.Hi.Ms \\ \dfrac{dMi}{dt} = \texttt{InfectionRateHtoM}.Hi.Ms \\ \dfrac{dHs}{dt} = -\texttt{InfectionRateMtoH}.Mi.Hs \\ \dfrac{dHi}{dt} = \texttt{InfectionRateMtoH}.Mi.Hs \end{cases}$$

Thus, we can observe the evolution of all four populations (healthy/infected, mosquitos/humans) over time (see Figure 5.28).

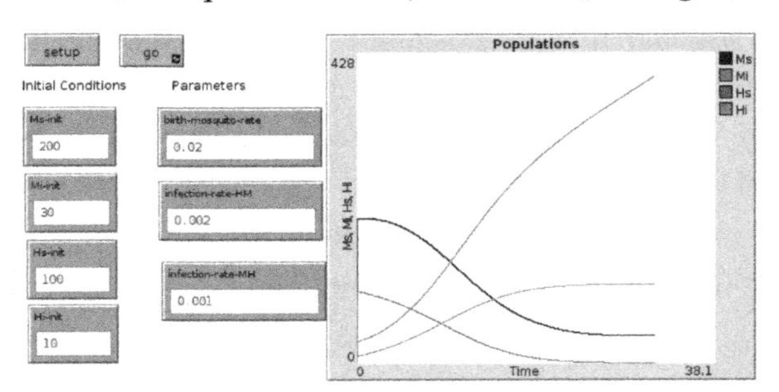

Figure 5.28. *Evolution of the populations of healthy mosquitoes, infected mosquitoes, healthy humans and infected humans in the running example. The parameter values are fixed as indicated in the* `inputs`*, with a mosquito birth rate of 0.02, a mosquito infection rate (by humans) of 0.002 and a human infection rate (by mosquitoes) of 0.001, and with initial populations of 200 healthy mosquitoes, 30 infected mosquitoes, 100 healthy humans and 10 infected humans. A large increase in the number of infected mosquitoes and a small increase in the number of infected humans can then be observed (with an obvious decline of healthy individuals of both species). These results are due to the fact that there is no mortality or cure. Note that the human population remains constant, whereas the mosquito population increases incessantly, due to mosquito births being taken into account. For a color version of the figure, see www.iste.co.uk/banos/netlogo.zip*

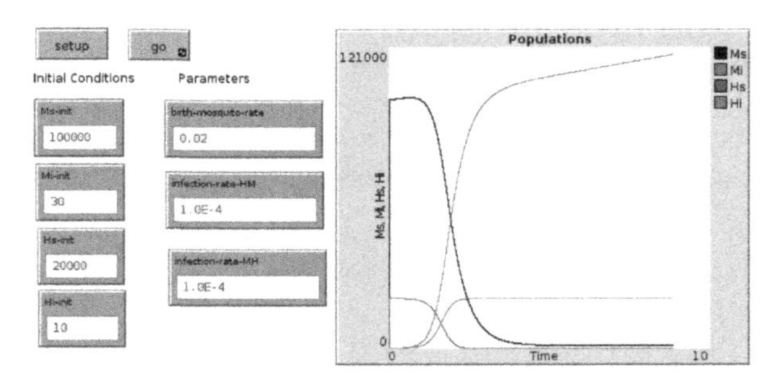

Figure 5.29. *Evolution of the populations of healthy mosquitoes, infected mosquitoes, healthy humans and infected humans in the running example. Note that the populations show similar behavior even when the initial conditions are modified. For a color version of the figure, see www.iste.co.uk/banos/netlogo.zip*

For this particular example, the importance of spatial spread should be noted, notably for the process that leads humans and mosquitoes to meet. In the "dynamic system" version of this problem, we implicitly assume that all of the mosquitoes are interacting in between each other and with humans. Thus, the actual "meeting" is not taken into account, whereas this plays an important role in the case of the agent-based model.

6

How to Involve Stakeholders in the Modeling Process

6.1. Introduction

The analysis of complex systems (CS) involves the use of different points of view so as to be able to understand the different aspects of the system's entities, and to characterize their interactions. Modeling and simulating CS are activities where collaboration between researchers is the rule rather than the exception. Indeed, as a result of the complexity of studied systems, it is often essential to bring together different perspectives from different fields of study. Thus, the popular idea of a solitary researcher that is able to collect data, put together conceptual models and use these with computing tools, is gradually being replaced with that of an interdisciplinary group usually composed of thematicians, computer scientists and mathematicians. For such a group, the model (or the simulation) is at once: (1) the reason for their coming together, (2) their collective objective and (3) the basis for their collective work.

Similarly, more and more uses for multiagent simulation emerge from laboratories and show that this approach has practical value: in

Chapter written by Nicolas BECU, Frédéric AMBLARD, Nicolas BRAX, Benoît GAUDOU and Nicolas MARILLEAU.

the field of decision-making (multiagent simulation allows for scenarios to be tested, and for their impacts and any implementation biases to be qualitatively identified), in the field of marketing (the tool allows for new product selling strategies to be put together), or to aid with the design of public policies (e.g. with respect to land use). Two main trends present relatively different epistemological positions relative to the use of such models by society. On the one hand, the first approach uses multiagent simulation to aid with decision-making, where the modeling process aims to create a product (the multiagent model), which would allow for a decision to be made based on elements that could not be taken into account with more traditional modeling methods. It is then seen as software which allows for scenarios to be tested, whether to support decisions, training, or to give an indication of reasonable expectations. On the other hand, the second approach is that of participatory simulations, which distinguishes itself from the first approach due to the fact that it integrates elements affected by the application's field into the modeling process and the framework of the tool's use [VOI 10].

A specific use of this process involves land use management, particularly to do with the collective management of renewable resources. The stakeholders tend to be all or some of the individuals affected by the management plan and may be involved in its proceedings, whether during the construction of the simulation or, subsequently, as users of it. Here, the tool serves as a substrate to help with the search for collective solutions (this could allow for management scenarios to be tested collectively), or as a tool allowing for individual management strategies and the ways in which they affect each other to be identified (usually, this requires the actor to be considered as a user of the simulation, a "player" if you will, which can subsequently be asked about any strategies adopted during the course of the "game".

Therefore, whether for the interdisciplinary group or for stakeholders involved in a collective project, there is an evident necessity to be able to bring several stakeholders together (modelers, thematicians and terrain stakeholders) into the modeling and simulation

(M&S) processes. This entails ethical and deontological challenges (such as how to integrate the knowledge of a third party into a group work), epistemological challenges (such as researchers from different disciplines that have different methods for the creating and processing of knowledge), organizational challenges (such as how to practically organize collective M&S work) and technical challenges (such as working out which tools will facilitate group work on a model). Only the last two organization problems, the methodological and technical aspects, will be discussed in this chapter. Readers interested in deontological aspects are advised to refer to works on companion modeling [COM 05]. As for issues related to interdisciplinary work, they will not be covered at all as they go beyond the limits of our subjects.

This chapter will focus on two principal methods for collaboration between several individuals working on a simulation model:

– The first method requires the interaction of users/stakeholders with a simulation. In this section, we will discuss the use of participatory simulation from the viewpoint of role-playing games, as well as NetLogo's HubNet tool that allows for several computers to connect to a single simulation and for their users to interact with it as a result [BLI 05]. This method aims to improve user cooperation.

– The second method requires the interaction of several modelers so that they may carry out experimentation upon a simulation model. We will present the PAMS technology which allows for NetLogo to be emulated within an Internet browser, which allows for several physically distant users to synchronously work on the development of a model and analyze its simulations. This method aims to improve collaborative work.

6.2. Diversity of multiagent approaches in modeling

6.2.1. *Participatory simulation*

Generally speaking, participatory approaches require dialogue between stakeholders founded upon mutual respect and recognition of the knowledge each individual entertains. So as to facilitate this dialogue, or at least to guide it, various types of consultation tools can be used. These tools serve to collectively develop supportive knowledge products, such as spatial representations (land mapping), decision trees (problem trees) and cognitive schemata (cognitive mapping). These knowledge support products express the "internal" representations of individuals and serve as intermediaries between them [VIN 99]. The dialogue between stakeholders can then be organized around this intermediate object and will be facilitated as a result of the fact that it structures, organizes and sometimes even creates knowledge. Thus, these are all knowledge sharing devices, which display representations of a given issue.

When the knowledge sharing tool used is a simulation model, we refer to it as participatory simulation. Very often, resorting to a model comes as a result of a necessity to represent temporal or spatial dynamics. Then the issue at hand involves multiple interactions between stakeholders or between stakeholders and resources, and we should look toward using multiagent modeling. Moreover, as with any participatory approach, different levels of involvement can be distinguished between stakeholders, from their consultation by a public organization to their role in the setup of projects and decision-making. As this is participatory modeling, the involvement of stakeholders can change at various different levels, such as: the prior identification of requirements, the construction of the conceptual model, the development of the operational model (IT implementation or other), the defining of indicators and different scenarios to be tested and the analysis of the simulation results.

Among the various participatory modeling approaches, companion modeling, or ComMod, uses a well-defined scientific framework that defines how stakeholders are involved in the M&S process and limits certain problems that are sometimes found in participatory approaches such as manipulation, not taking into account the points of view of some stakeholders or the deviation from the current issues of the intervention context. Apart from being a methodological framework, companion modeling has an ethical stance that defines the rules and responsibilities of the project's protagonists. This position has three requirements: a continuous and iterative confrontation between theories and grounds; accepting the legitimacy of different points of view, and taking them all into account even if they are contradictory; and reevaluating the project whenever a new element is introduced [COM 05].

The objective of a companion modeling operation is either the creation of knowledge (for researchers or local stakeholders) through a better understanding of a system of interactions, or to support negotiations during a process which explicitly requires a transformation of either resource management practices or socioeconomic interactions. In both cases, the method consists of using M&S tools to put together a shared (but not necessarily unifying) representation of the studied system, which also details its dynamics and provides a scenario analysis support tool. Two main simulation tools are used in ComMod approaches: computer simulation models and roleplay simulation. These two arrangements are similar: roleplay simulation – as its name implies – is a simulation where the stakeholders play a role, while computer simulations use virtual agents [BEC 10]. The aim is to share the various points of view about the studied situation, and to make them clearer. Specifically, the use of models is reflexive: the stakeholders learn collectively by creating, modifying or observing models. These tools allow for the stakeholders to suggest hypotheses to propose scenarios and to observe their consequences together. The use of such tools by stakeholders is done in an iterative manner and continues across participatory workshops spread over time (called Strong Collective Time) and interposed with period of laboratory work allowing for the previous session to be analyzed and for the next session to be prepared [BEC 08]. Thus, the experimentation presented in this chapter only represents a single brainstorming of a companion modeling approach. For more information on companion modeling, the readers may refer to the comprehensive synthesis [ETI 10].

6.2.2. *Collaboration within modeling and simulation (M&S)*

The project "tradition" that has become embedded within the scene of international research over the past several decades has increased the need for laboratories and researchers of different scientific fields and from different regions of the world to collaborate around complex issues. Even though this situation presents a much-needed opportunity for researchers who do not benefit from a sufficiently developed local scientific environment (in particular, researchers in developing countries), it remains nonetheless true that geographical separation, cultural differences and potential language issues often hinder international and interdisciplinary exchanges, which are less efficient than those that result from local interactions.

Collaboration plays an important role throughout the entirety of the scientific processes of M&S of a CS. It is therefore necessary to have methods and tools for both modeling and experimentation at our disposal. These two aspects will be covered in the two following sections.

6.2.2.1. *Collaboration within simulation*

The development of information technology that has taken place over the past 20 years allows for new collaboration methods that could partially solve these problems to be considered. They allow, among other things: (1) for researchers in laboratories in different locations, perhaps even on different continents, to be united within a single "platform"; (2) for resources to be shared no matter what their location; and (3) for the interactions between stakeholders as well as for the successive versions of their shared work to be stored. Thus, we meet the domain of "e-science", which is currently in increasingly rapid expansion. Within this domain, there are a plethora of studies, projects and platforms such as EGEE or GLOBUS [TAY 07, WAN 09]. This research deals with the sharing and management of distributed computing resources, most particularly relative to the provision of clusters and high-performance computing grids via the use of computer networks. Other studies do not define material resources, but instead refer to the simulator as an element subject to sharing [JAG 10]. KEPLER [BAR 10], VLE [QUE 09] and NetLogo's HubNet contribute to the domain. These tools ensure, to a certain extent, the sharing of models as they allow for simulators and their associations to be capitalized upon by creating new partnerships. However, these are not truly collaborative environments as they do not include any tools making possible direct interaction between users. Web-based simulation groupwares (WBSGs), such as PAMS [NGU 09] and BSCW [KOR 08], add a truly collaborative dimension by providing tools, thereby facilitating joint manipulation of simulators. Yet once again, these are focused exclusively on simulative aspects and omit the modeling process *proper*, which is however crucial for the study of a complex structure of natural system.

6.2.2.2. *Collaboration within modeling*

Besides the domain of collaborative systems, current platforms dedicated to the study of CS are better simulation tools than complete M&S environments, so much that they contain few or no modeling tools. As a result of this, developer communities working around popular platforms such as Repast [NOR 13], Cormas [BOM 14] and GAMA [DRO 13] have recently introduced graphical modeling tools such as Repast-Eclipse IDE, executable UML and GAMAGraM, respectively. In the fields of multiagent systems, many new languages and methodologies have also been proposed [CHI 13].

It is expected to develop tools dedicated to CS M&S from software engineering-oriented groupwares. However specific features of CS should be highlighted, as they result in the design of dedicated tools differing from these of "traditional" collaborative software engineering in several major aspects [GAU 11]:

– *Modeling process variability*: software engineering typically requires the use of a previously established and well-defined methodology. In the research world, even if a specific methodology exists, it is likely to considerably vary over the course of any project, most particularly due to the research subject requiring the emergence of facts and new developments to be integrated within the project if necessary. In this situation, methodological aspects are therefore often products of research work, along with all other initially defined goals.

– *Modeled system complexity*: in contrast to the world of software engineering, the inner workings of CS are often poorly understood by experts. Moreover, these systems have dynamics that are so complex that it can seem impossible or even idealistic to wish to display it as a comprehensible (analytical) model and for a simulation of it to give the predicted results. Depending on the modeling aims, different scales of time and space must be considered, which require the incorporation of multiple viewpoints.

– *Wealth of perspectives and skills*: the numerous interactions between researchers have the advantage of offering a significant richness of skills and opinions of the modeled system. Conversely, this wealth can be a source of misunderstanding as the concepts, terminology and aims can be different if not even conflicting. A CS modeling environment must be able to take advantage of this wealth in a controlled manner.

– *Model verification/validation*: although it is possible for certain properties of a model to be locally verified, complete model validation is most often impossible as a result of the complexity of the studied systems. Only simulative verification and the explanation of the observed behaviors allow for the validity of a model and subsequent simulators to be estimated.

To summarize, in the case of computational and/or mathematical modeling of a CS, researchers are faced with multiple difficulties: different disciplinary approaches, the distributed nature of projects, the complexity of the systems studied and the emergent aspect of the research method. It is to allow researchers to overcome these difficulties that tools for long-distance collaboration must be imagined and created. In addition to their ability to remotely manage projects, they must also allow for the specifics of CS modeling to be taken into account.

6.3. Simulating stakeholder games and learning about others: NetLogo's HubNet system

6.3.1. *The HubNet technology*

The technology of HubNet allows for NetLogo to be used in the context of participatory simulation [BLI 05]. Indeed, it proposes protocols and communication methods between users and the simulation conducted within the NetLogo environment. As such, users can directly act upon the simulation environment via terminals linked to the system.

Setting up such an activity requires the activation of a server in the NetLogo simulation that is to be used, allowing for other terminals, belonging to clients, to connect to the server via HubNet and to act upon the environment which is then presented to them.

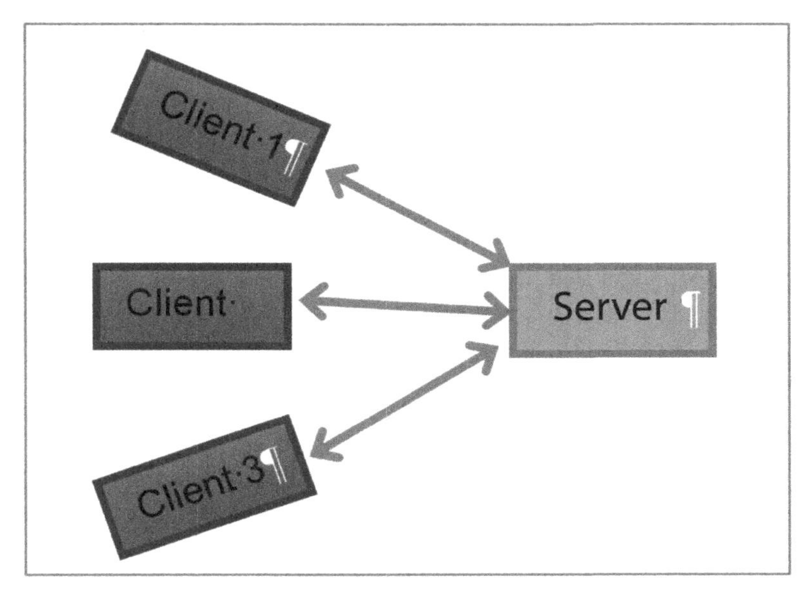

Figure 6.1. *Clients and Servers*

With the server, the operator will have the possibility to create a multiuser session, authorize the connection of clients and specify whether the 2D view and `plots` are displayed on their interfaces, all with the help of the *HubNet Control Center* tool.

The clients will have to launch the NetLogo's HubNet program, which is a software that runs separately from NetLogo's main program. Within this software, they must specify their username, which will be visible to the server, and then give the server's IP address or name, before connecting. Once the connection has been established, the client interface is displayed, and the user can then interact with the simulation currently being run on the server.

The content of this client interface is predefined by the modeler via the *HubNet Client Editor* tool. This tool is displayed as a likeness of NetLogo's main interface, allowing for buttons, fields, graphs, text and a workspace viewfinder to be added and defined. Buttons, pens and monitors are specified with the help of `tags`, not with the `command` or `reporter` as within NetLogo's primary interface (i.e. direct creation, movement, addition and removal of elements). These `tags` are information packages sent from the clients to the server in the form of messages. More specifically, when a user carries out an action within the client interface, a message is sent to the server, containing two elements: the source (name of the client sending the message) and `tag` (name of the effectuated action). `Plots` and the remote view are effectively mirroring elements that are already present within the main interface, and thus, a graphing pen can only be added to the client interface if it has previously been identified on the main interface. All of the primitives specific to HubNet are available online, on NetLogo's site.

Once the client interface has been defined, it is then possible to define how the client–server setup is used, as will be covered in the following section as part of a discussion surrounding participatory roleplay simulation.

6.3.2. *Participatory roleplay simulation*

6.3.2.1. *The concept of roles and forms of learning*

Participatory roleplay simulation is a form of hybrid simulation combining multiagent simulation and a role-playing game [LE 14] . In this system, some of the system's agents will be controlled by human players. These "controlled" virtual agents are therefore the players' avatars. Players may have one or more avatars; there are no specific rules on this subject. In certain participatory role-playing simulations, a player could thus control the avatar corresponding to the agricultural agent, whereas another player could control a population of bird agents that evolve upon the agricultural land represented by the simulation.

The concept of roles requires a precise interaction framework between the player and the simulation, as well as between the players themselves. A role is defined by a *personal aim*, a set *possible actions* and of *available information* [BAR 03]. Depending on these elements, the player will have to devise a strategy in order to reach their objective in order to collect information and analyze it, then take decisions and choose actions to perform. The actions that they make their avatar perform will affect the simulation (virtual entities will be modified). The simulation's new state will then influence the following choices made by players. In parallel with players modifying the simulation state, the simulation continues to run step by step, allowing for the evolution of all virtual entities following the set of rules defined by the modeler. Therefore, within participatory role-playing simulations, two main role-playing game concepts can be found, which are *turns of play* (equivalent to the simulation's time steps) and *rules* (equivalent to algorithms defined by the modeler to simulate the virtual entities' own dynamics) [BAR 03].

Within this methodological framework, the creator of such a simulation can then define different interaction modes between the players and the simulation. Interactions between players may be limited to the impact that each has upon virtual entities, including other players' avatars; for this the different players do not have to be in the presence of each other, at the same location. However, a setup where player can directly interact between themselves, before or during the decisions they take upon the simulation. A second level of interaction is then added to the interactions between virtual entities.

It is this type of setup, where players are gathered at the same location, which is usually chosen for companion modeling . The reason for this is that this type of modeling adapts participatory simulation in order to create social learning, that is to say, learning about others and how we interact with them [ASS 13]. To do this, the overseer of a participatory simulation session will make each participant experience a moment of interaction with the others (by making them play with participatory simulation), and will then ask each of them to explain to the other participants about why they made particular decisions and what was learnt from the experience. During this debriefing, the overseer plays on the experiential learning of the participants, that is to say what they “learnt by doing” [PRU 02]. This is a crucial moment of the learning process, as each one must analyze their own behavior and come up with new concepts that will change the way in which they perceive the world and their place among others [ETI 11]. Due to the fact that companion modeling seeks to create this form of learning, participatory simulation sessions are almost systematically done face-to-face and they are followed by a debriefing that can take as much time, if not more, as the simulation itself.

6.3.2.2. *Setting up and running a session*

Once the model and the HubNet client interfaces have been created, the setup requires as many computers as there are roles, with an additional computer running the server, and for all of these to be connected together in a network. The NetLogo model is then run on the server computer, the HubNet activity is started on the server (with the `hubnet-reset` command) and the server is then ready for clients to connect to it.

The individual who is in charge of setting the session up and beginning the server is often the person hosting the session (sometimes also known as game master (GM), as in role-playing games). In the room dedicated to the session, the GM sits at the server terminal whereas the other players use the client terminals. The GM is responsible for:

– the authorization of player connection and their subsequent monitoring throughout the session. In fact, an interface that shows the list of current participants, with options to invite new players or to kick current ones, is displayed to the GM. This interface also allows for communication with one or several of the participants, which means that individual or collective instructions can be issued at any time;

– managing the correct progress of the simulation. It is the GM who launches the simulation once all expected participants are connected, and he/she will then follow its operation. They can also act directly upon the environment by modifying parameters or emphasizing certain elements, and can send information to the players, etc.;

– conducting the debriefing session that follows the game.

Given the numerous duties of the GM, it can sometimes be useful to have a team of individuals conduct an animation session, which allows for the tasks to be given to different individuals. For example, one person could be in charge of setting up the session and other technical jobs, while another person leads the game and then conducts the debriefing session. Another example is that one person sets up the game and manages it until the end of the round, while the other person merely observes the game and only leads the debriefing session that follows. The second case is interesting as it allows for the debriefing leader to have a better overview of all the player interactions that occur during the game. This contrasts with the first example, as an overview is not always easy when one is managing the session.

As for the players, their roles are identical to that of the other agents: the participants' interface is constructed such that the actions and sensory information that are usually available to the simulation agents are also presented to them. As such, the simulation's stakeholders have, with respect to the environment, the same capacities as the agents as far as knowledge and action capabilities are concerned. They are also represented within the environment by a virtual avatar that is displayed, by default, as that of any other of the system's agents. This all shows that the interface is only made available to the players in order to allow them to visualize all information they have access to and to act upon the environment, to the extent that they are permitted and based on their own reasoning. It should however be noted that each stakeholder can have a role that differs from another, similarly to the agents with their own specific operative rules. In this case, the interface is the same for each participant except for certain elements that only certain players will be given access to during setup. Again, the stakeholders of a participatory simulation are at an equal level to the agents, and it is at setup that specific players will be given access to certain information or operative capabilities or not. In certain setups, players can have access to the main interface that is on the server, in addition to their client interface. This can be useful when the GM wants the players access to any information that cannot be displayed upon their client interface, and it is wished that this information should be made public, that is to say that all players are able to access it. In this situation, during game setup, the GM will take care to connect the server computer to a projector that can then display the model's main interface on a wall.

A session contains three separate parts. The first part is for setup of the game environment, for clients to connect to the server, and will also be used to cover the rules of the game. This is also when the individual roles will be distributed to the players and when these will be able to familiarize themselves with the computer interface. It is also often useful to play a "test round" in order to enable the player to try out different actions available on their interface and observe the effects these have on the simulation. Once this test round is over, the simulation is reinitialized and the game can start. The game round corresponds to the second part of the session. It can begin by a moment whereupon each player presents themselves orally to the rest of the group, based on their character role. This allows for each participant to better identify with their role and also serves the purpose of being an icebreaker, as players tend to caricature their roles during this public presentation, which never fails to incite laughter and relaxes the atmosphere. Then the GM begins the first turn and lets the players know how long they have to make decisions, discuss with others and carry out their actions. Once the turn is over, the GM moves the simulation forward by a step of time. At the beginning of the next turn, the clients will discover the new state of the system and they have to think of new actions to complete. This sequence repeats until the final predefined turn is reached. The number of total turns is usually announced by the GM at the beginning of the session. Once the last turn is over, the third part of the session, the debriefing, begins. This usually begins with a look at the results of the game, which the GM asks each of the players to comment upon. The results can take the form of graphs, simulated scores or a map of the 2D view of the main interface. Then, each of the participants is invited to express themselves about the strategy they chose to adopt during the game, the constraints they encountered (whether linked to their own role or to do with interactions with others) and how their strategy had to be modified as the simulation progressed. The other participants can respond to the given explanations and the resulting discussion is likely to produce new learning about how the others understand the impacts of their actions.

The debriefing often finishes by allowing each participant to propose solutions for the various encountered issues, whether of coordination between players, of prioritizing different aims or of inequalities between the different roles/players and their understanding of the system and its operation.

We will now present a specific example of a participatory roleplay simulation setup, with the help of the SimPAGE experiment which took place in the context of a partnership between EDF's R&D department (EDF is the French national electricity company) and the IRIT laboratory of Toulouse, surrounding an issue of water management in the Adour-Garonne watershed in the south-west of France.

6.3.3. *SimPAGE – learning from participatory simulation*

The issue covered by the SimPAGE process is the *management of minimum summer water levels* (from 1 July to 31 October) in the Adour-Garonne catchment basin in Midi-Pyrénées, France. In this large hydrographic basin of the south-east, water scarcity has been increasing for several decades as a result of two activities: first, between 1985 and 1995, the area of irrigated surfaces greatly increased despite an improvement of irrigation equipment: second, the available water tends to become rarer in summers with recorded global warming. Two terms were defined for use in this context: the lowest water level target flow rate (LTF) and crisis flow rate (CRF). The LTF corresponds to a level of satisfaction of all needs guaranteeing the correct functioning of the aquatic environment. The CRF is a value below which the drinking water supply and the survival of species within the environment are threatened. The aim in terms of quantitative management is achieving the LTF for at least 8 years out of 10. Thus, to achieve this goal, a management plan that groups the different stakeholders as well as restrictive measures exists. It is the departmental prefects who can issue restriction orders or temporarily suspend usage of the resource in the event of water shortages.

So as to make EDF's R&D team collectively think about this issue and the interdependencies between the various stakeholders involved in maintaining this minimum water level flow rate, a project to create and use a participatory roleplay simulation was put in place. EDF R&D's aims were:

– to develop a platform integrating the different resource, usage and management aspects and allowing for potential scenarios to be simulated;

– to analyze the behavioral dynamics of the stakeholders by using participatory simulation as a laboratory for social experimentation;

– to evaluate the tool's potential as a support for training water stakeholders (both internally, within EDF, as well as externally) so as to improve understanding of viewpoints of different users of the resource and of their interaction difficulties.

We will now describe this process, beginning with the multiagent model that has been developed, followed by the participatory simulation sessions that were organized, and finishing by describing what has been learnt from these sessions.

6.3.3.1. *Multiagent simulator*

6.3.3.1.1. The environment model

The model of the chosen environment therefore involves the Portet, Roquefort, Foix and Montréjeau watersheds. So as to define this environment based on a geographical information system (GIS), the followed steps are:

– tracing the boundaries of all the watersheds involved;

– importing the boundaries of each of the township areas for each of the watersheds;

– working out their centroids and linking it with the irrigated area and drinking water usage of the corresponding township;

– positioning existing dams and reservoirs;

– positioning the drinking water extraction points;

– positioning the irrigation water extraction points;

– importing river courses.

The hydrological model of the rivers was then created in the form of a hydrograph network. Each node of the network corresponds either to the confluence points of rivers or to the extraction point (of drinking or irrigation water). Once each of these points has been positioned, the hydrological network was reconstructed step by step by linking the nodes. This approach allows for the network complexity to be limited to only the data available and which is of use to the model. The flow mechanics have been modeled in the form of a flow circulating through this network, with a unique fictitious source upstream and going toward a common outlet. Furthermore, a function allowing for evapotranspiration in the network was added. As for the weather pattern, a linear model was used. It leads to the basin's diffuse inputs from rainfall to aggregate into a single source which enters upstream near the Pyrenees at each turn of the hydrological cycle. The model was calibrated using data that correspond to the average throughput of the Garonne over several years, with a min-max deviation, as issued by the Adour-Garonne Water Agency.

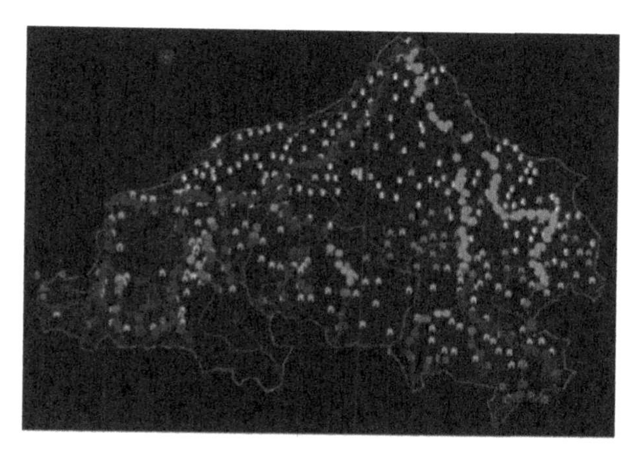

Figure 6.2. *Environment display of the model: the drinking water extraction points are represented by green houses, the irrigation water extraction points by yellow wheat, and dams and reservoirs by orange symbols. The nodes of the hydrological network are represented by blue circles, and the network itself is displayed in the form of links between these. For a color version of the figure, see www.iste.co.uk/banos/netlogo.zip*

6.3.3.1.2. The agent model

There are five categories of agents used in this model: farmers, hydroelectric dam managers, industries, drinking water managers and a prefect that represents the catchment's administrative authorities. The role and actions of each of these are detailed in the following table.

Prefect	The authority which can set a water consumption policy so as to preserve everyone's right as well as the environment.
Farmers (farmer) agents	They must irrigate their fields. They control an area that requires water, which can only be sourced from nearby rivers.
Hydroelectric dam managers	They manage the flow of water to produce electricity. They own dams with a certain reservoir capacity and valves to regulate the flow of water downstream.
Drinking water managers	They draw water from the river network for public needs. They are aware of the needs of the population within their zone.
Industries	They use water for manufacturing and their production levels depend on the amount of water they draw from rivers.

Table 6.1. *Description of the agent's objectives and available actions*

We will not describe all of the agent models in full detail in this chapter; instead, we will limit ourselves to that of the agricultural agent. Readers who are interested to know more details about this model are advised to refer to [BRA 10].

The agricultural agents represent uniform management entities at the scale of a township. Each one makes decisions about the water they source from the closest point of the river to the township, as well as irrigation decisions (relative to volume and dates). Their behavior is adaptive, which means that it evolves based on the state of the surrounding environment.

The above description of the agricultural agent's implementation shows that the model incorporates rules and algorithms that allow for the agent to autonomously evolve within the simulation. This is the same for all the other agents in the simulation. When the model has to be used in the context of a participatory simulation, the host will be able to decide which agents are to act autonomously (based on implemented rules) and which are to be controlled by players.

		Resource availability (incertitude)	
		Decreasing	Stable or increasing
Production level (stake affected by decision)	Decreasing	The agent searches for an *alternative solution* and adopts a behavior that is working for another nearby agent. If none are available, the agent experiments with new behaviors (*random behavior*).	*Rational behavior*, the agent follows technical recommendations (in this case, based on the graph defining water requirements for sweetcorn).
	Stable or increasing	The agent observes the behavior of nearby agents and adopts the *majority behavior*.	The agent's behavior is not put into question, all therefore everything operates as usual.

Table 6.2. *Behavior of agricultural agents depending on the incertitude created by the current availability of the resource and the difference between expected and actual production levels*

6.3.3.2. *The SimPAGE participatory simulation*

6.3.3.2.1. Roles and player immersion

The participants can take on the role of farmers, hydroelectric dam managers, drinking water managers, industrial tycoons or a prefect. Since there are actually a large number of farmers in the Adour-Garonne basin, the simulation was developed such that when a player controls one of the farmer agent-avatars all the other virtual farmer agents will adopt a behavior similar to that of the player (see Table 6.2).

The immersion of the participants in the roleplay setting is an important aspect to take into account during a participatory simulation because it will influence the quality of social interactions that occur between participants. The way that this immersion is achieved highly depends on the context and issue studied. For the study of the Adour-Garonne case, as for most of the cases linked to communal renewable resources, two types of objectives must be considered: individual and collective, which can occasionally be contradictory [OST 94]. These two aspects had to be explicitly defined in the introduction to the roleplay simulation. In order to make the participants aware of the issues surrounding water management in the whole watershed (collective objective), the game session begins with a slideshow displaying photos of different water uses and resource conditions (for example, rivers at low water levels). Furthermore, the main interface of the model is projected upon the wall for reference during the game. It displays information that is common to all player (river water level, rainfall, etc.). Finally, a public announcement is made throughout the game about changing hydrological conditions in the basin. These different elements all remind the players about the collective implications of their individual decisions. As for player immersion in their individual roles, the layout of the room and the role cards are important. Thus, the participants are seated at separate desks (each one with a computer allowing for interaction with the simulation) and receive an individual role card. The cards give information about the player's aims (for example, to store water in the case of the hydroelectric dam manager), the means to reach their goals (for example, water sources for the farmer role, setting up a meeting for the prefect role), as well as figures and tables summarizing the technical aspects of a role (for example, the graph showing how the hydroelectric reservoirs fill up). The role card aims to immerse the player in a specific role and provides guidance in the form of a set of rules and options that enable decision-making.

The interaction of players with the computer model requires custom computer interfaces that provide additional information (local resource conditions) and allow players to make their decisions at every turn.

6.3.3.2.2. Steps involved in a game turn

Once the environment is set up, the role cards have been distributed and the players are ready, the simulation begins. Each iteration of the simulation goes through the exact same stages:

– the farmer, industry and drinking water management agents indicate the quantity of water they wish to take for the next 10 days;

– the simulation runs one turn of the game (1 game turn = 10 days) by taking these indications into account and simulated 10 real days: crop growth, production levels, satisfaction of drinking water consumers, etc;

– during this time interval, the prefect monitors the flow in different rivers and raises an alert if necessary;

Dam Manager

Congratulations! You now control the hydroelectric dams of the Portet, Foix, Roquefort and Montrejeau watersheds in Midi-Pyrénées. This area contains __ hydroelectric power stations with a strategic role for EDF: that of ensuring a continuous production of electricity, especially in winter.

For this, the summer period is a crucial time, as you will have to fill the hydroelectric water storage (so as to be able to satisfy the winter production requirements) at a time when the water levels of the rivers feeding the reservoirs are at their lowest.

Moreover, part of the water stocked by the dams (51 million cubic metres across the entire period) will be used to maintain the water level downstream. This volume must satisfy the Lowest water level Target Flow rate (LTF) at the Portet station which is 52 m3/s. The prefecture can ask you to release water from this storage at any time, to ensure that this flow rate is maintained.

For your information, here is the optimum fill curve for EDF across the 4-month period that the game time corresponds to (each turn is equal to 2 weeks of real-time).

Theoretical fill rate of a dam

Your goal is to reach a fill of 72% or higher after this period of time.

For this, at each turn of the game:

- you will have access to information about the total amount of water retained by the hydroelectric dams (1, in m3) and the flow rate at the Portet station (D, in m3/s);

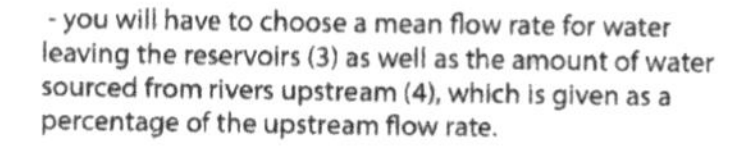

- you will have to choose a mean flow rate for water leaving the reservoirs (3) as well as the amount of water sourced from rivers upstream (4), which is given as a percentage of the upstream flow rate.

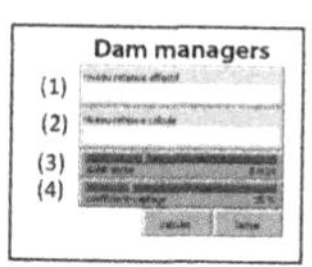

The Calculate button allows for you to calculate the total volume of water you will obtain based upon the values given. When you are happy with these, click on the Release button to confirm your decision for the game turn in question.

Figure 6.3. *Example of a role card.*

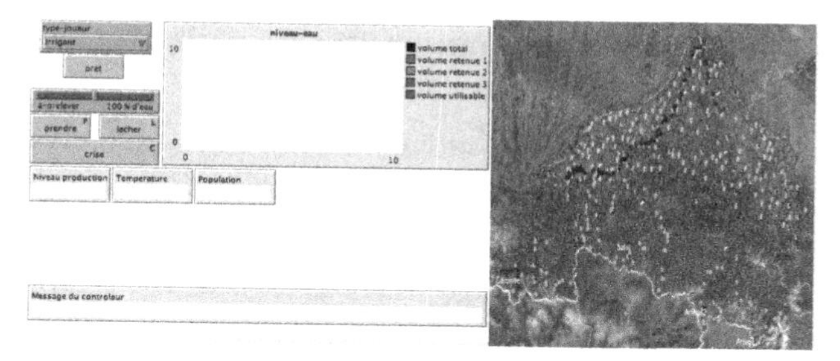

Figure 6.4. *Client interface for each role. For a color version of the figure, see www.iste.co.uk/banos/netlogo.zip*

– at any instant, depending upon the scenarios that we wish to test by simulation, an agent or a hydroelectric dam manager can decide to release some of the stored water to increase water levels downstream;

– the hydrological model used allows us to avoid the issue of having to apply a water sharing rule, due to each stakeholder having access to different extraction points and the flow dynamics of non-extracted water that is in place between extraction points;

– the simulation continues for another 10 days, as long as the period of low water levels has not ended.

During the eight game rounds, players are free to put together a strategy that can either attempt to satisfy both collective and individual aims, or follows a more individualistic path. The role of prefect has a clear collective strategy because its individual goal directly depends on the decisions made by other roles. It is also the only one with the ability to call all participants together for a meeting.

6.3.3.2.3. Sessions conducted and recording of results

The SimPAGE participatory simulation was developed and used in the context of a partnership with EDF R&D. It is within the company that the gaming sessions were held. During each session, a number of recordings were made so that the events of the game and the resulting learning could be analyzed later. Four recording methods were used:

– an automatic recording of all the manipulations carried out on the custom interface (including comments that the participants could type to explain the decisions they were making);

– a video recording of the moments when the prefect asked for a meeting between players to discuss their collective management of water;

– the use of an individual whose role was to observe the attitudes and interactions of the participants during the session;

– and finally, an audio recording of the debriefing during which the participants are invited to explain the reasons behind their decisions.

It is from these recordings that we carried out a retrospective analysis of any induced learning.

6.3.3.3. *The induced learning*

6.3.3.3.1. Learning about constraints and individual impacts

The sessions enabled participants to better understand the challenges that water users face while trying to meet their water needs. For example, participants who played the role of a farmer had to repeatedly adapt their decisions during the turns of the game so as to reach their production goal. One reason is that they had to understand the technical aspects of this role (none of the participants had previous experience in the agricultural sector). The second reason is that they had to take the decisions of other water users into account. Another example is the case of the role of drinking water manager for which one of the participants complained to the others that his actions had little or no impact on the system. The relevance of having this role in the participatory simulation was questioned as a result. [BAR 07] suggested that the roles with little impact upon the system should not be included in a participatory simulation due to the lack of interest for participants. However, in such a case the role is useful because it allows them to become aware of the reality that drinking water has a low impact compared to other water use. In addition, the role-playing game highlights the duality between the individual goals and collective interests. The actors sometimes have difficulties when trying to respond to both at once. The role of the hydroelectric dam manager clearly illustrates this problem. During the sessions, participants in this role had to produce energy (and for this they had to fill their reservoirs), and, at the same time, had to follow the orders of the prefect player, who was asking them to release water to maintain a minimum water level downstream. Despite the participants being all employees of EDF, and the fact that those who embodied the role of dam manager had actual dam management skills, the difficulty to meet the electricity production goal as well as maintaining the LTF generated many debates and negotiations that sometimes became very heated.

6.3.3.3.2. Learning from the interactions between stakeholders and power relations

The case of the dam manager mentioned above illustrates how participatory simulation highlights the power relations between the different roles. For example, during a session, the participant with the role of prefect made many attempts to convince the dam manager to release water from the dam following the quantities that they had fixed, not only using various technical arguments, but also using their status as state authority to impose their choices. These negotiations took place during the consultation meeting between participants organized at mid-game as well as during face-to-face discussions. The prefect player attempted to apply the same strategy with the farmer players, but without success. Thus, this example illustrates how participatory simulation can reveal power relationships and gives the ability for us to learn from it. During another session, we simulated a climate change scenario to reinforce the difficulty for the dam manager to maintain a minimum water level. This also had the effect of increasing tensions and power relationships among participants. In this way (by adjusting the parameters of the simulation), it is possible to orient the path of a session and bring attention to particular aspects such as the negotiation process, for example. In summary, participatory simulation induces an individual learning process about the constraints that each user has to face, about the non-triviality of combining different objectives, and the importance of power relations in the negotiation process. Relative to this last aspect, the SimPAGE experiment was particularly useful for showing the participants to which point collective decisions are not only affected by technical criteria, but also by social pressure, power relations and lobbying processes. Participatory simulation then becomes an arena within which stakeholder interactions occur and can be observed. The participant plays a role, but due to the distance from the reality represented by the simulation, it is also an observer of social interactions [DAR 03].

6.4. Exchanging and questioning knowledge: the PAMS collaborative portal

The experiment shows that exchanges during a modeling–simulating activity are, more often than not, carried out via a variety of independent tools. The use of instant messaging tools and/or video-conferences are the easiest methods of communication. The participants then communicate either by voice or by text such that, each on their own, they may replicate the model or execute the simulator. Thus, to eliminate any comprehension or distortion problems, the use of screen sharing tools or remote control is often necessary. Collaborative Portal for Aiding Modeling and Simulation (PAMS) (*Portail collaboratif d'Aide la Modélisation-Simulation* in French) is one of the very few initiatives that introduces collaboration into the center of the process of modeling and simulation. This tool's originality lies in its placement of the simulator at the center of the collaboration. It then becomes an exchange support and media, shared by the research group. PAMS therefore facilitates researchers to work upon a simulator together by manipulating, configuring (especially by modifying the input parameters) and analyzing the results.

6.4.1. *Sharing the PAMS simulation*

PAMS supports several generic simulation platforms including NetLogo [NGU 09]. PAMS's architecture has the advantage of being modular and thus allowing easy integration of new simulation platforms (like Repast [CHA 09] for example) or *ad hoc* simulators. In addition to the main tool for collaboration with the simulator, PAMS also provides all the generic, standard and essential collaboration tools for easy communication (messaging, video-conferencing, forums, etc.).

PAMS is based on free and open-source technology. Particularly, we use OpenMeeting[1] for creating synchronous collaborative tools such as video and messaging, and asynchronous tools such as forums, file sharing, etc. It presents the advantage of being able to be integrated within most Content Management Systems (CMS) such as SPIP[2] which manage the web interface.

From a technical point of view, PAMS uses a combination of standard web application technologies: a web application server based on JSP, AJAX and Servlets (on a Tomcat server), an application server based on distributed components (Java Enterprise Bean (EJB) on a

1 http://openmeetings.apache.org.

2 http://www.spip.net.

Jonas server) notably, to execute the simulations and a MySQL database server to record the results. PAMS was developed with a modular architecture in mind, so that it could be easily extended. The architecture is detailed in [NGU 13].

As mentioned in the previous paragraphs, PAMS was designed to easily integrate new models and simulators. For existing platforms in PAMS (including NetLogo and GAMA), all that is required is to upload the template on the PAMS server via a dedicated web interface. Regarding new simulators, they can be easily integrated as long as they have a certain architecture, that is to say, they all have a function that initializes the simulation, advances to the next simulation iteration, recovers or fixes the value of local variables and parameters of the simulator.

6.4.2. *Usage example: the MIRO project*

As a reminder (see section 1.6), the MIRO project (financing PREDIT 2004–2007, ANR 2009–2013, MEDDE 2014–2015) sought to explore the possible impacts of urban policies on the spatiotemporal accessibility of the town for its citizens and the results of this on their daily mobilities by computer simulation. It also aims to establish territorial (losses and gains of localized accessibility) and social diagnostics (populations privileged and disadvantaged by the different policies tested).

Finally, it explores the possible global impacts of individual behavior changes, less focused on the maximization of individual utility and taking greater account of global issues.

Three models were developed from this perspective (see Figure 6.5).

GaMiroD is a descriptive model which was applied to the towns of Dijon and Grenoble. This model was developed within the GAMA platform [DRO 13]. The purpose of these two case studies was to test scenarios involving a change in the urban environment that also relate to local public policy actions promoted by sustainable development goals (construction of a collective transport infrastructure on its own site; establishment of an urban zone with traffic regulation to reduce the effects of pollution).

In parallel, the SMArtAccess model was developed with the NetLogo platform. This is an explanatory model facilitating the user to build a city, placing commercial and public services, as well as places of work and residence, and then to populate it with autonomous agents performing various sequences of activities using different modes of transport (walking, public transport and cars). The aim of the user is not only to test urban models (compact cities, urban villages, etc.) but also to define, in an iterative and interactive manner and based upon a large number of macroscopic and microscopic indicators, urban configurations satisfying certain sustainability criteria. The aim of this game is to get users to become aware of the difficulty of controlling a complex urban system, especially when we seek to achieve several goals, some of which are mutually incompatible.

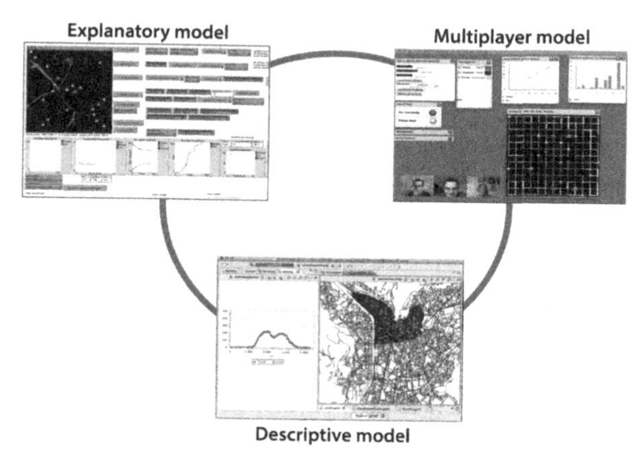

Figure 6.5. *The 3 models developed by the MIRO project. For a color version of the figure, see www.iste.co.uk/banos/netlogo.zip*

Then, the SMArtAccess model was deployed on the PAMS platform with the aim of constructing a participative, multiplayer model. Via a web interface (see Figure 6.6), this version of the model (called SM2A2) allows for five people to play collaboratively to identify adopted scenarios. Each of the participants takes on a role (developer, carrier, citizen, etc.) and can only act within one part of the model and the environment created as part of this role (e.g. the developer player defines the road network, the Action Priority Zone for air, etc.). The aim of this serious game is to get the players to be aware of the difficulty of acting sectionally on a CS, driven by its own dynamic and subject to the uncoordinated yet interdependent actions of other actors.

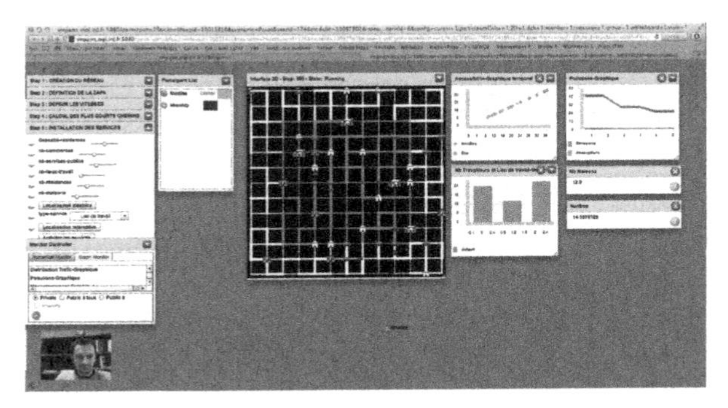

Figure 6.6. *Smart Access within the PAMS portal (SM2A2)*

SM2A2 was the subject of many experiments which involved masters students, researchers, communities and administrative governments (City of Dijon, Grenoble City, World Organization of Health, Ministry of Ecology) as well as industrial organizations.

6.5. The issues to which multiagent models may provide answers

We have now covered two large areas of modeling and multiplayer simulation: participatory simulation and collaborative M&S. We will now conclude this chapter by describing how these tools can address three major issues of the multiagent modeling community.

6.5.1. *Revealing behaviors and joint model building*

Participatory simulation allows for the processes and dynamics of a human player's behavior to be observed (in sociological, cognitive and psychological aspects). Indeed, it is possible to follow the evolution of the logic behind their actions and reasoning by analyzing their operations on the computer, their oral exchanges with other players, their behavior during group discussions and their individual choices. It is then possible to establish hypotheses about the individual and collective behaviors related to how the situation evolves. This prospective aspect can then be used to establish collective strategies that will be tested through simulation. Participatory simulation therefore acts both as an indicator of individual behaviors and as a place of experimentation with implementing strategies constructed from interactions with others.

6.5.2. *Tools favoring interdisciplinarity*

Participatory simulation appears to be unifying and encourages the integration of different skills and disciplines. Role-playing allows for actors with different profiles (farmers, dam managers, etc.) to be brought together within a same setup. In a broader perspective, the development of an application such as SimPAGE initially requires the integration of expert knowledge about the modeling of water networks, then uses computer skills to develop a simulation platform and finally uses social science knowledge to define a participatory framework and analyze the results of participatory simulations. During the participatory simulation sessions, the scientists discover the integrated platform and the work carried out by each of the participants in the project. An interdisciplinary learning process then occurs. Each scientist took the time to understand the work of the others and to explain their own work. Discussions on the methodological approach took place about inconsistencies of the model related to interdependencies between disciplines. As scientists played the role of different actors of the system, each of them could use the tool by interacting with the computer and could see the consequences of their decisions on the part of the system they had developed. In the case of the SimPAGE experiment, the collective learning process was therefore also a way to validate the model and to detect its limitations.

6.5.3. *Mediation and training*

Participatory simulation is a technological device highly effective at producing exchanges between participants. It provides a framework that favors the sharing of knowledge and collective action [BEC 10]. Thus, the use of such tools in the context of training professional individuals (industrial sector employees, environmental managers, elected officials) is entirely possible. When participatory simulation is used with a single stakeholder category (such as with a group of dam managers), sessions can be a good way to raise awareness of the impacts their decisions can have on water resources and other water uses. When sessions are organized with a mixed professional group whose interests may conflict, participatory simulation can facilitate and improve the exchange of information between stakeholders by comparing perceptions and explicitly showing the logical reasoning behind different actions.

Similarly, during the collaborative development of a model, a learning process takes place between the scientists involved: each specialist provides part of the solution to the problem from their own scientific field and can gain a better understanding of other scientific disciplines (related to their questioning, methods and approaches). When business people are also involved, scientists can better understand the issues related to a particular objective or physical constraint. For the group, collaborative modeling is therefore a good way to build a shared representation of the model so as to better define the interactions between different activities and to anticipate potential difficulties related to the complexity of the studied systems. However, such applications are conditioned by the participation willingness of professionals and of scientists. This willingness may even be more difficult to achieve in the context of participatory simulations, which often have similarities to games, which may put some people off. In these conditions, the use of other forms of collaborative simulation has to be favored.

Bibliography

[ANS 98] ANSELIN L., BERA A.K., "Spatial dependence in linear regression models with an introduction to spatial econometrics", *Statistics Textbooks and Monographs*, Marcel Dekker AG, vol. 155, pp. 237–290, 1998.

[ASS 13] ASSOCIATION C., "La modélisation d'accompagnement: fondements et éthique d'une démarche de concertation pour un développement durable", *Proceedings of ComMod*, 2013.

[BAN 15] BANOS A., LANG C., MARILLEALU N., *Agent-based Spatial Simulation with NetLogo Volume 2: Implementation*, ISTE Press and Elsevier Ltd, London and Oxford, 2015.

[BAR 03] BARRETEAU O., "The joint use of role-playing games and models regarding negotiation processes: characterization of associations", *Journal of Artificial Societies and Social Simulation*, vol. 6, no. 2, 2003, available at http://jasss.soc.surrey.ac.uk/6/2/3.html.

[BAR 07] BARRETEAU O., LE PAGE C., PEREZ P., "Simulation and gaming in natural resource management", *Simulation and Gaming*, vol. 38, no. 2, pp. 181–184, 2007.

[BAR 10] BARSEGHIAN D., ALTINTAS I., JONES M.B., *et al.*, "Workflows and extensions to the Kepler scientific workflow system to support environmental sensor data access and analysis. Barseghian, Derik and Altintas", *Ecological Informatics*, vol. 5, no. 1, pp. 42–50, 2010.

[BAT 76] BATTY M., *Urban Modelling: Algorithms, Calibrations, Predictions*, MARTIN L., MARCH L., (eds.), Cambridge University Press, 1976.

[BAU 01a] BAUER B., MÜLLER J.-P., ODELL J., "Agent UML: a formalism for specifying multiagent software systems", *Proceedings of the 1st International Workshop on Agent-Oriented Software Engineering (AOSE'00)*, Secaucus, NJ, Springer-Verlag New York, Inc., pp. 91–103, 2001.

[BAU 01b] BAUER B., MÜLLER J.P., ODELL J., "Agent UML: a formalism for specifying multiagent interaction", CIANCARINI P., WOOLDRIDGE M., (eds.), *Agent-Oriented Software Engineering*, Springer, pp. 91–103, 2001.

[BEC 03] BECU N., BOUSQUET F., BARRETEAU O., *et al.*, "A methodology for eliciting and modeling stakeholders' representations with agent based modelling", HALES D., EDMONDS B., NORLING E., *et al.*, (eds.), *Proceedings of Multi-Agent-Based Simulation III*, Springer, Heidelberg, pp. 131–148, 2003.

[BEC 08] BECU N., NEEF A., SCHREINEMACHERS P., *et al.*, "Participatory computer simulation to support collective decision-making: potential and limits of stakeholder involvement", *Land Use Policy*, vol. 25, no. 4, pp. 498–509, 2008.

[BEC 10] BECU N., BOMMEL P., BOTTA A., *et al.*, "Technologies mobilisées pour l'accompagnement", ETIENNE M., *La modélisation d'accompagnement: une démarche participative en appui au développement durable*, Quae Editions, Versailles, France, pp. 183–201, 2010.

[BER 05] BERNON C., COSSENTINO M., PAVON J., "An overview of current trends in European AOSE research", *Informatica*, vol. 29, pp. 379–390, 2005.

[BLI 05] BLIKSTEIN P., ABRAHAMSON D., WILENSKY U., "Netlogo: where we are, where we're going", EISENBERG M., EISENBERG A., (eds.), *Proceedings of the Annual Meeting of Interaction Design and Children,*, Boulder, CO, 2005.

[BOM 09] BOMMEL P., Définition d'un cadre méthodologique pour la conception de modèles multi-agents adaptée á la gestion des ressources renouvelables, PhD Thesis, Université Montpellier II-Sciences et Techniques du Languedoc, Montpellier, France, 2009.

[BOM 14] BOMMEL P., DIEGUEZ F., BARTABURU D., *et al.*, "A further step towards participatory modeling. Fostering stakeholder involvement in designing models by using executable UML", *Journal of Artificial Societies and Social Simulation*, vol. 17, no. 6, 2014, available at http://jasss.soc.surrey.ac.uk/17/1/6.html.

[BON 03] BON G.L., *Psychologie des Foules*, Presses Universitaires de France, December 2003.

[BOO 91] BOOCH G., *Object Oriented Design with Application*, Benjamin Cummings, 1991.

[BOU 98] BOUSQUET F., BAKAM I., PROTON H., *et al.*, "Cormas: common-pool resources and multi-agent systems", *Tasks and Methods in Applied Artificial Intelligence*, Springer, Berlin, Heidelberg, pp. 826–837, 1998.

[BRA 10] BRAX N., AMBLARD F., BECU N., *et al.*, "When predictive modelling meet participatory simulation: a feedback on potential and issues of a combined approach", ULM E., (ed.), *Proceedings of the MAPS2: Teaching of/with Agent-Based Models in the Social Sciences*, Paris, France, 2010.

[BRE 04] BRESCIANI P., PERINI A., GIORGINI P., *et al.*, "TROPOS: an agent-oriented software development methodology", *Journal of Autonomous Agents and Multi-Agents Systems*, vol. 8, no. 3, pp. 203–236, 2004.

[BRI 00] BRIASSOULIS H., *Analysis of Land Use Change: Theoretical and Modeling Approaches*, Regional Research Institute, West Virginia University, 2000.

[CAI 13] CAILLAULT S., DELMOTTE S., KDOWIDÉ C., *et al.*, "Assessing the influence of social and economical networks on land use and land cover changes: a neutral model based approach", *Environmental Modelling and Software*, vol. 45, pp. 64–73, 2013.

[CER 07] CERVENKA R., TRENCANSKY I., *The Agent Modeling Language – AML: A Comprehensive Approach to Modeling Multi-Agent Systems*, Whitestein Series in Software Agent Technologies and Autonomic Computing, Birkhuser, Basel, 2007.

[CHA 09] CHARLES M., MACAL M.J.N., "Agent-based modeling and simulation", *Proceedings of the Winter Simulation Conference*, pp. 86–98, 2009.

[CHA 13] CHASSET P., RK4: Runge-Kutta 4th order method for the simulation software NetLogo, 2013. Available at http://flow.chasset.net/netlogo-rk4/.

[CHI 13] CHIPEAUX S., Génération automatique de Systèmes Multi-Agents à partir de modèles pour la simulation à large échelle de systèmes complexes de grande taille, PhD Thesis, University of Franche-Comté, December 2013.

[COA 97] COAD P., NORTH D., MAYFIELD M., *Object Models: Strategies, Patterns, and Applications*, Yourdon Press, 1997.

[COM 05] COMMOD C., "La modélisation comme outil d'accompagnement", *Natures Sciences Sociétés*, vol. 13, pp. 165–168, 2005.

[COQ 96] COQUILLARD P., HILL D.R.C., FRONTIER S., *Modélisation et simulation d'écosystemes des modèles déterministes aux simulations à évènements discrets*, Masson, Paris; Milan; Barcelona, 1996.

[DAM 94] DAMASIO A.R., *Descartes' Error: Emotion, Reason, and the Human Brain*, G.P. Putnam, 1994.

[DAR 03] DARÉ W., BARRETEAU O., "A role-playing game in irrigated system negotiation: between play and reality", *Journal of Artificial Societies and Social Simulation*, vol. 6, no. 3, 2003, available at http://jasss.soc.surrey.ac.uk/6/3/6.html.

[DEM 95] DEMAZEAU Y., "From interactions to collective behaviour in agent-based systems", *Proceedings of the 1st European Conference on Cognitive Science*, Saint-Malo, pp. 117–132, 1995.

[DEM 97] DEMAZEAU Y., "Steps toward multi-agent oriented programming", *Proceedings of the 1st International Workshop on Multi-Agent Systems (IWMAS '97)*, 1997.

[DEM 03] DEMAZEAU Y., "Créativité Emergente Centrée Utilisateur", *11èmes Journées Francophones sur les Systèmes Multi-Agents*, Hermès, Hammamet, pp. 31–36, 2003.

[DRO 13] DROGOUL A., AMOUROUX E., CAILLOU P., *et al.*, "GAMA: multi-level and complex environment for agent-based models and simulations", GINI M.L., SHEHORY O., ITO T., *et al.*, (eds.), *Proceedings of AAMAS*, IFAAMAS, pp. 1361–1362, 2013.

[EDM 04] EDMONDS B., MOSS S., "From KISS to KIDS – an 'anti-simplistic' modeling approach", DAVIDSSON P., LOGAN B., TAKADAMA K., (eds.), *Proceedings of MABS*, vol. 3415 of Lecture Notes in Computer Science, Springer, pp. 130–144, 2004.

[ETI 10] ETIENNE M., *La modélisation d'accompagnement: une démarche participative en appui au développement durable*, Quae Editions, 2010.

[ETI 11] ETIENNE M., "Pédagogie active et enseignement de la biodiversité par la modélisation d'accompagnement", *Actes du Colloque: Education au développement durable et à la biodiversité: concepts, questions vives, outils et pratiques*, publication électronique, Réseau francophone international de recherche en Education à l'environnement, Université du Québec à Montréal, available at http://www.refere.uqam.ca/, Digne-les-Bains, France, 2011.

[FAI 13] FAIVRE R., IOOSS B., MAHÉVAS S., *et al.*, *Analyse de sensibilité et exploration de modèles: Application aux sciences de la nature et de l'environnement*, Collection Savoir-faire, Quae Editions, 2013.

[FAP 00] FAP, FIPA KIF Content Language Specification, Report, Foundation for Intelligent Physical Agents, Switzerland, 2000.

[FER 95] FERBER J., *Les systèmes multi-agents: vers une intelligence collective*, Informatique, Intelligence Artificielle, Interéditions, 1995.

[FER 98] FERBER J., GUTKNECHT O., "Aalaadin: a meta-model for the analysis and design of organizations in multi-agent systems", DEMAZEAU Y., (ed.), *Proceedings of International Conference on Multi-Agent Systems (ICMAS '98)*, IEEE Press, pp. 128–135, July 1998.

[FER 03] FERBER J., GUTKNECHT O., MICHEL F., "From agents to organizations: an organizational view of multi-agent systems", GIORGINI P., MÜLLER J., ODELL J., (eds.), *Proceedings of Agent-Oriented Software Engineering IV 4th International Workshop*, Melbourne, Australia, pp. 214–230, July 2003.

[FER 04] FERBER J., MICHEL F., BARRANCO J., "AGRE: integrating environments with organizations", *Proceedings of the 1st International Workshop on Environments for Multi-Agent Systems,* Springer, pp. 48–56, 2004.

[FIN 94] FININ T., FRITZSON R., MCKAY D., *et al.*, "KQML as an agent communication language", *Proceedings of the 3rd International Conference on Information and Knowledge Management* (*CIKM '94*), New York, ACM, pp. 456–463, 1994.

[FOR 61] FORRESTER J.W., *Industrial Dynamics*, student ed. edition, Productivity Pr, 1961.

[FOR 68] FORRESTER J.W., *Principles of Systems*, Pegasus Communications, 1968.

[FOR 69] FORRESTER J.W., *Urban Dynamics*, MIT Press, February 1969.

[FOU 05] FOURNIER S., Intégration de la dimension spatiale au sein d'un modèle multi-agents à base de rôles pour la simulation: application à la navigation maritime, PhD Thesis, University of Rennes, France, 2005.

[FOU 97] FOUNDATION FOR INTELLIGENT PHYSICAL AGENTS, FIPA '97 Specification Part 2: Agent Communication Language, 1997. Available at http://www.fipa.org.

[FOU 02] FOUNDATION FOR INTELLIGENT PHYSICAL AGENTS, Geneva, Switzerland, FIPA Communicative Act Library Specification, 2002.

[FRI 86] FRIJDA N.H., *The Emotions*, Cambridge University Press, 1986.

[GAU 11] GAUDOU B., MARILLEAU N., HO T.V., "Toward a methodology of collaborative modeling and simulation of complex systems", *Intelligent Networking, Collaborative Systems and Applications*, Springer, pp. 27–53, 2011.

[GLO 04] GLOOR C., STUCKI P., NAGEL K., "Hybrid techniques for pedestrian simulations.", SLOOT P.M.A., CHOPARD B., HOEKSTRA A.G., (eds.), *Proceedings of the 6th International Conference on Cellular Automata for Research and Industry*, vol. 3305 of Lecture Notes in Computer Science, Amsterdam, Netherlands, Springer, pp. 581–590, 2004.

[GRI 99] GRIMM V., "Ten years of individual-based modeling in ecology: what have we learned and what could we learn in the future?", *Ecological Modeling*, vol. 115, nos. 2–3, pp. 129–148, 1999.

[GRI 06] GRIMM V., BERGER U., BASTIANSEN F., *et al.*, "A standard protocol for describing individual-based and agent-based models", *Ecological Modeling*, vol. 198, nos. 1–2, pp. 115–126, 2006.

[GRI 10] GRIMM V., BERGER U., DEANGELIS D., *et al.*, "The ODD protocol: a review and first update", *Ecological Modeling*, vol. 221, pp. 2760–2768, 2010.

[GRI 13] GRIGNARD A., TAILLANDIER P., GAUDOU B., *et al.*, "GAMA 1.6: advancing the art of complex agent-based modeling and simulation", *Proceedings of the Principles and Practice of Multi-Agent Systems (PRIMA'13)*, vol. 8291 of Lecture Notes in Computer Science, Springer, pp. 117–131, 2013.

[GRI 14] GRIMM V., AUGUSIAK J., FOCKS A., *et al.*, "Towards better modelling and decision support: documenting model development, testing, and analysis using {TRACE}", *Ecological Modelling*, vol. 280, pp. 129–139, 2014.

[HAG 73] HAGGETT P., *Analyse spatiale en géographie humaine*, Armand Colin, Paris, 1973.

[HAY 84] HAYNES K., FOTHERINGHAM A., *Gravity and Spatial Interaction Models*, Sage Publications, 1984.

[IRW 02] IRWIN E.G., BOCKSTAEL N.E., "Interacting agents, spatial externalities and the evolution of residential land use patterns", *Journal of Economic Geography*, vol. 2, no. 1, pp. 31–54, 2002.

[JAG 10] JAGERS H., "Linking data, models and tools: an overview", *International Congress on Environmental Modeling and Software*, Ottawa, Canada, 2010.

[JEA 97] JEAN M.R., PESTY S., "Emergence et SMA", *Intelligence Artificielle et Système Multi-agents (JFIADSMA '97)*, La Colle-sur-Loup, Hermès, France, pp. 323–342, 1997.

[JEN 00] JENNINGS N., "On agent-based software engineering", *Artificial Intelligence*, vol. 177, no. 2, pp. 277–296, 2000.

[JUD 88] JUDGE G., *Introduction to the Theory and Practice of Econometrics*, Wiley, 1988.

[KER 39] KERMACK W.O., MCKENDRICK A.G., "Contributions to the mathematical theory of epidemics", *The Journal of Hygiene*, vol. 39, no. 3, pp. 271–288, 1939.

[KER 91] KERMACK W.O., MCKENDRIC A.G., "Contributions to the mathematical theory of epidemics III. further studies of the problem of endemicity", *Bulletin of Mathematical Biology*, vol. 53, no. 1–2, pp. 89–118, March 1991.

[KLE 07] KLEINBAUM D.G., *Applied Regression Analysis and Multivariable Methods*, CengageBrain.com, 2007.

[KOR 08] KORICHI A., BELATTAR B., "Towards a Web based simulation groupware: experiment with BSCW", *Information Technology Journal*, vol. 7, no. 2, pp. 332–337, 2008.

[LAN 89] LANGTON C., *Artificial Life 1*, Addison-Wesley, 1989.

[LAN 13] LANGLOIS P., BLANPAIN B., DAUDÉ E., "MAGéo, une plateforme de simulation multi-agents pour tous", *Proceedings of SimTools*, 2013.

[LE 90] LE MOIGNE J.-L., *La modélisation des systèmes complexes*, Bordas, 1990.

[LE 05] LE PAGE C., BOMMEL P., *A Methodology for Building Agent-Based Simulations of Common-Pool Resources Management: From a Conceptual Model Designed with UML to Its Implementation in CORMAS*, IRRI Press, 2005.

[LE 14] LE PAGE C., ABRAMI G., BARRETEAU O., *et al.*, "Models for sharing representations", *Companion Modeling*, Springer, pp. 69–101, 2014.

[LEG 97] LEGAY J.-M., *L'expérience et le modèle. Un discours sur la méthode*, Collection Sciences en questions, INRA Editions, Paris, 1997.

[LEP 12] LE PAGE C., BECU N., BOMMEL P., *et al.*, "Participatory agent-based simulation for renewable resource management: the role of the cormas simulation platform to nurture a community of practice", *Journal of Artificial Societies and Social Simulation*, vol. 15, no. 1(10), 2012.

[LUK 04] LUKE S., CIOFFI-REVILLA C., PANAIT L., *et al.*, "Mason: a new multi-agent simulation toolkit", *Proceedings of the SwarmFest Workshop*, vol. 8, 2004.

[LUM 04] LUMINET O., VERMEULEN N., "Personalité et psychopathologie cognitive", *Traité de psychopathologie cognitive*, VAN DER LINDEN M., CESCHI G., (eds.), Marseille: Solal, 2004.

[MAR 08] MARILLEAU N., CAMBIER C., DROGOUL A., *et al.*, "Multiscale MAS modelling to simulate the soil environment: application to soil ecology", *Simulation Modelling Practice and Theory*, vol. 16, no. 7, pp. 736–745, 2008.

[MAS 07] MASSE D., CAMBIER C., BRAUMAN A., *et al.*, "MIOR: an individual-based model for simulating the spatial patterns of soil organic matter microbial decomposition", *European Journal of Soil Science*, vol. 58, pp. 1127–1135, 2007.

[MIN 96] MINAR N., Burkhart R., Langton C., *The Swarm Simulation System: A Toolkit for Building Multi-Agent Simulations*, Report, Santa Fe Institute, 1996.

[NAI 10] NAIVINIT W., LE PAGE C., TRÉBUIL G., *et al.*, "Participatory agent-based modeling and simulation of rice production and labor migrations in Northeast Thailand", *Environmental Modelling & Software*, vol. 25, no. 11, pp. 1345–1358, 2010.

[NGU 09] NGUYEN K.T., BENOIT G., VINH H.T., *et al.*, "Application of PAMS collaboration platform to simulation-based researches in soil science: the case of the Micro-Organism Project", *Proceedings of the IEEE-RIVF International Conference on Computing and Telecommunication Technologies*, IEEE-RIVF, 2009.

[NOR 13] North M., Collier N., Ozik J., *et al.*, "Complex adaptive systems modeling with Repast Simphony", *Complex Adaptive Systems Modeling*, vol. 1, no. 1, p. 3, Springer, 2013.

[OCC 01] Occello M., Koning J.-L., Baeijis C., "Conception des Système Multi-Agent: quelques éléments de réflexion méthodologique", *Technique et science informatique*, vol. 20, no. 2, pp. 233–263, 2001.

[ODE 00] Odell J., Parunak H., Bauer B., "Extending UML for agents", Wagner, G., Lesperance E.Y., (eds.), *Proceedings of the Agent-Oriented Information Systems Workshop at the 17th National Conference on Artificial Intelligence.*, pp. 3–17, 2000.

[ODE 01] Odell J., Parunak H.V.D., Bauer B., "Representing agent interaction protocols in UML", *Agent-Oriented Software Engineering, First International Workshop*, Lecture Notes in Computer Science, Springer, vol. 57, pp. 121–140, 2001.

[OMG 03] OMG, Unified Modeling Language: Superstructure version 2.0, 2003.

[OMG 05] OMG, UML 2.0 Superstructure Specification, Report, Object Management Group, August 2005.

[OST 94] Ostrom E., Gardner R., Walker J., *Rules, Games, and Common-Pool Resources*, University of Michigan Press, 1994.

[PAD 02] Padgham L., Winikoff M., "Prometheus: a methodology for developing intelligent agents", Giunchiglia F., Odell J., Weiss G., (eds.), *Agent-Oriented Software Engineering III*, vol. 2585 of LNCS, Springer-Verlag, pp. 174–185, 2002.

[POL 08] Polhill J.G., Parker D., Brown D., *et al.*, "Using the ODD protocol for describing three agent-based social simulation models of land-use change", *Journal of Artificial Societies and Social Simulation*, vol. 11, no. 2(3), 2008.

[POL 10] Polhill J.G., "ODD updated", *Journal of Artificial Societies and Social Simulation*, vol. 13, no. 4(9), 2010.

[PRO 05] Provitolo D., "Un exemple d'effet de dominos: la panique dans les catastrophes urbaines", *Cybergeo: Revues européenne de géographie*, vol. 328, 2005.

[PRO 07] Provitolo D., "A proposition for a classification of the catastrophe systems based on complexity criteria", *Proceedings of Emergent Properties in Natural and Artificial Complex Systems (EPNACS '07)*, 4–5 October 2007.

[PRU 02] PRUNEAU D., LAPOINTE C., "Un, deux, trois, nous irons au bois. L'apprentissage expérientiel et ses applications en éducation relative à l'environnement", *Éducation et francophonie*, vol. 30, no. 2, pp. 241–256, 2002.

[QUE 09] QUESNEL G., DUBOZ R., RAMAT E., "The Virtual Laboratory Environment – an operational framework for multi-modelling, simulation and analysis of complex dynamical systems", *Simulation Modelling Practice and Theory*, vol. 17, pp. 641–653, April 2009.

[RAI 11] RAILSBACK S.F., GRIMM V., *Agent-Based and Individual-Based Modeling: A Practical Introduction*, Princeton University Press, 2011.

[RAO 91] RAO A.S., GEORGEFF M.P., "Modeling rational agents within a BDI-architecture", *Proceedings of Knowledge Representation and Reasoning*, Morgan Kaufmann Publishers, 1991.

[REN 02] RENNARD J.-P., *Vie Artificielle. où la biologie rencontre l'informatique*, Vuibert, 2002.

[RES 96] RESNICK M., "StarLogo: an environment for decentralized modeling and decentralized thinking", *Proceedings of Conference Companion on Human Factors in Computing Systems*, pp. 11–12, 1996.

[RES 97] RESNICK M., *Turtles, Termites and Traffic Jams Explorations in Massively Parallel Microworlds*, MIT Press, Cambridge, 1997.

[REU 13] REUILLON R., LECLAIRE M., REY-COYREHOURCQ S., "OpenMOLE, a workflow engine specifically tailored for the distributed exploration of simulation models", *Future Generation Computer Systems*, vol. 29, no. 8, pp. 1981–1990, 2013.

[RYK 96] RYKIEL E., "Testing ecological models: the meaning of validation", *Ecological Modelling*, vol. 90, pp. 229–244, 1996.

[SAL 09] SALTELLI A., CHAN K., SCOTT E., *Sensitivity Analysis*, vol. 2008, Wiley, 2009.

[SAN 05] SANDERS L., "Simulation des systèmes urbains", *Ecole thématique CNRS: modélisation et simulation multi-agent de systèmes complexe pour les SHS*, Poquerolles, 2005.

[SCH 65] SCHLAGER K.J., "A land use plan design model", *Journal of the American Institute of Planners*, vol. 31, no. 2, pp. 103–111, 1965.

[SCH 99a] SCHERER K.R., "Appraisal theory", DALGLEISH T., POWER M., (eds.), *Handbook of Cognition and Emotion*, pp. 637–663, 1999.

[SCH 99b] SCHERER K.R., "On the sequential nature of appraisal processes: indirect evidence from a recognition task", DALGLEISH T., POWER M., (eds.), *Cognition and Emotion*, vol. 13, no. 6, pp. 763–793, 1999.

[SCH 02] SCHWEITZER F., "Brownian agent models for swarm and chemotactic interaction. Abstracting and synthesizing the principles of living systems", *Proceedings of the 5th German Workshop on Artificial Life*, Nerlin, Germany, pp. 181–190, 2002.

[SCH 03] SCHWEITZER F., FARMER J.D., *Brownian Agents and Active Particles: Collective Dynamics in the Natural and Social Sciences*, Springer, 2003.

[SIL 03] SILVA V., GARCIA A., BRANDÃO A., *et al.*, "Taming agents and objects in software engineering", *Software Engineering for Large-Scale Multi-Agent Systems: Research Issues and Practical Applications*, Springer-Verlag, LNCS, vol. 2603, pp. 1–25, 2003.

[SIN 00] SINCLAIR T., SELIGMAN N., "Criteria for publishing papers on crop modeling", *Field Crops Research*, vol. 68, no. 3, pp. 165–172, 2000.

[STU 03] STURM A., DORI D., SHEHORY O., "Single-model method for specifying multi-agent systems", *Proceedings of the 2nd International Joint Conference on Autonomous Agents and Multiagent Systems (AAMAS '03)*, New York, NY, ACM, pp. 121–128, 2003.

[TAY 07] TAYLOR I.J., DEELMAN E., GANNON D.B., *et al.*, *Workflows for e-Science: Scientific Workflows for Grids*, Springer, 2007.

[TIS 04] TISUE S., WILENSKY U., "NetLogo: a simple environment for modeling complexity", *Proceedings of the International Conference on Complex Systems*, pp. 16–21, 2004.

[TRE 05] TRENCANSKY I., CERVENKA R., "Agent modeling language (AML): a comprehensive approach to modeling MAS", *Informatica*, vol. 29, pp. 391–400, 2005.

[US 83a] US LIBRARY OF CONGRESS, Fatal Panic on the Bridge, Twelve persons killed and many injured, http://chroniclingamerica.loc.gov/lccn/sn83030214/1883-05-31/ed-1/seq-1/, 31 May 1883.

[US 83b] US LIBRARY OF CONGRESS, Terrible Disaster, http://chroniclingamerica.loc.gov/lccn/sn82014381/1883-05-31/ed-1/seq-1/, 31 May 1883.

[VAR 13] VARENNE F., SILBERSTEIN M., *Modéliser & simuler. Epistémologies et pratiques de la modélisation et de la simulation, tome 1*, Editions Matériologiques, 2013.

[VIA 11] VIAL G., Le système proie-prédateur de Volterra-Lotka, website of l'Ecole Centrale de Lyon, 2011.

[VIN 99] VINCK D., "Les objets intermédiaires dans les réseaux de coopération scientifique", *Revue Française de Sociologie*, vol. 40, no. 2, pp. 385–414, 1999.

[VOI 10] VOINOV A., BOUSQUET F., "Modeling with stakeholders", *Environmental Modelling & Software*, Faculty of Geo-Information Science and Earth Observation (ITC), University of Twente and Cirad, UPR Green, vol. 25, no. 1, 2010.

[WAL 77] WALLISER B., *Systèmes et modèles. Introduction critique à l'analyse des systèmes*, Editions du Seuil, 1977.

[WAN 09] WANG L., JIE W., CHEN J., *Grid Computing: Infrastructure, Service, and Applications*, CRC Press, 2009.

[WAT 92] WATSON D., CLARK L.A., "On traits and temperament: general and specific factors of emotional experience and their relation to the five-factor model", *Journal of Personality*, vol. 60, no. 2, pp. 441–476, June 1992.

[WIL 74] WILSON A., *Urban and Regional Models in Geography and Planning*, Wiley, 1974.

[WOO 97] WOOLDRIDGE M., "Agent based software engineering", *Software Engineering*, vol. 144, pp. 26–37, 1997.

[ZAM 03] ZAMBONELLI F., JENNINGS N., WOOLDRIDGE M., "Developing multiagent systems: the Gaia methodology", *ACM Transactions on Software Engineering and Methodology*, vol. 12, no. 3, pp. 317–370, 2003.

List of Authors

Frédéric AMBLARD
IRIT
University Toulouse 1 Capitole
France

Arnaud BANOS
Géographie-cités
Panthéon Sorbonne University
Paris
France

Nicolas BECU
LIENSs
University of La Rochelle
France

Fabrice BOUQUET
FEMTO-ST
University of Franche-Comté
Besançon
France

Nicolas BRAX
IRIT
University Toulouse 1 Capitole
France

Philippe CAILLOU
LRI/INRIA TAO
University Paris Sud
Orsay
France

Sébastien CHIPEAUX
FEMTO-ST
University of Franche-Comté
Besançon
France

Nathalie CORSON
LMAH
University of Le Havre
France

Eric DAUDÉ
IDEES
University of Rouen
France

Benoît GAUDOU
IRIT
University Toulouse 1 Capitole
France

Arnaud GRIGNARD
UMMISCO/IRD
UPMC
Bondy
France

Guillaume HUTZLER
Laboratoire IBISC
University of Evry-Val d'Essonne
France

Christophe LANG
FEMTO-ST
University of Franche-Comté
Besançon
France

Nicolas MARILLEAU
UMMISCO/IRD
UPMC
Bondy
France

Claude MONTEIL
DYNAFOR
INP-ENSAT
Toulouse
France

Jean-Marc NICOD
FEMTO-ST
ENSMM
Besançon
France

Damien OLIVIER
LITIS
University of Le Havre
France

David SHEEREN
DYNAFOR
INP-ENSAT
Toulouse
France

Patrick TAILLANDIER
IDEES
University of Rouen
France

Index

N, O

P, R

S, T

U

V